YOUR
FAC OR E
MINE?

The adventures of a professional
Tom Cruise lookalike

For George enjoy
Cheers Gores

Memoirs of Gary Strohmer
working as Tom Cruise

Grosvenor House
Publishing Limited

The right of Gary Strohmer to be identified as the author of this
work has been asserted in accordance with Section 78
of the Copyright, Designs and Patents Act 1988

The book cover picture is copyright to Gary Strohmer

This book is published by
Grosvenor House Publishing Ltd
28-30 High Street, Guildford, Surrey, GU1 3EL.
www.grosvenorhousepublishing.co.uk

A CIP record for this book
is available from the British Library

ISBN 978-1-78623-003-4

CONTENTS

* * *

INTRODUCTION

He could see the London Eye, now less than a hundred yards away. Could he make it? He had to try he thought as he started to run with all his might. But it was too late! The mob was upon him baying for blood (and the odd autograph or two!) All in a day's work for Tom Cruise (Well, his lookalike anyway!)

CHAPTER 1

B.C. BEFORE CRUISE

My first awareness of anything at all about Tom Cruise was back in 1983 when, still living at my parents' house in Bibby Close, Corringham in Essex, a film came out called *Risky Business*. I was 21 at the time and, coincidently the same age as Tom Cruise himself. I had never heard of him back then but, a few short years later, I was to know *all* about it! Although this was not Tom's first film, it was the first film that I ever saw him in. I went to see it at the local cinema with my girlfriend of that time and all throughout the film she kept nudging me saying, " 'ere 'e don't 'alf look like you", much to the annoyance of the other patrons. My thoughts at the time were 'can you stop poking me in the ribs' and 'looks like we use the same barber' as we seemed to have a similar haircut. My girlfriend started to make it her mission to tell everyone and anyone who would listen how much I looked like this new actor, Tom Cruise. People did look at her rather peculiarly as, for the most part, no one really knew who he was back then. I found it all rather embarrassing at the time and as a result of her endeavours, we split up shortly after. This, was ironic as later on, when he was Mr. Hollywood famous and I was in my singleton days, I did use it to my advantage with the ladies. Plus, of course, several years later, I managed to earn a living as a lookalike for him. And then *Top Gun* came out.

Top Gun was released in 1986 and it catapulted Tom into mega stardom. He was now a house hold name. I went to see the film with my new girlfriend who promptly sat through the whole film nudging me in the ribs with her elbow saying, " 'ere 'e don't 'alf look like you." Now because Tom was a famous actor by now, she proudly started telling everyone how her boyfriend looked like Tom Cruise. She really got into this, bought me a leather flying jacket for my birthday and even cut my hair in to the Top Gun look, telling me at the time she was just going to give me a trim. I got a bit miffed at this because it had taken me a long time to grow my hair into the famous '80's mullet which I was rather proud of. She started to try and make herself look like Kelly McGillis, the leading lady and had her hair done in the style of the actress in the film. She even wanted me to get a motorbike. This time, however, people knew who he was and did sometimes stare at me. In the end, however, once again I found it all rather embarrassing - and time for a new girlfriend.

Time went on and Tom carried on making very successful films, *The Colour of Money*, *Cocktail* etc and I started to notice that with each film that Tom released, people would go through a spate of telling me how much I looked like him. At first I didn't take a lot of notice but after a while I realised that the ladies were mostly the ones saying it to me and given the fact that at this time I was single, I started to embrace the idea a bit more. This was when I started to move from being a little embarrassed about it to starting to enjoy some adventures with it (before I became a professional lookalike, that is).

In 1988 I was looking for a new home to live in. I already left home a couple of years before but the house I was living in, I lived in the downstairs lounge as a bed sit and rented the upstairs 3 rooms out. Multiple occupation they call it so, basically, I was living for free. I had a day job at the time as well as gigging a lot at weekends so I had a few bob in my pocket and I bought myself a car, an Audi 100, top of the range. So, with a nice car, a couple of bob and my Tom-ish looks, I would grab a few mates and we hit the town as often as we could. Good days they were. Further to this, my mates, mercenary as they were, would use my lookalikeness to their full advantage! We would often hit the night clubs. It would be *Kings* night club at Canvey Island on a Thursday then *Talk of the South* in Southend on a Friday evening and *The Ilford Palace* on a Saturday night. So we would get into the club, be standing at the bar then one of our mates, Glen, would just disappear. At first we couldn't figure out what he was doing. Now Glen was a philanderer; he had a good eye for the ladies and the gift of the gab. He would turn up a while later, having tracked down whatever girl took his fancy and bring her back to where we were standing, 'bla bla'ing' her all the way. After getting her to look me up and down for a bit, (preferable when I was having a beer and chatting to my mates so as I wouldn't notice), he would disappear off with her and we wouldn't see him for the rest of the evening. We used to think he knew all the lines but we soon cottoned on to what he was doing. It turned out his best chat up line was nothing special after all; just him wandering up to a girl he fancied saying, "Oi darling, my mate looks like Tom Cruise. Come and 'av a look"! He later said, "Tom becoming famous was the best thing to happen for me with women; glad you're my mate, Gal".

Didn't always work though; not everyone's a Tom Cruise fan and not absolutely everyone thought I looked like him either. This fact came to the fore one night when Glen, me and a few other mates were in a bar having a few drinks and he did his usual disappearing act. One mate said, "Looks like Glen's on the pull again. Better Tom yourself up, Gal." However I fancied doing a windup that night and so deliberately made myself look as un 'Tom-ish' as I could. Tipping a little beer in my hands, I rubbed it into my hair and pushed it all forward. A mate grabbed a cushion off a chair and we stuffed it down my shirt, smoothed it out and I put my jacket on over the top. Made me look well fat. I then pulled my trousers up as high as I could so the bottoms were halfway up my calf and proceeded to slouch in a chair. I looked like a right wally and certainly nothing like Tom. Anyway, a little time went by and sure enough, Glen turns up with his latest conquest and she was stunning! The best looking girl I had ever seen him with and well above his station. He had that look on his face like the cat that got the cream. As he approached, the rest of us heard her saying to him, "You better not be pulling my leg. I've just dumped my mates to come over here and have a look." It was so hard to keep a straight face but I did my best. As they approached our table she said, "Well, which one is it?" Glen pointed to me and with a bit of a scowl on his face said, "It's that one." Silence fell. Our other mates where sniggering so hard that beer was coming out of their noses. She stared at me for a bit, gave a little squint then, with a face like thunder, turned to Glen and said, "You 'aving a laugh?!! This is a wind up. You're taking the piss out of me!" followed by a few choice expletives. He was none too pleased but trying to save face, said, "Honest babe, it's him". Her response was priceless; she slapped his face so hard he fell over. Then with a few more expletives, she stormed off, followed by an echoing, "And don't call me babe!". I can't tell you how much we rolled up. I was laughing so hard that my guts hurt. Glen would not speak to us for weeks after that and I can't say as I blamed him; ruining his chances with one of the best looking girls we had ever seen. In the end, we made up but he never did the 'Tom' thing again.

At this point I have to say, although I did take advantage of my lookalikeness sometimes and so did one or two of my mates, I can't blame them. However whenever I had a proper girlfriend or a long-term relationship, I would always put the Tom antics to bed. Now, I'm not saying I'm a handsome man or I'm an ugly one; I'm probably about average and I think Tom Cruise is too. Now I know that beauty is in the eye of the beholder; it's just lucky for me that Tom's success has made him attractive. Let's face it, there's nothing like success to do that. Look at, say, Mick Jagger; is he a handsome man? But because of his status, he's been able to be one of the biggest womanisers on the planet. Would Jerry Hall have married him if he was a regular guy like us? However, you have to bear in mind that some of my friends actually met their ladies whilst out with me on a "let's take advantage of who Gary looks like" night as they used to say. Usually the first thing to happen would be they were not allowed to go out with me anymore unless accompanied by their ladies or, for the more headstrong mates, their ladies would cook them dinner and load it with garlic! Wow, they did stink sometimes. So looking like someone famous can have its down side too. It does seem to provoke a bit of jealousy in some people and that did happen on occasions. The usual one would be, "Ha! You don't look anything like him" whether they think you did or not and I would just agree with them and that would be that. But sometimes it went a bit further. Most of my mates were cool with it and, as I say, used it to their advantage, but Ray, whom I'd been friends with for a long time, would really put the boot in. He was not a looker by anyone's standard and not having much success with the ladies, he would try to undermine me whenever I met someone with whom I wished to take things a little further. He would pull them aside and tell them they were just another notch in my bed post. Most of the time they would just tell him to fuck off but occasionally it would ruin my efforts with a girl I was interested in. In the end I got wise to him and told him to 'sling his hook' in no uncertain terms! So very occasionally it has cost me a friendship but, then again, how much of a friendship was it if that's how they are?

In the late '80's I started working as a salesman for an American vacuum cleaner company called Kirby. I started as a door to door salesman, selling this very good (but very over priced) vacuum cleaner. I noticed there was a very high turnover in staff; not surprising these things where practically impossible to sell and being on commission only, guys were just not earning a living unless you had an edge e.g. looking like someone famous! Ladies loved Tom Cruise and ladies usually were the ones to be interested in vacuum cleaners. I sold loads of these things. Got top salesman of the month in only my second month there. I would go into a house, do my demonstration ('dem' for short we would call it), have a little flirt with the lady of the house and voila - another deal done. Word got about that 'Tom Cruise' was selling cleaners and these customers would tell all their mates about it. The office would get a call from customers saying, "Can you send Tom round. My mates want to buy a Kirby from him." The guys in the office started to call me 'Tom Kirby' which I thought was quite funny. It was a great summer until one day things went a little too far. After having done a 'dem' for an older lady, she had told all her mates about me. Then came the inevitable phone call to the office; "Send Tom round, my mates want to see him". Now I took pride in my work; although theses Kirbys were very expensive, they did do an outstanding job and lasted for nearly ever (I still use one, or my wife does, to this day. She inherited it when we got married.) So I felt that I was helping these folk and not just being some ruthless salesman. So off I went, suited and booted, and with my nice polished 'dem' kit. I rang the doorbell. The lady answered the door stinking to high heaven of granny perfume, eye watering it was, and ushered me into the lounge where I was confronted with another 4 or 5 of them. A "gaggle of grannies" if you will. I noticed a few half empty wine bottles about the place and that they were all rather drunk! 'Mmmm,' I thought to myself, 'probably wasting my time here' but I was there anyway and thought, 'what the hell, let's give them a quick 'dem'; you never know I might sell one'. With that started to unpack my 'dem' kit, only to be met with, "Ooh, young man" and, "Phwoar, if only I was 40 years younger" which quickly descended into yobbish cries of, "'Oi darling, getting your kit out? Ha ha ha." And, "Get your kit *off* more like!" Well, things went from bad to worse as they all rose up from the settees and, with arms out stretched, proceeded to stagger towards me. I went from feeling a little intimidated to downright terror at this point. My memory of this scene was like something from an early '80's video nasty; the zombies were gonna get me! I was edging towards the door to make a hasty retreat only to be cut off in a pincer movement from the gaggle. At this point I did the only thing a boy could do, I abandoned my 'dem' kit, climbed out the window and legged it to my car to a rousing chorus of, "Tom, Tom, come back and make some old ladies happy." I drove back to the office (eyes wide with some kind of post traumatic shock and clothes a little dishevelled) and relayed my harrowing tale to the guys in the office... who just fell about laughing. The boss, after recovering his composure, came over and said, "That's an expensive piece of gear you left there. You're going to have to go back and get it." I replied, "Fuck that; you go and get it, I quit" and they all fell about laughing again. They talked me into staying and I was glad I did as went on to open my own office to sell Kirbys and put my own salesmen on the road. But never again would I do a sales pitch to a woman (or women) unless the husband was there. These Kirby days were full of things happening like that; both good and bad but nearly always funny. They are another memoir I've been asked to write which I must get round to at some point.

Another amusing incident took place one weekend when, as I was lead guitarist in a band, (my band/music stuff are a whole big bunch of other adventures, to say the least). We had a recording studio booked for the weekend in Colchester. We had spent all day Saturday recording the instruments and vocals and were going to do the mixing on the Sunday. So Saturday night, we all decided to hit the town in our inimitable style. We tracked down the local night club; The Windmill. It was getting late in the evening when the bass player, Del, came up to me and said, "You gotta come and meet these two girls, Gal. They're big Tom Cruise Fans." So off we went over to them and sure enough after the usual, "You look like Tom" platitudes, we started hitting it off. Now thinking that our luck was in, we offered the two girls a lift home. At this particular time I had a nice orange/red ford Capri that I was proud of, *The Flame Red*, we used to call it. When we got to my car, the girl I was with said, "Ooh, that's flash. Is it a Porsche?" I looked at her a bit odd and said, "Err... yeah". So off we went and as it turned out they both lived in farm houses miles from anywhere, down the dark country lanes, just outside of Witham in Essex. I dropped Del and his girl off first and said I'd pick him up in an hour or two. Then my girl directed me to her place. I pulled up outside and we had a bit of a snog. Thinking she was going to invite me in, we got out of the car but then she said, "Thanks for the lift. Here's me number. See you around." With that, she walked off into her house leaving me leaning on the bonnet, feeling a tad frustrated! I decided that I ought to pick Del up so got into the car and turning around headed back the way I came... only to realise that I didn't have a clue where to go. Dark country lanes at 2 in the morning have a tendency to all look the same. I drove for a while, hoping to retrace my steps, but to no avail. I was getting worried by now; not only could I not find Del, I was hopelessly lost to boot. I decided the best thing to do was head in the general direction of Colchester and just hope and pray that I eventually came across somewhere I recognised. In the end I managed to negotiate my way back to the recording studio, worrying about my mate all the way. I started to bang on the door, waking up the studio owner who was none too pleased by this, and explained the situation to him. In the end I managed to talk him round and persuaded him to help me look for my mate as he knew those back roads quite well; so he said. We set off in his car. It was a great big top of the range Rover, the type of car the villains would use in the old '70's gangster movies. Off we trundled and after about an hour of driving around, against the odds, we drove past Del jogging along an unlit country road. How lucky was that? He didn't recognise the car, having never seen it before and certainly did not realise it was us so feeling rather mischievous, not to mention relived having found him, we drove past him slowly and menacingly. Now being about 4 in the morning by now, it must have been rather scary for him; he certainly gave us a few furtive glances. We just couldn't resist it. We turned the car around and started following him down this dark road. He stared speeding up until he was in a full run. I wound the window down and as we drove past him I shouted, as loud as I could, "OI!" to which he fell down into the bushes and we fell about laughing. Poor old Del! Luckily for us, he saw the funny side, got in the car and off we went. On the way back, we passed the *Windmill* night club and noticed the drummer's car still in the car park. Now the other members of our band; the singer and drummer, had got drunk and decided to sleep it off in the back of the car. Again, feeling a little mischievous, we pulled into the car park. Realising they were asleep in the back, we plastered posters of the band all over the windows of the car and quietly drove off, back to the studio to sleep for the rest of the night. We got up rather late the next day and started to do the mixing of the recordings we had done the previous day. At about 4pm that afternoon, the other two turned up a bit miffed about what we had done to their car saying, "We didn't realize what the time was. We kept waking up thinking it was still night cos it was so dark!"

I mentioned earlier that back in 1988 I was looking for a new home to live in and I settled on a nice little house in a place called Pitsea, part of Basildon in Essex. After living there on my own for a few months my sister, Petina came to lodge with me. This was, as my sister glibly reminisced with me recently, really the start of when she noticed that other people paid me a lot of attention whenever a new Tom film came out. This was particularly prevalent, as she pointed out, when they showed films of his on the telly. I was young and single and, having no particular 'someone special' in my life at that time, was playing the field and enjoying every moment of it. I tried not to upset anybody as I do care about other people's feelings but being a young red blooded male at the time, I felt it would be rude not to! So we would sit there watching a Tom film and I remember her commenting, with somewhat of a grim resolution, "And let the phone calls begin!" ...and they did. One particular instance I remember, we were watching a rerun of *Rain Man*, the best film he ever made in my opinion, when just before the end the phone started ringing. Now we'd been through this lots of times before so I knew what was coming. However, this particular call was from a young girl called Helen. I was fond of her but she was a bit too young for my palate, me being in my twenties and her being a teenager. Think she had a crush on me and she would talk so fast you sometimes couldn't get what she was saying. So anyway the phone rang and Tina answered it, "Hello?" Within what seemed about 2 seconds, Tina said, "Ok" and put the phone down, "Helen?" I said. "Helen" was the reply and we carried on watching the film. Later I asked. "What did Helen say?" Tina replied "She said I was just watching a Tom Cruise film and I thought of your brother. Haven't seen him for a bit can you get him to give me a call please? Any way how are you etc etc....." To which I replied, "All that in 2 seconds?" "Yep" came Tina's reply. I think Tina was the only person in the world who ever understood what Helen said! So the film ended and I dashed off to the pub to a rousing chorus of, "Oi! don't leave me fending off the phone calls" just as the phone started ringing again. I came home to a very pissed off sister who promptly stated, "Bloody phone. Next time there's a Tom film on the telly, I'm moving out" This was, of course, long before the days of mobile phones but, hey, who needed one? I had a handy size sister!

I have had a lot of experiences like above both before, after, and mostly when I was a lookalike; these particular stories are the ones that come to mind as I write. I wasn't particularly a Tom fan at the time but neither did I dislike him. He was, and is, a very good actor and considered a handsome man so if you have to look like someone he's not a bad bet for people to think who you might look like. I personally have not seen the resemblance myself; he's purportedly only something like 5' 6" tall and I'm 5' 11" for a start. This is not me being modest; I just think, at best, we have only a passing resemblance and if other people hadn't said anything, I would not have noticed. I would say that, before I started my lookalike days, the only thing that was the same was our hair cut; we shared a similar style back in the '80's. Although I could take him or leave him, I have always liked his films; he rarely makes a bad one in my opinion, so hey, so much the better for me when I was a lookalike. I do have to say having a resemblance to a famous Hollywood actor has certainly given me a more colourful life than I might have otherwise had. Cheers Tom I owe you one!

CHAPTER 2

AND SO IT BEGINS

It all came about in the mid nineties. Some time had passed and I was now a family man having settled down a few years earlier and I had, at that time a couple of children called Ben and Samuel and was later to have a daughter called Mollie. I had since moved out of Basildon and, with my new family, bought a house for a family home in a place called Benfleet in Essex. Nice little three bed semi. I had settled into being a father and enjoyed every moment of it. I was working as a full time musician, gigging evenings and weekends, my Kirby vacuum cleaner days were behind me by now and as my partner back then didn't work I would drop in and out of either part time or temporary work contracts during the days to supplement the income as and when needed. However, as I say, being a dad was, and is, for me the most important thing to tend. I really love my kids. So despite working hard to support my family I always made time for the children and tried to be the best dad I could be for them. All this family life totally absorbed me and I had not thought about the Tom Cruise thing for a long time. Now at this time I had a 6 month contract working for a local firm selling electrical instruments into the industry as well as gigging. I worked in a typical office environment having a desk, phone, computer etc. 9 to 5 and all that. I hated it. Don't do the 9 to 5 thing very well and can't do the boss thing either. So there I am thinking about chucking the job in when one day I walk into the reception to find that they had recruited a new receptionist, a middle aged lady by the name of Lynn. I got on well with her, we would regale each other with family life stories and generally chit chat about whatever on our breaks. Well one day we we're chatting away when I happened to mention that my musical duo partner, had let me down for a gig at the weekend and I wasn't sure where to get a replacement at such short notice. She mentioned that her son, who was an actor and singer, might be able to help me out. His name was Tim and she gave me his telephone number. So I gave him a call and sure enough he was free that weekend so we arranged to meet up and run through a few songs. When we met up one of the first things he said was "Wow! How much do you look like Tom Cruise?" to which I replied "Boring! How much 'av I been told that?" But he was adamant. He said that as an actor he had a lot of contacts up London and knew of one or two lookalike agencies that might be interested in me. He then said something that intrigued me. Now given as I was just about ready to chuck my day job in he mentioned that lookalikes can earn some really good money for just having a laugh and pretending to look like someone famous. At first I was a little dismissive about it given the fact that for quite a while now that's what people had said to me and I was like "Yeah ok if you say so" and also the fact that I had never particularly seen the resemblance myself; I wasn't really open to the fact that I might be able to take things a little further. Anyway as I'm glad to say now, he was insistent and decided that If I didn't mind could he take a few photos of me and send them off to these agents. Given that I was about to leave my current job and could do with a replacement income, I agreed. He came over to my place with the biggest camera I'd ever seen. Wow; talk about a Willy compensator this thing had a lens extension on it like I'd never seen! He proceeded to take a few photos of me and although I gave it my best shot, I was a little reluctant about all this. He had the photos developed and sent them off to the agents. He also covered a couple of gigs with me and ever since, we have remained good friends. Meantime I was just cracking on with my life when out of the blue, I get a phone call. It was from an agency called

'Susan Scott Lookalikes'. Although the lady on the other end of the phone was not the head honcho, she was the talent scout for the agency. She had seen the photos of me that Tim had sent in and would I like to pop up London and meet with them? It took me by surprise a little bit because all the time Tim was 'givin it the biggun' as it were, I had just thought that he was another 'You look like Tom' merchant and it was all a windup. I gave Tim a call and asked if this was for real to which he replied "Sure is, man, and you should go for it." So I went to London to investigate this lookalike agency. At this point I had no idea what to expect, but I did feel a little apprehensive. Anyway I wore my best suit and tie, stuck a little bit of gel in my hair and, upon arriving, knocked on the door. As it turned out, it was the owner of the agency herself, Susan Scott, who answered the door. Now obviously, at that time, I didn't know who she was so I just said, "Hi, my name's Gary Strohmer and I was asked to pop down" to which she replied, "You really *do* look like him, don't you!" All I could say was "Er, I guess". She looked me up and down a bit and said "You look more like Tom Cruise then the guy we're currently using. How'd you like all his work?" That was the first time I was introduced to the business and how cut throat it could be!

Susan was a no- nonsense business woman and certainly quite mercenary. In fact, a few years later, I was to fall foul of in the same manner as the previous Tom Cruise lookalike she replaced with me. But I don't blame her; I understand business is business and whilst she looked after her lookalikes whilst they were in her camp, her loyalties lay in her purse. The same mercenary streak also made her the best lookalike agency to be with and over the course of my lookalike career, over 50% of all the lookalike work that I did came from her. So bless you, darling! However, mercenary or not, I did quite like her and we got on well in the beginning. So there I was on her doorstep, feeling a bit awkward. She invited me in; I met a few members of staff and she made me a nice cup of tea. Tea, my favourite drink! I drink gallons of the stuff; so much so, that given the fact that I suffer a bit with insomnia, I always have decaff . As it turned out, so did she so we got off to a good start. She asked me a bit about myself, my background and my musical career, which seemed to impress her. I think she liked that I was a bit of a showman; doing lots of gigs in front of sometimes quite large audiences, which of course, held me in good stead for lookalike work. I did adopt the attitude of treating a lookalike gig the same as a band gig but without my guitar which worked well for me through my time as a lookalike. She told me about the business; how much fun it could be, some of the pit falls and how I'd meet lots of interesting 'weird and wonderful' people – and boy, did I! She said about getting some proper photos done in various Tom guises so she could show them to prospective clients. As we concluded, she said something that particularly grabbed my attention. She said that although she couldn't stop me going with other agents, if I was good to her, she would be good to me. I hadn't thought about that as this was all new to me. Other agents? That sounded like a very good idea. If I was going to do this, I might as well get on with as many agents as I could – which was exactly what I did. Maybe being mercenary is infectious!

The first thing I did when I got home was to phone a photo studio that the function band I was in used for our promo photos. The studio had done an excellent job for the band and I felt they would do a good job for me too. Next I went to the local video shop and hired a few Tom films to check out his attire, his mannerisms, his accent etc. You have to bear in mind that this was the days before things like 'Youtube' and 'Netflix'; the internet was only in its infancy back then. Now I've never been good with doing accents and I couldn't really pinpoint any particular inflections or twangs to his voice. But, luckily for me I realised quite soon that this was not going to be a problem as majority of my jobs were things like corporate do's; 'meet and greet, mix and mingle' that sort of thing. For the most part, folk knew they couldn't hire the real thing so they had lookalikes and I soon learnt that as long as you put on the show, that's all they really wanted. So I would always make myself a gregarious, outgoing, almost caricature, portrayal of Tom and they seemed to lap it up.

It's all just entertainment at the end of the day; I was there to entertain and that's what I did best. As I said, a gig but without my guitar. Not all jobs were 'meet and greet, mix and mingle' type things although they were my favourite ones. I did television, adverts, photo shoots etc and occasional modelling jobs; things like catalogue photo shoots such as "Tom wears the latest leather jacket" kind of thing. I didn't like the modelling jobs; they were rather boring and involved a lot of hanging around. However, I digress; back to my promo photos. I went down to the local fancy dress shop and hired a few outfits such as a navel uniform, flying jacket and any other bits and bobs that I thought would look good. I headed off to the photo studio and I was in there for hours; the photographer had my photo taken every which way and when I saw the proofs, I have to say they looked good. He'd done an excellent job on making me look like Tom. So I chose what I thought were the best ones and had them blown up into 6x4's and sent them off to the agency. Within a couple of days, not only was I was up on her website (bearing in mind this was the mid-nineties so the internet was still a newish thing) and I was given my first job. I've dug out a thick folder containing a lot of stuff from when I first started, as memory joggers, and I've found some of the photos that were taken of me that got me started as a lookalike.

I also took the opportunity to ingratiate myself with the other lookalike agencies. There were a few about at the time; Derricks Doubles, Splitting Images, Class Act UK, Celebrity Lookalikes, Business Development Promotions and Debbie's Doubles, to name but a few. I sent my photos off to all of them and one by one, they took me on. Although, as I said, Susan Scott lookalikes got me the majority of the jobs, there was another good one called A List Lookalikes, who got me practically everything else; they even sent me to Italy for a few days once! They came from up north so I didn't get to meet them for a while but the other agencies would filter the odd job my way and in the end, I worked for all of them. In the beginning, it all happened so fast. From my friend Tim sending off a photo of me to me doing my first job was literally

15

only about two weeks and it hadn't really sunk in that I was a real life lookalike. I hadn't had much of an opportunity to tell anyone about it and when I did, they thought it was a Gary wind up; except my kids and they were really excited. The first thing they did was to tell their mates at school and it spread like wild fire 'cos when I went to pick them up that afternoon (given the fact that I had only just told them that morning) all the kids came out pointing at me calling, "Oi Tom, can I have your autograph? Ha ha!" My kids were dead proud of their dad and that really made me feel good. Can't beat being a dad.

And so, onto my first lookalike job.

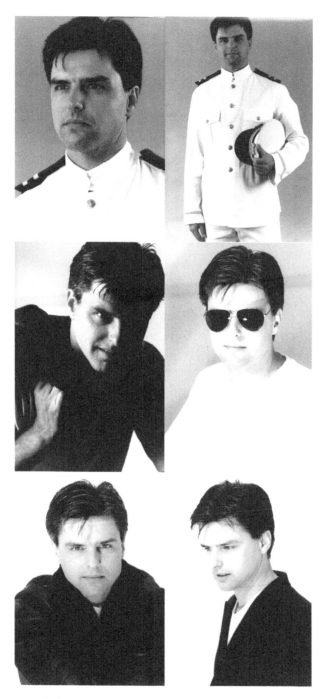

Some of the Tom Cruise pictures of me that the agents
used to promote me as lookalike.

CHAPTER 3

EASY DAYS

What I'd like to say here is that it's one thing to be told you look like someone famous and have a laugh with it but it's an entirely different beast to be booked and paid to pretend to be that person. The pressure was on, or so I thought. However, I soon got into the swing of it and thoroughly enjoyed myself but I always held in the back of my mind that I was getting paid so always tried to be as professional as I could. Some jobs were more unusual than others, although having said that, no two jobs were ever quite the same. However, they did fall into broad categories; the 'meet and greet mix and mingle' which were my personal favourite, the television and filming work, where a lot of my mishaps happened, or the openings ceremonies etc. Here's a few of my more memorable one's for you to enjoy:

The phone call came through from the agent; would I do a job in Wales? It was to open a new UCI cinema in Cardiff town centre. This job was to be done with a Mel Gibson lookalike, a guy by the name of Kim Carron. We were to do a meet and greet and then a question and answer session to give away tickets for the premier showing of their film showing and free tickets for the whole of the next year to one lucky winner. The local press were going to be there as well as the local radio station and the whole event was well promoted. I've done a lot of gigs and spent a lot of time on the stage so I don't frighten or get nervous easily. But this was my first time doing anything like this and to be honest, I did feel a little apprehensive; the fear of the unknown. So I was very glad that I was doing my first job with Kim who had been a lookalike for a couple of years and knew what to expect. He lived round by Hounslow and the agent had given me his telephone number so we could make our arrangements and travel down together. We had to be there by 11am on the day so I got up real early, about 4am (and being a muso, that's often the sort of time I would go to bed!) I drove round the M25 and met Kim at his place. We transferred to his car and made our way to Cardiff down the M4. He drove so that gave me time to catch up on some sleep. It was a long ol' drive but we got there in good time; in fact we were a little too early and so had time for a spot of breakfast. This was handy because, having been asleep most of the way, I hadn't really had the chance to get to know him or pick his brains about what to expect. So over breakfast, that's what I did. It turned out he was a van driver for a living so, apart from a few lookalike jobs, he had no experience in showmanship other than what he had picked up along the way. He had just split up with his wife so his head was up his arse and, although he was a smashing bloke, wasn't able to be of much help at the time. So I kind of thought 'Well Gal, your just gonna have to wing it'. Luckily for me, having done more than a few dodgy gigs in my time, I can be quite good at that!

My brief was to go in the character of Jerry Maguire which basically involved me wearing a suit jacket and trousers over a tee-shirt kind of look (which was very common for Tom.) Kim did his Mel Gibson thing in the changing room that we were given and so we prepared. After having a chat with our contact and the organiser, we were ready to go. We stepped out of the door to be met with a barrage of flashes from all the press cameras that were there. There were loads of them; far more than we expected. It was all a bit overwhelming to be honest as people kept shouting "Tom, Mel!" It put us on the back foot; it was all too much and we certainly were not prepared for all this. We found out later that it had actually been put out that the real Mel and Tom were going to be there hence the "over the top" reaction. I wasn't sure what to do or how to handle it and neither was Kim. I thought that, as this is my first job, what I do now is either going to make or break me in the lookalike world. So I thought, 'Fuck it, let's have it' and with that I stepped forward and in my loudest (and phoniest American accent) I boomed, "Hi, how you doing? Tom's the name, promotion's the game!" They lapped it up! Phew, I thought, that worked so off I went and did 'a gig without my guitar'. I really enjoyed myself and luckily, Kim backed me up and followed suit. It was a bit like the blind leading the blind but we just followed our instincts and soon got into the flow of things. We were signing autographs, shaking hands, posing for the press, kissing all the local girls; it was great! After about 30 minutes, we were ushered into the back of the cinema, ready to come out onto the stage in front of the cinema screen where there was a plush table with a red silk cloth on and microphones as well as a couple of seats for us to plonk ourselves in. Things had calmed down by now, probably because most folk had realised by now we were not the real thing. But, hey, they seemed to like to pretend anyway and, enjoying ourselves as much as we were, who were we to deny them? It's amazing the power of suggestion, isn't it? People had been told that the real articles were going to be there so they just seemed to believe it and for a little while, that's how they treated us. It was fun for us, because of it not being real, but can you imagine living your whole life like that? At least we could play our parts and then go home; the real Tom has to live with that every day. Sounds good but not if you can't ever get away from it. No wonder these guys become reclusive. Anyway, we did a question and answer session in front of a large cinema full of the local folk. We would ask pre-set questions that we had been given about who starred in what film or who directed what and a chap with a cordless microphone would dash about the audience to whoever had their hand up. There were a lot of people so it was just the luck of the draw who got to answer and I'm glad to say, not down to me. Then they would come up onto the stage. After about ten minutes of this and a stage of about twenty people, we finished the questions. There was a final show down; Kim had to ask a sudden death question and the quickest to answer would be the winner. God knows what the question was because as he stood up with his mike and started to speak, a rather large woman dashed up on stage, grabbed hold of me and proceeded to try and snog my face off! I was sprawled out on the floor as she pinned me down using all her weight. I could hardly breathe, let alone call for help, when a couple of burly blokes seemed to appear out of nowhere and pulled her off me. How does that always seem to happen? Whenever I've got into a fight or trouble on a gig or something, which was not often, there are always some burly blokes who just appear out of nowhere and pull us apart! They sort it all out, usually shouting the words like, "Leave it! Leave it!" and then disappear. I don't get it. Weird but true. So there I was sprawled out and prostrate on the floor, as this woman was being lifted off me, she was saying "Sorry mate, I'm such a Tom fan and this is the nearest thing I'm ever going to get to kissing him". Bless her; imagine being such a Tom Cruise fan that you are driven to do something like that. I almost felt sorry for her. I'm such a sucker for a hard luck story which, as it turned out, was the case with the old geezer who actually won the competition. His story was that his wife had died the year before and between them they had raised their only granddaughter because their daughter, the girls mother, had died of cancer some 5 years before. The granddaughter was only 7 so we got her up on stage. She rushed up, hugging her grandfather with tears in her eyes and I heard her say "We never win anything, do we Grandpa?" It was so moving. We had lots of photos taken with them and the day came to a close. What a great day and my first experience as a lookalike. I remember sitting in the dressing room afterwards when Kim turned to me and said, "Wow, I never had a job go like that. How about that bloke and his granddaughter!" to which our eyes started to fill up. As this was my first experience doing a lookalike job and given how it ended so overwhelmingly, I did wonder how things would go from then on. But how perfect for the cinema promoters? It couldn't have been a more fairy tale ending if it had tried. The local press lapped it up and the promoter sent a glowing report back to the lookalike agent saying that the boys they sent down did an absolutely wonderful job. And so ended my entry into the world of the lookalikes.

Many years later I went to Cardiff. My sister Tina had long ago got married, had a family and moved to Abergavenny in South Wales. I like to go and visit her when I get the chance with my daughter, to keep in touch with her cousins. Recently on a trip there I took my daughter Mollie, and my niece and nephew, Amy and Joe, to the Doctor Who exhibition on a day trip out. We visited that cinema (which has now become a VUE cinema) and on the wall there was a plaque with a picture of when the place was opened and there at the bottom, is a photo of me and Kim cutting the ribbon that opened the place. Gosh, I looked young!

My first solo gig as a lookalike, although a little less traumatic, was no less memorable. All lookalikes jobs, by their very nature, are eventful and this being the first on my own, it will always stick in my mind. Bit like remembering your first kiss. Nothing particularly bad or untoward happened, (as did on a few other occasions that I shall be writing about in the following chapters.) It was just that this was my first solo flight without any help or back up from other, more experienced lookalikes to give you a little nudge in the right direction. So I kind of felt like I was performing without a safety net. One thing I will say is that us lookalikes did watch out for each other. There was always quite a degree of camaraderie amongst us and when I first started, not knowing much about it all, getting a pointer or two when needed did come in handy. The more experienced looked after the newbies as did I later on when I had a few miles under my own belt.

This first solo gig was up in Dewsbury near Leeds and was for a company called 'Principles Public Relations' which, as the name suggests, was the public relations arm of its parent company, 'Cable Tel Kirklees' . They are a large cable T.V. provider in and around that area. They were launching a new film channel called 'Front Row' and were promoting it using the local press and radio stations. To help get people's attention, they had decided to run a lookalike competition they were calling 'Search for a Star' and invited the local folk to send in photos of themselves. Then they had hired a Hollywood lookalike for the day (me) to spearhead the campaign. The whole competition was going to be judged by a soap star, Emmedale's Malandra Burrows, who played the character of Kathy Glover. She was in the show from 1985 to 2001 and according to what I was told, she was one of the highest paid soap stars at the time. This was the first time, or so I thought, that I was going to meet a real celeb during my lookalike career but the problem was (and no offence to Malandra), not being a watcher of the soaps, I didn't know who she was. So the first thing I had to do when I accepted the job was to do a little bit of research on her so that when I got there, it looked like I knew what I was talking about. Always loved a bit of bluff and bluster when I didn't really know what I was doing. We musos call it busking and to be honest, I've busked my way through most of my life. The winner of the competition would be spending an all-expenses paid weekend in London. This included being taken to Planet Hollywood in a chauffeur driven limousine and generally getting a full on pampering. They would also meet Malandra Burrows and get to spend a little time with her, having their mug shots splashed all over the local papers and stuff. Sounded good to me and if I wasn't already a lookalike, I would have probably entered the competition myself, just for a bit of a laugh. Now it was a long drive from where I lived and an early start so I booked myself into the local Travel Inn up there and drove up the night before. The next morning I drove to the address given and met my contact, a lady by the name of Suzanna Johns, who gave me my brief for the day. It turned out that Suzanna was quite the Tom Cruise fan which is why, after a little persuasion on her part (as they had originally planned to use the Jack Nicholson lookalike,) they chose to use me instead which I was most grateful for. I did feel a little nervous. Not because of the gig that lay ahead of me but, and this might seem a little strange given as I had already done that job in Cardiff and given that for all parties concerned I had been accepted and taken on as the Tom Cruise lookalike by the agencies. But as I mentioned earlier, I personally never really saw anything but a passing resemblance to dear old Tom myself so was a bit worried that the client upon seeing me might feel the same way. I have to say it took me a few jobs back then when I first started to overcome that particular feeling of apprehension. But in the end, I accepted that other people thought that I did indeed look like him; well, they kept telling me often enough and employing my services to pretend to be him and at the end of the day that was all that mattered I suppose.

This event had been getting heavily promoted by the local radio station all week as well as in a couple of the local rags so they were expecting a good turnout. They had hired a shop front in the local shopping mall and I was allowed to use the shop's changing rooms to get into character. It was getting on for 9am by now, show time, so I didn't have long and I could hear the hustle and bustle of the crowd gathering outside. It was quite a big crowd as it turned out. The local press where there with their photographers as well as the radio station who had set up a P.A. system and, using one of the DJs doing a live broad cast, were working the crowd. As I was not displaying myself as a character from one of his films, more playing the part of Tom Cruise the actor himself, again I used the suit jacket and tee-shirt look that was popular with him back then. Suzanne popped her head around the changing room curtain seeing if I was ready and it was all systems go. I just had time to gel my hair when I heard the call "And now ladies and gentlemen please would you welcome..... Mr TOM CRUISE!" I stepped out from behind the certain to be met with a rousing cheer and a thunderous round of applause. Putting on my biggest Hollywood smile, I stepped out from the shop door and on to the platform where I shook hands with the DJ. We were live on the radio at this point and in front of this live audience, he started asking me questions such as what it was like to be a lookalike, how long I had been doing it for and did I have some advice for any of the budding wannabe lookalikes out there? Well, this was only my second ever job as a lookalike so I had virtually no experience at all to draw upon and as I hadn't been prepped for this part of the gig, I was totally unprepared. What I was meant to say? The crowd fell silent in anticipation of my response. I stared blankly at him for what seemed like forever while the cogs where turning in my head. In reality it was probably only a few seconds but long enough for him to want to start to repeat the question. Just in the nick of time, I cut him off at the pass. The busker in me kicked in and I launched into an animated regalia of how I had started many years ago and a few funny anecdotes of jobs past. God knows how, but I managed to make the DJ chuckle and pass a few laughs in to the crowd and it all went down rather well. Little did I know back then that it wouldn't be the last time I would have to bluff myself out of a sticky lookalike situation! I then went in to a rehearsed script about the benefits of the new 'Front Row' channel, which of course was what the whole event was about in the first place, and wound down with a few handshakes. After the interview I stepped down to the side of the stage and signed a few autographs for a while and had lots of photos taken with various people for the benefit of the local press who were lapping it up. Then off for a tea break (of course). Now Malandra Burrows, the soap star, was on her way apparently to do the same as I had done up on the stage but I was asked if I could go on to another local radio station, the B.B.C's one this time, to do another interview. It meant that I had to go to their studios down the road and Suzanne, my original contact, not wanting to miss an additional opportunity for a bit more 'Front Row' promotion, asked me if I would. So I left in a taxi before Miss Burrows turned up and as I did not return till after she had gone, I completely missed her. The second interview was pretty much along the lines of what I had been asked on the first interview on the stage so this time I was a little more prepared. The only thing was, because I had made it up on the spot, I couldn't always remember what I had said the first time. However, I think I got away with it as they all seemed happy enough. I was beginning to realise by now that this line of work was defiantly not for the timid! When I arrived back to the shopping mall, the crowd had dispersed and the stage was being dismantled ready for transport back to base. Suzanne and I had a bit of lunch with some of the rest of the crew after which, being finished for the day, I made my way back to my car and set off on the long drive home. With my first solo lookalike gig under my belt, I had a great sense of job satisfaction and had a big grin on my face all the way home.

This was a really nice thing, I thought. A few days later I got a letter in the post from Suzanne which read as follows:-

Dear Gary,

I just wanted to write and thank you on behalf of everyone at CableTel Kirklees and Principles Public Relations, for making the launch of Front Row in Huddersfield and Dewsbury, such a successful event. We are anticipating some good coverage in the local press and will make sure you get a selection of copies of whatever comes through.

We were all very impressed with the way you handled both radio interviews – just took it in your stride as if you'd been doing it for years! But seriously, your contribution to the interviews formed a vital part of raising the awareness of Front Row.

I have been in touch with Susan Scott and passed on our comments, so hopefully, even more bookings will come your way. As I said to Helena, at Susan Scott, I certainly won't hesitate in recommending you to anyone looking for a Tom Cruise lookalike, and will keep you in mind for any future events or press calls we may have.

Thanks once again for all your help – hope you had a good journey home, and we wish you all the best in your future lookalike career!

Kindest regards. Yours sincerely,

Suzanne Johns Manager

How nice was that?

CHAPTER 4

THE LIMELIGHT CLUB/
HIPPODROME INCIDENT

One of my earlier jobs was a gig at the Limelight night club, Shaftsbury Avenue in London. I had a few jobs under my belt by now and was settling into my lookalike role quite comfortably. My agent contacted me; was I free on such and such a date to do a 'mix and mingle' for a rather important client called Unique Entertainment Productions and Design Ltd? I was told that they were a TV production company that did a lot of work for the independent channels. It was the managing director's birthday which also happened to coincide with the firm's annual do. The M.D. was a lady called Sue Bradbury and apparently she was a real Tom Cruise fan. The company had also hired the Limelight night club and had organised a casino evening and then a disco later that night. This was in addition to a reception room at the Hippodrome, which was located around the corner from the Limelight club. All sounds a bit longwinded and complicated and, I believe, might well have contributed to the forth coming mishap. It all must have cost a fortune but then again this M.D. lady, Sue, was rather a V.I.P. and well known in the business circles. The day was to start at the Hippodrome club where the event Co. WWAV, were going to kick off the day's events with a champagne reception then move events over to the Limelight club later on. My remit was to turn up at the Hippodrome and meet up with a lady by the name of Ann Williams, at 6pm and get my briefing as to what they wanted from me for the evening events. Over a glass of champagne, she told me that Sue would be turning up at 8pm and although she would know about the evening's events, she would have had no idea Tom was going to be there. It was to be a surprise for her as a little birthday treat. After a drink or two, I was then to escort her round the corner to the Limelight club making it look like we were on a date. She also told me that the lady in question liked a man in uniform. Well, it just so happened that one amongst the couple of outfits I had fetched along with me that evening was a bright white naval officers uniform so I wore that. Once at the Limelight, I was to mix and mingle for a couple of hours with the guests and then I would be done. At the end of the brief she added that it had "accidently" been leaked out to the Paparazzi that the real Tom was in town and out on a secret date at the afore mentioned clubs with an unknown female. The real Tom, at this time, was married to Nicole Kidman so, look out, a scandal brewing! However it didn't quite all work out as planned.

So the scene was set and by half past seven I was suited and booted looking as Tomish as I could, chatting with the other guest's waiting for the M.D. to arrive. At ten to eight I was ushered into a side room, (after all I was supposed to be a surprise,) where I waited, and waited, and waited, and waited some more. By about 8.30 I poked my head around the door and whispered to Ann, "What's happening? Has Sue turned up yet?". "No, she's not here. Go back inside and I'll find out what's going on" came the reply from a flustered and slightly panicking Ann. So after about another half an hour Ann pops into the room I'm still waiting in, pulls me out and announces to everyone, "Sorry people, it doesn't look like Sue is coming to night. Better all make your way round to the Limelight club and we'll continue from there." So off everyone shuffled... everyone that is, except me. Ann grabbed me by the arm saying, "Hang back for a bit Gary, let them disperse first; the Paparazzi are still waiting outside the main entrance and have been for a while now so they're baying for blood!" I would imagine so having been told Tom Cruise and his secret girlfriend were supposed to have been and gone about an hour ago. I think I would be pissed off too. "Go out the side door next to the main entrance and make your way round to the other club. Hopefully, they won't notice you" said a very embarrassed and stressed Ann followed by, "I'm really sorry about this. Apparently she has had a better offer". A better offer? Wonder what it was that could have been better than *this*? The Hippodrome and Limelight night club all laid on for your birth-day, a Tom Cruise lookalike, in a uniform, for an escort, (especially if you are a Tom fan,(granted she didn't know about the Tom bit,) and even the Paparazzi there to take her photo for the morning papers. What more could a woman ask for? I never did find out what the better offer was. It must have been bloody good though; maybe she really had gone on a secret date with the real Mr. Cruise and this was her way of deflecting the attention. Clever girl! So I slipped out of the side door, only to realise that it was only a few yards away from where the Paparazzi were standing when I heard one of them shout, "Look there he is! Tom, Tom, give us a smile!" At which point they all started to run for me. I legged it as fast as I could, heading in the direction of the Limelight club. Luckily it wasn't too far away, just up the end of the road and round the corner. Man, these guys were fast; I suppose they had to be given their line of work. I was struggling to keep ahead of them and it was all a bit scary. As I rounded the corner, I noticed a couple of door men had the main entrance door held open for me but, unfortunately, they had realised what was going on and even though they knew I was not the real article, decided to join in the fun. "Tom, Tom, over here, son!" they shouted with big smiles on their faces. "Hurry up or they're gonna get ya"! Good grief, this was the last thing I needed; it whipped the Paparazzi into even more of a frenzy. They really were like a pack of hounds and unless you have ever been in that situation, it's hard to describe how scary it becomes. I glanced back over my shoulder and noticed that one of them had broken ahead of the rest of the pack and was gaining on me fast. As

I approached the entrance, which by now was only a few feet away, the guy caught up with me grabbed me by the shoulder, span me around looked me straight in the eye and said, and I quote, "Oh fuck!.... I feel like a right mug now!" It completely changed the atmosphere in an instant, and as he uttered those unforgettable words, I could see the look on his face as he realised I was not the real deal; it went from glee to utter disappointment as he spoke. It was hilarious! And, of course, it ended the chase immediately. I was laughing so hard I couldn't catch my breath as I staggered into the club with the doors closing behind me. I can see why they call the Paparazzi "sharks"; I certainly thought I was going to be eaten alive at the time. Apparently, that little incident made one of the national papers the next day; I wish I could have seen it.

The rest of the evening pretty much went as planned. Once I had composed myself, I stepped out into the crowd at the Limelight club and, during my mix and mingle duties, proceeded to regale the folk with the story of what had just happened. It helped the rest of the evening go smoothly and at one point, I had a little crowd around me as I retold the story for the umpteenth time. They loved it as it made them laugh. I felt like the story teller in Jackanory except it wasn't just a Jackanory, it was true. The night came to a close and after I got changed back into my 'civvies', I made my way to Fenchurch Street station and caught the train home to Benfleet. All the way home I had an enormous grin on my face as I recalled the evenings events and I remember thinking to myself, 'All that – and I got paid'!

It's funny; you don't realise it at the time but some of the best times you have in life are when things don't go to plan, or things happen unexpectedly, and you have to kind of wing it. And so it was with the lookalike stuff as well. That's probably why I remember this particular story so well. Sometimes when life's getting me down, as it does to all of us from time to time, I think of this incident and it never fails to put a smile on my face.

CHAPTER 5

THE BIG BREAKFAST SHOW

Back in the Nineties, there was a television program that used to be on 7am on Channel Four each day called The Big Breakfast show. It was done as a live broadcast and was a very popular program at the time, attracting something like eight to ten million viewers depending on what day of the week it was. One of the reasons it was so popular was because back in the day when Sky TV was not so prevalent and we didn't have digital T.V. there wasn't a 24 hour news channel, just rather bland morning shows. Now, as I say, this show was transmitted live and, not taking itself too seriously, was just fun to watch. So it made a good back drop for the nation when everyone was getting up and getting ready for work. It was hosted by Johnny Vaughan and, originally Denise Van Outan who was later to be replaced by Kelly Brook. The set was made to look like the inside of a house and they would sit at a table at one end of the room and 'strut their funky stuff' so to speak, from there. We used to have it on in our household whist the kids were getting ready for school and I would be getting ready for work. I enjoyed it a lot; it was off the cuff and funny and I loved Johnny Vaughan's sense of humour. He was always taking the piss out of something or other, never in a nasty way, but very humours. My kind of guy. Now around the same sort of time, there was a burst in popularity of the Jerry Springer type talk shows. I'm sure you know the type of show

I'm talking about; they would advertise and invite members of the audience out there in TV Land to come on the show and air all their dirty laundry in public, in front of an a live audience. The show guests would always be rather inarticulate, attention seeking low lives who had not a lot to say and said it far too loudly. They never seemed to have a job and always on benefits of some kind. Slobby, fat single mums with half a dozen kids by half a dozen different blokes who never seemed to be sure which kid matched up to which parent and all that sort of thing. We would always moan about the different guests each week, being judgemental of them and listening to them swearing their heads off to each other, yet for some strange reason it was very compelling viewing and became enormously popular. I used to watch them myself sometimes. Then came the English version popularized by the likes of Robert Kilroy-Silk. Being English, they were a little tamer than the American version but no less moronic; yet it still was compelling viewing, (the modern version is the Jeremy Kyle show.) It was kind of the start of the reality show phenomenon which overwhelms us today. Everyone jumped on the band wagon and they sprang up all over the place. The TV and radio show host, Vanessa Feltz, started doing one that became popular and being Mr. Average TV Audience Man, I watched a few of her shows myself. Then came an article in one of the national newspapers questioning whether the guests were actually real. The article was specifically targeting the Vanessa show and, unfortunately for Vanessa, as the story ran, it gathered momentum. The British public love a good scandal and a gossip and it all ended in being a big deal in the public eye. Looking back, I think we viewers didn't like the idea of being duped in such a manner and fuelled by the papers lust for sensationalism, it seemed to put an end to her show. It quickly went off air never to be heard from again. I remember at the time feeling a little sorry for Vanessa because although she was the presenter of the show, it wouldn't have been specifically her fault. It would have been the producer's idea but she was the one who got it in the neck because *she* was the one the viewers saw. However, as always in these cases, it soon and became yesterday's news and was quickly forgotten; the press and collective public consciousness moved onto the next latest scandal and Vanessa moved on to hosting another TV show. Now back to Johnny Vaughn and his big breakfast show. Apparently he had a lot of say in the content of his show and given the fact that he had this lovely 'take the piss' sense of humour, decided that he would have a few 'real' guests on his show and so came the phone call to me from my lookalike agent.

The phone rang. "Hi Gary are you free on this particular Friday to appear on the Big breakfast show for Channel Four?" to which I of course replied, "Yes" and we started to talk about the details. I was to be there at 5am, *how early*? We musicians don't do early; that's not too far past our bed time, let alone getting up at silly o'clock! Often I'd gig 'till midnight and wouldn't get home until 2ish in the morning and even then you couldn't go straight to bed because it takes a while to unwind. So the ol' body clock gets very out of sync with the rest of the world. They were going to send a car to pick me up at about 4am to get me to the studios so that they would then have a good couple of hours to set everything up, makeup, get the studio ready for the days shoot etc. They were going to be using a couple of other lookalikes as well; a George Clooney and an Elton John. The day before, I happened to be watching the Big Breakfast show whilst having a lay in when Johnny Vaughan started talking about his special guests that they were having on the show the next day in a very tongue in cheek manner; hinting that it had something to do with what had been in the papers recently. He was funny but listening to him, I realised that I hadn't really thought about this beforehand; the show was going to be broadcast live and in front of *how many viewers*? I didn't actually know how many at this point but I knew it was a lot and this was going to be going out all over the country. Although I'm not a nervous person by nature, I did start to get a few butterflies in my stomach. So that day I reminded my kids about it on the way to school; they were getting all excited and couldn't wait to tell everyone at school about their dad being on the telly tomorrow. They were so proud of me bless them, I was their hero for the day. That night, I set up the video recorder to record the program in the morning and tried to get an early night. But as I said, my body clock was so out of sync, I didn't actually manage to get off to sleep 'till about 2am only to rudely awoken by the alarm at 3! Don't know what's worse; not bothering to go to sleep at all or waking up after only an hour. I really couldn't gather myself together. I had a shower and a little breakfast. God, breakfast at 3am! I gathered my 'Tom' clothes that I was going to be wearing that day; I had been asked to do the "Top Gun" look so I had the leather flying jacket, sun glasses, tea shirt and jeans with boots. I sat on the settee waiting for the car to pick me up and promptly fell asleep. I could have only been a matter of minutes when I was awoken by the sound of a car horn outside. I staggered outside with my clothes bag over my shoulder, all bleary eyed, to be met by the biggest and shiniest limousine I had ever seen. Wow, I thought, this will get the neighbours gossiping, especially next door. They were always going on about how well off they were and they had a thing about their cars in particular and how they could afford much better than the rest of us down the street. Like I gave a toss; but I did give a little smile when I saw their curtains twitching, having a nose at me. I couldn't resist giving them a sarcastic wave as the chauffeur opened the door. I settled in the back, yawning my head off. The driver noticed this, turned to me and said, "Want a little something to wake up mate?" "What?" I said. "Here you are, have one of these". He held out what looked like a little white pill. "No thanks" I replied "that's not my thing, a kip will do for me". "No worries" came the response and with that we set off for London. By the end of the road, I was fast asleep.

We arrived at the studios about an hour later and I was feeling more refreshed by now and met up with the other two lookalikes down in the canteen. I knew these guys, having worked with then once or twice before and, over a cup of strong coffee to help wake us up, we had a catch up. If you're in the business for long enough, you do get to know all the other lookalikes. Although one or two of them do get up their own asses sometimes (prima-donnas who think they're really stars) most of them are friendly enough;

just ordinary folk like me taking advantage of a quirk of nature. I offered to pay for the drinks but when I got to the counter, I realised I had forgotten my wallet, as well as my door keys and my phone, (even though mobile phones were big clunky things back then, I had still managed to leave it behind.) Ever had that sinking feeling when you have thought you lost your wallet? I realised that what had happened is when I picked up my lookalike costume bag, I then forgot my jacket with everything in it and hadn't noticed 'till then. It's always a little embarrassing when that sort of thing happens but, hey, we've all done it. I started to think, 'How the hell am I going to get home later?' but before I had a chance to start worrying about it, one of the programs gofers came and fetch us. Off we went to the makeup room where we got changed and had our hair and makeup done. After this we were ushered into a kind of anteroom where any guests on the show get briefed before they go on about what's happening and what they need to do. One of the producers, as well as Johnny Vaughan himself, popped in to have a chat with us lookalikes. I found him to be really personable and friendly and not at all like one or two of the celebrities that I have worked with over the course of my lookalike time. Most were OK but some could be quite arrogant and, on occasion, downright obnoxious. They would appear to be nice guys in front of the camera but behind the scenes; all I can say is that it is the fans that put them there, not their god given right to be where they are. Now we had no idea what Johnny and Kelly (as in Kelly Brook, the female host of the show at the time) were going to be like but as it turned out, they were great. He was chatty and made us feel right at ease, asking us about our lookalike work and jobs we had done when I happened to mention about the forgotten wallet/jacket saga and didn't know how I was going to get home. He said, "Where do live?" "Benfleet, in Essex" I replied. "Hang on a mo" he responded and disappeared, only to reappear a minute later saying, "No worries, Tom." I nearly always got called Tom on my lookalike jobs. It was rare to be called by my real name but you get used to it, "I've had a quick word with my driver and he will drop you off home in my car". How nice was that? I didn't really get to talk to Kelly very much but I got the impression she wasn't there for her brains. But, wow, what a stunner; she was beautiful. It was about 6.30 in the morning by now and things were winding up ready for the day's show. He explained to us about the false guest wind-up thing they wanted to do, although we pretty much knew that was the case anyway, and how he wanted us to play it. I was to be the first one out from behind the curtain and was look as much like Tom as possible (and I have to say the makeup crew did a fantastic job,) but then to obviously not be him by greeting everyone in the best cockney accent I could muster. Then the other two were to follow suit. I asked Johnny how many people they expected to have viewing the show and he said that he couldn't be certain but it would be around the ten million mark for that day, explaining that Fridays were always the highest viewer days. "My word" I said in a rather loud voice, "how many?" Well, actually it was rather more of an expletive than that; I didn't mean to say it but it just came out. I didn't know what I was expecting but ten million people; it kind of took me by surprise. It was a far cry from gigging down the local social club in front of an audience of 50 – and that was on a good night. Luckily, no one took offence; in fact it made ol' Johnny chuckle. Seven o'clock came around and time for the show to start. So there we were, waiting in the wings, when we heard the set director shout, "Quiet on the set please. We are on in 10, 9, 8, 7, 6, 5, 4, *, *, * …" (that was the silent count at the end of the countdown) "Good morning, Britain!" said Johnny in a nice booming voice, "How we all doing today?" followed by, "We've got a delight for you today, ladies and gentlemen. In a couple of minutes we have some very special guests coming on the show; world famous with a sprinkling of Hollywood to boot." Then in a very tongue-in-cheek voice, "and they are the real deal" and with a wink at the camera, "if you know what I mean". It's just the way he said it in his inimitable style; it cracked us all up, including the camera crew and the rest of the support staff. "But before that over to you, Kelly" who started talking about what was on the rest of the show. After a couple of minutes we were up. "Now ladies and gentlemen," piped up Johnny, "as promised, our very special guests for the day......" he left it hanging for a moment, "A nice big hand if you will, please welcome Mr. TOM CRUISE!" and with that I stepped out from behind the curtain to a huge round of applause and whooping from everyone. I stood there posing, as much like Tom Cruise as possible, with the biggest Hollywood smile I could muster. As the applause started to die down, I took another step forward, stuck my thumbs up, and in the roughest, loudest Cockney accent I could manage boomed, "Ol 'right everybody 'ows it going?" to which everybody started laughing and a whooping once again and I have to say I was finding it hard not to laugh my myself. I was invited forward to have a seat on the guests' settee. As the laughing subsided the camera focused back to Johnny and Kelly where, with furrowed brows, they started looking first at me then back to the camera a few times in quick succession. Sort of doing double takes. I found it all very funny and felt myself having to suppress a fit of the giggles as I was supposed to sit there with a straight face which of course, made it all the harder. "Erm....... ok" came a pseudo perplexing cry from Johnny as the camera panned back to the entrance curtain. Johnny carried on. "Ladies and gentlemen, please welcome Mr. GEORGE CLOONEY!" to which the George lookalike stepped out from the curtain to a similar reception as me, again waited 'till it all died down and said in the campest voice I have ever heard, "Why, hello" to which everyone cracked up again. I know I was instructed to sit there with a straight face but I just couldn't hold it in any longer and I burst out laughing. Luckily for me, the camera wasn't on me at that point so I got away with it. As with me, George was directed to the settee, so mincing his way over, he sat down next to me in the middle to a similarly perplexed Johnny and Kelly. It was a similar thing with the Elton John lookalike and ended with all three of us sitting on the guest settee. As it happened, I was sitting at the end where the actual settee camera was and it was only about a foot from my face. Johnny said "Wait a minute! You're all fakes!" and with that, I noticed out of the corner of my eye, a little red light come on this particular camera which meant it was the one filming at the time. I didn't show it but the thought that went through my head at that moment was, 'Shit! There's about ten million people looking at me right now'. I leave it to your imagination as to how that felt. At that point, we lookalikes were met with a rousing chant of "Fake! Fake! Fake! Fake! Fake!" from every one there as Johnny stood up and with great arm gesticulation and gusto in his voice, shouted, "Get out, you fakes!" At that point, as was our brief, we three lookalikes stood up and, with great pretend indignation, marched off the set.

When we were off set and out of sight of the cameras and everybody working there, we all breathed a sigh of relief and received a pat on the back from the producers who were saying, "Nice job, boys. We're well pleased with that; it couldn't have gone any better if we tried." We all shuffled back to the changing rooms, feeling very full of ourselves and discussing what had just transpired with great glee. With a nice cup of well-earned tea in our hands, we had our makeup cleaned off, changed back in to our normal cloths and prepared to bid our goodbyes to each other 'till the next time our paths crossed. At which point, I felt a tap on the back. I turned around and found myself staring right at the chest, (which was at my head height and I'm five foot eleven,) of an enormous mountain of a man who said in the deepest of voices, "ello, Tom". Well I did not know what to make of this so I took a step back, arching my neck up to look him in the eye. "I'm 'ere for you" came that gruff voice again. "Bloody hell," I cried "who have I upset?" A great big grin crossed his face as he replied "Nah, you're all right. Johnny sent me; had a word with me earlier said you might need a lift home? I'm his driver, Dave". "Oh right" I said heaving a sigh of relief for the second time that morning. So I grabbed my stuff and he led me out of the building to the poshest Jaguar I had ever seen. He kindly opened the rear door and I stepped inside. It was lovely inside; plush leather seats, a little TV and even a drinks cabinet. Dave somehow managed to squeeze himself into the driver's side, started up the car and off we went. I asked him if he needed directions to Benfleet but he reckoned he knew where it was and we headed out of London and east along the A13 road toward home. I asked would he mind if I had a little kip to which he replied with a chuckle in his voice, "Yeah, I have that effect on people" followed by, "Go for it." I sprawled myself out right across the back seat and dosed off. I awoke about 9am and just before the Benfleet area so I directed Dave to where I lived. As we pulled up outside my house, I noticed the net curtains twitching from the nosey neighbour next door once again. Dave come around to the rear door and opened it for me. I grabbed my stuff and as I stepped out I said "Cheers, Dave". "No worries" came the reply, "See you around sometime" and with that I strolled to my front door with a great big cheesy grin on my face; giving the next door's another little sarcastic wave as I went. And so ended one of my favourite TV lookalike jobs.

Later that afternoon at about 3pm it was time to pick my kids, Ben and Samuel, up from school. It was within easy walking distance and quite a nice day so I walked down there and waited at the gates with all the other parents. If you're a parent, you'll know that you tend to get to know some of the other parents. For the most part, its mums and mums being mums, often like to have a little girly chat between themselves about whatever the latest gossip is for that day... and that day, it was me! They were all looking at me , pointing and chatting, when a couple of the mums that I had got to know through my kids being friends with their kids, came up to me and said, "We watched you on the telly this morning. It was good. Don't you look like him? How long have you been doing lookalike work for?" and other such stuff. One or two of them, the ones that I had got to know over the course of time, already knew I was a lookalike but a lot of them didn't so it was all a bit of a novelty for them; a nice bit of gossip but I didn't mind, bless them. Now one woman, a single mum, who happened to be a bit of a George Clooney fan, started asking me about the George lookalike. What was he like, where did he live, did he really look like him in real life and of course was he single? To which I replied, "As far as I know, he is". Then she said, all red faced and embarrassed, "Don't suppose you could give him my telephone number, could you?" and pushed a bit of paper into my hand. I felt really awkward. I didn't really like being put into this position and didn't know what to say to her but, as luck would have it, the school bell went and all the kids started rushing out. Talk about being 'saved by the bell'! Now kids, being kids, would usually rush up to their parents, excitedly chatting about their day but today they were rushing up to me, all excited and loud, thrusting bits of paper and pens at me shouting "Ben's dad" or "Sam's dad, can I have your autograph please?" They obviously thought I was some kind of celebrity 'cos I'd been on the telly. I was surrounded by them. Apparently, I had been the talk of the school that day and most of the kids had seen me. This was nice for my two because a little while back, their classes had done a little topic about what their parents did for a living and all the different jobs people had and who's dad had the most unusual job. So my kids had mentioned about their dad being a lookalike but most of the other kids hadn't believed them – until now. So after about twenty minutes of this, the children and their parents started to disperse and me and my two walked home with beaming smiles on our faces. I had made them feel proud and I felt good about that. On a personal note, that was the real high light of the day for me, making my kids proud because as I've said before, you can't beat being a dad and I felt proud of them too.

As a little foot note to this chapter here the local paper by the name of the Evening Echo picked up on this story of a lookalike in our midst. I don't know how, someone must have told them I guess. The paper does have a story line telephone number for members of the public to phone in with an interesting anecdote so best guess would be that's what happened. My guess would be it was the woman who had asked me to give the George Clooney lookalike her telephone number. Anyway it sparked off a little local lookalike competition; they wanted people to send their photos in and who they were supposed to look like with any stories attached. The paper also contacted me and asked if they could do an article about it and me and could they come round for an interview and take a picture or two of me dressed up as Tom to help get it all started. So I said yes that will be fine and we fixed a date. Couple of days later they turned up and the woman interviewed me asking the usual sort of questions of how did I first become a lookalike and what jobs I had done recently as well as wanting to know about the Big Breakfast show to which I duly regaled her with the information. Then, as requested, I got dressed up as Tom and the photographer took a few snaps. I used the Rain Man and Jerry Maguire look which was the tee shirt under the suit and trousers type thing with lots of gel in my hair. They ran the article a couple of days later and they got a huge response. The next week they did a centre page spread with a few of the very close lookalikes and also a few of the ones that didn't look anything like who they wanted to be but a little bit of wishful thinking never hurts. The best one, I thought, was a guy called Tom who looked just like Victor Meldrew as did the paper. They asked me if I could help them put him in touch with the lookalike agencies which I was happy to do and one of them took him on. How nice was that for him. I met him on a lookalike job a couple of years later and he bought me a beer by way of a thank you telling me that he had had some of the best times of his life doing lookalike stuff. I knew how he felt.

CHAPTER 6

VALUE FOR MONEY?

Being a lookalike was, for the most part, a part time job for me as it was for most of the lookalikes. One or two lookalikes said that they worked all the time and made a living out of it which, to be honest, I took with a pinch of salt. May be they did, I don't really know but most of us we all had day jobs; well for me an evening job as I was working as a musician/entertainer which was my full time occupation and my main source of income. Some other lookalikes hardly worked at all; maybe only two or three jobs a year, often because there was more than one lookalike for their particular character. For example back in the nineties when Victoria and David Beckham were always in the public eye, there was about five or six of that couple that I met in my travels so obviously they competed for the work and therefore didn't do as much as they might have otherwise done. It was a very competitive business. So different lookalikes worked different amounts depending on how popular they were at the time or whoever was in vogue. Now, luckily for me, the only other Tom Cruise lookalike around at that time, (I never met him myself,) was young chap who by all accounts wasn't really very good and not very gregarious as you would need to be to be a popular lookalike. So apparently didn't get much work and didn't last very long either. Therefore for most of the Tom Cruise jobs the agents would try and use me as much as possible, resulting in me working roughly about four to six jobs a month. This usually panned out to one, occasionally two, a week during a normal run of things which, although part time, was actually quite a lot compared to most of the others.

About two weeks after I had done the 'Big Breakfast Show' the call came though from the agent about another television appearance. In the meantime, I had done a couple of not especially eventful 'Meet and greet, Mix and mingles' but none the less enjoyed them anyway as I did all my lookalike jobs. Then I was asked to do a programme for the BBC called "Value for Money". This was a prime time television show that aired early evening on BBC One on Friday nights and was hosted by none other than Vanessa Feltz. After she had had her talk show cancelled, thanks to the false guest scandal in the papers, this was the next project she had moved onto and she was the main host. It was a show that, as the name suggested, explored various items; stuff for sale to the public and whether or not it was good value for money. Now around that time there was a new piece of legislation passed for the black cabs of London that they had to be more disabled friendly than they currently were. This meant that the existing taxies in use had to be replaced with a new style cab that disabled people could use more easily than the old ones, things like being able to have wheel chair access and such like. So this lead to all the older style taxies having to be replaced and therefore they were going to be sold off at auction and also made available to the general public as family cars (although whoever would want to drive around in a London black taxi as a car for the family was a bit beyond me.) That was one of the articles the show wanted to do so, and it was good for me of course as it meant another job. All work gratefully received and all that. Also, around this time, it was rumoured that Tom Cruise owned a black cab and whenever he came over to good old Blighty, he would travel around London in it which allowed him to drive practically anywhere he wanted as of course, black cabs are allowed to drive in places that ordinary traffic was not allowed to go, Tottenham Court Road for example. Another reason he purportedly did this was because it afforded him some anonymity in his efforts to get around the city; nothing like climbing in and out of limousines dragging a bloody great big entourage around with you to attract attention to yourself if you don't want it. After all who really takes any notice of the black taxies, unless you want to flag one down of course, let alone who's driving them? These taxies are just a back ground feature of our fair city, part of the furniture so to speak. Bloody good idea, Tom. Now although this would never actually be the case as I'm sure his taxi would show 'not in service' but what would happen if you tried to flag down the taxi driven by Tom himself? This was going to be part of the twist in the story for the Value for Money show as was explained to me by the agent when she offered me the job and that is why they wanted me. I was going to be given the full detailed brief by the producers when I got there but basically after Vanessa had done her article and price feature on said taxies, she was going to be filmed hailing down a cab that just happened to be the one driven by Tom, aka me, and whisked off into the sunset by her dream boat man Tom. This sounded like a laugh, not to mention a handsome day's pay, and so I took the job. It did strike me as odd at the time though that they wanted me dressed in the full 'Top Gun' outfit shades and all. Did they really think that Tom would drive about in a London black cab and then deliberately dress up as one of his most famous film characters he has ever done? Hmm strange, however it was supposed to be all tongue in cheek so I suppose poetic licence was the order of the day. Incidentally, they reckoned they were going to fetch a price of around fifteen hundred pounds for one of these things which upon seeing and driving one did actually seem rather cheap for what they were. I guess they were good value for money after all!

A few days later I arrived at the BBC studios early in the morning, bright eyed and bushy-tailed ready for a day lookaliking, my costume bag with my Tom stuff in it slung over my shoulder, to be met at the entrance by one of the shows team. She was a young petite Indian girl and spoke very softly. I got the impression she was new to this and came across as a little shy. She led me through the reception area explaining on the way the details of the days shoot and what they wanted from me. It was going to be an outside shoot at two or three different locations around London, starting off at Trafalgar square by Nelsons column and ending up along the Embankment under the bridge quite near Embankment tube station. This was going to be the location at which Vanessa was going to hail down the cab that I, as Tom, would be driving and would be the final shoot of the day. Although she went into quite a lot of detail about what was going to be happening, it did seem to be that they were going to 'wing it', so to speak a lot of the time which in my experience, was often the case. Things often did not go as planned, cock ups and unwanted members of public trying to involve themselves in the back ground, trying to get their face on the telly, always a problem in an uncontrolled outside environment. Not to mention, it was Nelsons column they were first filming at with all those pigeons, pooing on members of the cast during filming or even on the cameras themselves, as happened to us that day. Any number of things could happen or go wrong, usually with the usual hilarious consequences. Now there was a lot of stuff to be done in between takes but most of it didn't seem to concern or involve me and apart from the final shoot, all they wanted from me was the odd furtive shot of Tom driving past the different locations in his black cab. All sounded pretty easy to me and I was actually going to get to drive one of these things which, as it happened, turned out to be a lot of fun. They had hired a taxi for the whole day and I was going to be getting my hands on it at Trafalgar Square. In the meantime, it being still quite early in the day, the film crew and equipment was not quite ready to go. We were going down to the staff canteen to have a nice cup of tea and to wait until everyone was ready, so me and this Indian girl met up with one of the low level producers and headed off to meet with Vanessa who was standing outside the canteen entrance waiting for us. As we approached her I couldn't help but notice how, to put it politely, rotund she was. She looked much larger in real life than she did on the telly. They introduced me to Vanessa who stuck out her hand and said "Hi, you must be Tom pleased to meet you" and with that I shook her hand saying "Hello Vanessa, how are you? Seen you lots on the telly, nice to meet you in person" to which she replied "yes I'm sure". 'Mmm o...k...', not sure if I like you' was my first thought, first impressions and all that but let's not prejudge I was thinking. She then turned to the other two and said, rather rudely, "where the bloody hell have you been? I've been waiting here for ages, keeping me hanging around like this, who do you think you are?" 'Mmm' I thought again 'I defiantly don't like you'. The other two seemed to react rather subserviently to her remark and the producer said in a 'let's calm things down' kind of voice "well never mind, why doesn't every one sit down and I'll get us all a nice cup of tea" to which Vanessa let out a rather loud 'humph' and plonked herself down at the nearest table. I followed suit with the other girl, being not sure on how to handle things. I tried making polite conversation but I wasn't getting much response and found it all rather hard work. While Vanessa was talking to this other girl about something or other, now I can't remember what she actually said, but I do remember thinking that it didn't ring true to me. So I piped up saying to Vanessa "that doesn't sound right, you sure about that?" trying to make conversation, to which her indigent response was "of course its bloody right man, it was on the telly!".This really and instantly got my back up, there was no need to be like that. She obviously, and mistakenly, thought she was being challenged and didn't like it. What really irritated me about her comment was the hypocrisy of it, not to mention the rudeness. Not so long ago she had had her own talk show cancelled for the false guests thing so how's that for untrue? I just couldn't resist it and with a little mischievous look in my eye, I leaned forward to her and said "now that's not necessarily so Vanessa is it!" She glared at me with this real indignant look for a few seconds which suddenly changed to one of recognition. "I recognise you. You're that lookalike off of the Big Breakfast show aren't ya?" and with that she pushed her chair back, stood up shouting "I'm not working with him, who does he think he is! This is outrageous!" The girl who was sitting with us started fumbling and stuttering poor thing "erm, well, erm, I,I,......." but as luck would have it one of the more senior producers had come down to fetch us and witnessed what was happening. He went over to Vanessa with some authority in his step, telling her that she needed to calm down and that she was contractually obliged to work with me for the day whether she liked it or not, as was I. She didn't talk to me, off camera anyway, for the rest of the day. I didn't take it personally at the time and thinking back on it now I find it all rather amusing.

We all piled into a couple of large vans; a couple of camera men, sound guys, the director and producers, me, Vanessa, (she made sure she went in the other van to me,) and drove away from the BBC centre heading off to Trafalgar Square where we all piled out and stood on the pavement next to the Nelsons column. The black cab was already there. It had been washed and valeted and look quite pristine. The driver hadn't been there long and when we pulled up, he got out, walked over to the van that I was getting out of and passed the keys to me saying "there you go, Tom, enjoy yourself". 'How cool is that' I thought to myself having never driven one of these before. The director suggested that I have a little drive about in it to get used to it, (apparently it was a little different to a car,) whilst they set up and did a few takes of scenes that they needed to do for that particular area. I had been told not to go too far as they wanted to do a couple of shots of me driving it past so they could incorporate those shots into the scenes for effect when editing. These taxis had smallish sized diesel engines in them for maximum economy. They where not very fast, (they didn't need to be going around the streets of London,) but they had a really great turning circle being able to turn in virtually their own width and they were well fun to drive. I promised myself that, as and when the opportunity presented itself later on, I was going to have a good drive about in it. So after being directed to do those drive bys whilst they filmed me I pulled up next to the vans and got out. I wanted to watch the filming for bit. I'm glad I did because someone had gone off and got a bunch of teas for everyone and I do like my tea! Vanessa was standing there with a scowl on her face; I don't think she really wanted to be there after what had transpired earlier, but when a sightseeing open top bus drove by bibbing its hooter and the folks on board waving and shouting "Vanessa, Vanessa!", she instantly put a big smile on her face a gave an exuberant wave to them. I have to say she was quite professional (when needed.) The crew then set up the scene whereby she was interviewing a member of public, who had previously been approached and had given the ok to be interviewed. As the interview progressed, talking about their views on the subject at hand, a great big dollop of bird poo fell out of the sky straight on to the microphone that Vanessa was holding. Out take number one. We all laughed. I wasn't sure how Vanessa was going to take this given what a foul mood she had been in so far but luckily for all concerned, she saw the funny side of this and laughed along with us. I could see the director breathe a sigh of relief. So whilst I stood there drinking my cup of tea, it was time for take number two. The interview started up again pretty much along the lines of what it had done before when right near the end another dollop of bird poo came flying out of the air and landed on the bloke being interviewed, right on his head. How's your luck? It was even funnier the second time around and we all fell about laughing once again. Out take number two. It was a good thing that happening because up until then there had been a somewhat unpleasant atmosphere about this shoot since the canteen incident, a stress in the air that I felt was partly my fault to some degree. I could have not said anything back to Vanessa I suppose but at the time I just could not resist it. You understand. Anyway we managed to get through the rest of the shoot at that location and all took a well earned lunch break. However despite the mood having been lifted and Vanessa seemingly in better spirits she still would not talk to me, but by now nobody seemed to care, least of all me. It is not likely she would ever want to work with me in the future so the chances are I was never going to be seeing her again after this anyway and that suited me too.

After lunch the whole ensemble trundled off to the second location somewhere around the Strand but I was not needed for the shoot at this locale having done most of the drive-by shots that they wanted to use already at Trafalgar Square. However I was under strict instructions to be at the third and final shoot at the Embankment a little later on. 'Result' I thought to myself I've got a bit of time to kill and a new toy to play with; namely this black cab. I decided to treat myself to my own personnel sightseeing tour for the next couple of hours.

I had got to know my way around the capital quite well from sometime back when I used to work there. Years before, back in 1978, I was a sixteen year old lad and had just left the senior school, Gable Hall, that I had been attending for the last five years and had managed to secure myself an apprenticeship, which back in that day was the usual path boys took to start their working career off. The only alternative at the time being sixth form college which I really didn't fancy as I wanted to get out into the big wide world and spread my wings. Now just out if interest, this apprenticeship was in electrical engineering with what was then the Post Office, later to become British Telecom International; they were based in London and so the training for the most part was in London in the city. After three years training, I had qualified for the job I was employed for and so I went on to work for British Telecom as a maintenance technician for a total of about Ten years in all. My job was what they called building control which involved the maintaining of electrical generators, lifts, air conditioning and that sort of thing and I worked as part of a team, we were the maintenance department. Although we were primarily based at a building called St. Botolphs House, a place that no longer exists having been knocked down and replaced with a newer and more modern building a few years ago. It used to stand in Aldgate above the old post office there, We had several buildings all over the city to take care of back then. We also had vans that we used to get about in, (bright yellow things they were,) and we drove around the capital quite extensively doing our maintenance work. I liked driving and driving these vans in particular, (they were a lot of fun to drive,) I usually got to be the designated driver so hence I knew my way around the streets reasonably well.

So pedal to the metal, as much as you could in these small diesel engine vehicles, I think they did nought to sixty in about an hour and a half, (black cabs are not exactly known as performance cars,) and headed off for a drive about. I first drove to some of the places and areas that I used to work at, treating myself to a little reminisce from my younger days, but being as this was now about ten years after I had finally left my old maintenance job, things had changed somewhat. Upon having a drive by, I noticed that one or two of the buildings had been knocked down to be replaced by newer more modern premises and the other ones that were still there were no longer owned by my old firm and had changed beyond recognition. Feeling a little disappointed, I treated myself to a drive down Oxford Street for no other reason than I could by virtue of the fact I was in a black cab and no cars were allowed, (it is funny what can give you a sense of power, it's the little things,) after which I headed off to Denmark street, where there were a lot of good music shops and a favourite hangout of mine from back in the day. I used to while away many a lunch break there, or bunk off work if I could get away with it, which wasn't too hard as I was always out and about going to some building or another. Cruising the music shops popping in and out availing myself of a tinkle on whatever was the latest keyboard out at the time or having a strum and zipping out a lead break or two on the most expensive Gibson Les Paul guitar that they had in the shop. Typical grandioso dreams of a teenage lad that one day soon me and my band were going to be famous rock stars, have lots of fame and money and then I would come back down Denmark Street and buy up all these fantastic instruments that the shop managers begrudgingly let me used to try out and play, usually at the loudest volume they would allow me to. They knew full well I was never going to be able to afford to buy one, being an eighteen year old apprentice and all, but understanding that I was a young budding musician that once upon a time they had been themselves. Oh the enthusiasm of youth eh? One of my favourite music shops at the time was called Argents, named after the famous keyboard player Rod Argent who owned it as the name suggests. He used to play in the Zombies, back in the sixties penning such greats as 'She's Not There' and one of my personal favourites 'Hold Your Head Up'. He was one of my musical heroes, which was one of the other reasons I used to go in there lots, hoping to meet him but sadly never did. The other reason was all the latest gear they had; it was a treasure trove to a young lad like me. So some years later arriving to Denmark Street in my taxi, (which incidentally also allowed you to stop just about anywhere for a pick up,) to my great delight there was Argents. It was still there. 'Oh yeah nice one' I thought to myself . I just had to go in there I just couldn't resist it. So pulling up outside and putting on the hazard flashing warning lights so as to make it look like I was picking up a passenger, I leaped out and dashed into the shop. It looked as I remembered it, crammed full of all the latest gear and technology. I was in hog's heaven. After looking around for a bit, I spied a good looking keyboard with all the latest trappings that technology could muster for the nineties. It was jaw-droppingly expensive but what a sexy piece of kit. I just had to have a go. I wandered up to the counter and said to the bloke "'Ere fella, any chance I could have a little play on that?" pointing to the sexy beast only to be met with the response "oh no not you again! I remember you. You back in town are ya?" "Yep and I wanna have a play just like the old days" I laughed to which he fortunately had a little chuckle as well. It turned out to be the same bloke I used to harass when I was a lad and he had recognised me. I didn't recognise him initially having rather grey and receding hair by now and a beard, (well it had been at least Ten or fifteen years ago from when I was last in there,) but once he had uttered his initial words, recognition came back to me. We had a laugh and a chat for a while explaining to him about my Tom Cruise lookalike work and why I was up there for the day. I asked him "Did Rod ever come in?" "Nope never did, least not when I was here" he replied. I did get to have a play, and I played and I played and plum forgot what the time was I was so immersed in this great piece of kit. Oops! In the middle of twiddling a few knobs changing the sounds around and stuff an alarm bell went off in the back of my head and with a panic I shouted over to the desk "what's the time fella"? "About half three", "Bloody hell!" I cried. Not only had I left the taxi out on the curb for god knows how long, I had completely forgotten I was supposed to be at the Embankment for three o'clock for the third and final shoot of the day. How could I forget something like that? That's what I was up London for in the first place. "I got to go and quick" I shouted with rather a large degree of alarm in my voice. "No worries mate, nice to see you again" he replied. "Yeah you too fella" I hollered as I started to leg it out of the door my mind full of thoughts of 'what if the taxi's been clamped? Or even worse what if it has been towed away! Ahh!' Luckily, none of the above had happened which was surprising really as I had left it there far longer than just a few minutes. To this day I don't know how I got away with that one but thank god I had. I jumped in the cab and started her up. Nothing! Just the whirr whirr whirr of the engine trying to turn over. "What!" I cried and tried again. Whirr whirr whirr. Still nothing. "No no no, bollocks" I cried, banging the steering wheel in frustration, as you do in these situations. I tried a third time but still to no avail. 'What the hell was I going to do'? I thought taking a deep breath. Looking up at the heavens I pleaded "please God come to my rescue" not expecting any kind of response but, oh my lord, right at that moment, out popped the guy from the music shop. "Having a little bit of trouble there are we, Tom?" he said rather condescendingly as he leaned in through the open window of the drivers cab, resting his arms on the open ledge. "Fuck off!" I cried. "Serves you right for making me get all those keyboards and guitars down for you to play over the years" he said, laughing his head off. Now looking back I can't say as I blame him for enjoying the moment; I was an annoying little shit back then as a kid and although I used to exasperate him he was very patient with me. But back to the now. "What am I gonna do?" I said. I was proper panicking by now. "Let's give it a push" he said in a rather calm manner, still enjoying the moment. As he started to walk round to the back of the cab, I climbed out of the cab door and with one hand on the wheel and the other on the door post we began pushing with all our might. We got the taxi up to a bit of speed which did take some effort, (those things were quite heavy), and I jumped back into the driver's seat, slid it into second gear and popped the clutch. With a huge sigh of relief, the engine burst into life. "Thank god" I cried and thanked the shop manager too. I stopped the taxi, revved the engine to make sure it was running ok as the guy came round to the cab once again. "All good then, Tom?" he enquired, "Yeah thanks very much fella, I really appreciate it. I will pop in sometime and buy something from you sooner or later" I said placatingly to which he started walking away in the direction of his shop waving a hand in the air laughingly saying "Yeah sure you will, Tom, sure you will". As he disappeared from view, I revved the engine and pulled away, heading in the direction of the Embankment as fast as I could. I never did get to know his name, I wish I had, I just never thought to ask. As it happened I did go back to that shop some months later. I wanted a new keyboard and I knew exactly which one I wanted so I headed off to Argents and purchased a brand new Rowland E 15, latest thing out at the time and I still play it to this day. It was still the same bloke who served me and he nearly fell over backwards when I pulled my credit card out to pay for it.

So back to the story. I was driving like mad to get to the embankment as fast as I could,feeling rather anxious about being so late and letting the film crew down, my head doing ten to the dozen, when I was suddenly struck by the thought of how absurd it must have looked; a bloke dressed up like Tom Cruise in all his Top Gun outfit, pushing a taxi for all he was worth! It certainly dispelled my worries because I burst out laughing, ending up having a fit of the giggles all the way there. The whole day was turning into a comedy fest. I actually got there quite quickly luckily enough as there didn't seem too much in the way of traffic or hold ups in the way, arriving about a quarter to four making me about forty five minutes late. I came tearing down Northumberland Avenue, turned left on to the Embankment, driving under the train bridge, ending up beside Victoria embankment gardens, where we were supposed to meet – only to realise there was no one there. 'Oh shit' I thought 'had I missed them? Had they been and gone?' I didn't know what was going on.

At first I thought I must have got the location wrong and maybe they meant somewhere else along the Embankment so, as they definitely were not about here, I decided to take a little drive along the road up to Temple and back, see what I could see, which, is exactly what I did. Now, you may ask yourself, why not just give them a ring? See where they are? But you have to bear in mind this was the mid nineties and although mobile phones were out by then, and I had one myself (poser that I was) they were more like fashion accessories and were not very prevalent back then. Most people did not bother carrying one about with them if indeed they even owned one, and likewise so it was with me. I rarely had mine with me or even had it switched on for that matter. I turned around at Temple and headed back down the Embankment the other way only to be met by the BBC vans pulling up at the other side of the road under the train bridge just as specified. 'Phew' I thought 'what a welcome sight'; they had arrived even later than me I said to myself as I turned around and pulled up behind them. I got out of the cab and was approached by one of the crew who promptly said "sorry we are late Tom. Madam decided to pop into a shop on the quick, which turned into half an hour, and then got caught behind some bus that had broken down". "That's alright. I got here and you weren't about so I had a little drive up and down the Embankment to get the lay of the land" I lied. "Nice one, Tom. Nice to see you're on the case, mate" he replied, 'Phew' I thought for the second time in as many minutes 'my bacon is saved'. I mentioned to him about the flat battery problem I had endured a little earlier and having to get a push and all that to which he replied "Oh yeah, I forgot to mention the bloke we hired it from said the battery got a little sticky from time to time so probably a good idea not to turn the engine off if you can avoid it Tom, you know, just in case, don't want you breaking down now do we"? With a rather incredulous stare I said "Gee, thanks for heads up mate, we wouldn't want that now would we"? But I don't think he got the sarcasm because he said as he was turning away, "Yeah, no worries, Tom" preoccupied with what he had to do next. All's well that ends well. And so we did the third and final shoot for the day. They placed a camera man and a sound engineer on the back seat. Don't know how they managed in the final shot to make the inside of the taxi look like there was just the two of us in it; me and Vanessa and she was a rather large lady. We had a cab full of gear and everywhere I turned, I seemed to be knocking into something. We then drove back to Temple, which was the nearest place there was to turn around and back along to where we were going to be picking up Vanessa, being filmed along the way. As we drove past the spot where she was supposed to be hailing us down, she wasn't there and I accidently drove right past only to be told to go around again so that they could do a retake. So that is what we did. Apparently what happened was she was going to be filmed striding across the pavement stepping out into the road a little with her hand up to be hailing us down but as she was told "action", the heel of her shoe had got stuck in the crack of the pavement and had caused her to trip over, falling flat on her behind. I don't mean to sound nasty here but I bet that was a sight to behold! As I said earlier, lots of mishaps can happen when you are out on location and today was certainly no exception. The next, and fortunately the last, mishap of the day was when we were coming around for the third time for the pickup. There just happened to be, unnoticed by us inside the taxi, another cab driving alongside us and, yes you've guessed it, as Vanessa stuck her hand out, he accelerated past me and then nipped in front, pulling over to pick up what he obviously thought was a fair. He must have got a shock when he realised who it was and what was going on because I saw the director shooing him away in no uncertain terms and him looking through his back window doing the two fingered salute. Another chuckle to be had. So off we went again around the now quite familiar circuit, only this time it all went to plan, thank god. It had been a long day and we were all getting a little bit frayed around the edges. As she stepped inside, Vanessa was filmed giving an over-exaggerated gasp when she supposedly realised who had picked her up. I was told to turn around then with the best smouldering Tom look I could muster and let her settle down into the back seat with a nice big smile on her face and a doe-eyed wink at the camera. And that was the end of that. After we had finished, I got changed in the back of the van, handed the taxi keys back over and said my goodbyes to everyone, who all seemed happy with what I had done, (except Vanessa of course). She still wasn't talking to me! As we were right near the Embankment tube station, I caught the circle line from there round to Tower Hill, jumped on the train at Fenchurch Street and off home for me. Reflecting on the day's events on the rather packed train ride home, (it was rush hour by now), my thoughts wandered back to the events down Denmark Street earlier that day and I found myself chuckling rather loudly at the absurd scene of a fully Top Gunned Tom Cruise pushing a taxi for all he was worth. Having a fit of the giggles in a crowded train carriage was rather embarrassing I have to admit, even for me and I don't embarrass easily. It was hard to stifle and so I got more than a few odd glances but laughter is rather infectious and the person sitting next to me enquired, "What you laughing at?" to which I responded, "You wouldn't believe me if I told you".

They had given me the date of when this particular Value for Money article was going to be broadcast which was to be about a month later. So that Friday night, me and my family huddled around the telly, my kids all excited 'cos daddy was on the telly again and they set the video recorder up so they could show their mates, bless'em, (they were eight and six years old at the time). Then there I was, all smiles on the screen, "Yea Dad" the kids screamed and then it was over. There was in total three separate shots of me and all added up together, it couldn't have lasted more than 30 seconds or so as is often the case with these things, but it had been a very enjoyable day.

CHAPTER 7

THE BUPA JOB.
A MISSION IMPOSSIBLE

Back in November 2000 I was asked to do a Mission Impossible job for a company called Flying Colours. They were a film production company, quite high profile at the time, and they had been commissioned by BUPA to do a scripted fifteen minute spoof of the Mission Impossible films. The films were proving very popular at the time and having a good run at the cinemas to the extent that they have ended up making five of them so far and counting. Every couple of years they seem to bring a new one out and with it a nice little earner for "Tom". At this point in time we were up to Mission Impossible Two and in my opinion, the best one they have made so far. This second film in the series was directed by action filmmaker John Woo and in the film Tom Cruise plays the part of a character called Ethan Hunt; a secret agent working for a covert organization killing all the baddies, as usual. Hunt is given the task of retrieving a deadly genetically engineered virus, known as 'Chimera', from a rogue IMF agent, Sean Ambrose, played by Dougray Scott. Hunt attempts to infiltrate Ambrose's inner circle through Ambrose's former girlfriend, Nyah Nordoff-Hall (Thandie Newton), an accomplished thief. During their mission Hunt and Nordoff-Hall engage in an affair that complicates the mission. Well, that is a surprise then, isn't it? At the climax, Nordoff-Hall is forced to infect herself with the last virus in order to save Hunt, with Hunt having destroyed the only other traces of the virus, she was thus able to shield Hunt until he could escape. Subsequently racing against time, (the virus becomes incurable twenty hours after infection), Hunt manages to acquire the cure and kill Ambrose. Yeah, Cruise does it again; good old Tom. Now the reason for this little film synopsis is that the honchos at BUPA wanted their little promo film script to be loosely based on this second film. BUPA, as I'm sure everyone knows, are one of, if not *the,* major players in the private medical insurance world. They are a worldwide company and make a tidy profit every year so with lots of cash to splash, they wanted a no- expense- spared production done with all the trimmings – and of course a nice little earner for me. Well, I did have a family to support after all. Cheers Tom!

As always, the usual type of phone call came through from the agent, outlining the nature of the job and checking my availability. I liked to make myself available as much as possible as I loved doing this stuff; these gigs were always an adventure of some kind. It was to be a two day shoot in and around London and I was going to be working in the city once again at various locations. I was to use my Mission Impossible look as I've said but this time they were going to be supplying the various outfits they wanted me to wear which was nice as it meant I didn't have to cart my own clothes bag about, just my face this time. On the majority of lookalike jobs I would usually be expected to take one of my own outfits and it could be a pain in the arse if it was a London job as it meant I would have to use the train. Lugging a bloody big clothes bag on and off a train, especially during rush hour, was a royal pain at the best of times.

To digress a moment, although I had assembled quite a few different Tom guises that I felt I would need when I first started out as a lookalike and on the advice of the agents, I only ever seemed to need to use four of them. There was the 'Top Gun' look which consisted of a faded pair of blue jeans, the obligatory white tee-shirt, brown leather boots, a nice pair of mirrored aviator sun glasses and a black leather flying jacket complete with furry collar and adorned with various military badges (although I took them off after a while as I could never really get them to look quite right and decided it looked more authentic without them). Then there was the navel officer's uniform; bright white complete with officer's cap and a very well-polished pair of leather shoes. The girls especially liked that one; man in a uniform and all that. Once or twice on a private party, job, they thought I was a stripper gram, (a Tom a gram if you will) but that's another tale. Then there was, as I mentioned before, the white V-neck tee shirt under the suit jacket and trouser outfit, the Jerry Maguire and Rain Man type of look. Tom used that look quite a lot in his late eighties and early nineties films. I liked this attire because it was a kind of a generic Tom look so was useful when the client did not quite know how things were going to go or I wasn't sure what was wanted. Got me out of trouble on a few occasions. Then of course the Mission Impossible look which consisted of a pair of black combat trousers, a black tee shirt, a pair of black boots although I sometime used black trainers as sometimes this role would involve a lot of physical activity like running and stuff, and topped off with a replica pistol complete with side holster, (which got me into trouble on more than one occasion), and sometimes a pair of headphones with a little microphone coming around the side.

The scenario for this particular job was for four secret agents, (the baddies), to be chasing the goody secret agent, (me as Tom Cruise aka Ethan Hunt), all over London city. They were trying to catch him so that they could get their hands on a secret computer disk I was carrying as it contained a secret formula; a deadly computer virus by all accounts. To what end I was carrying it, or where I was supposed to be taking it in the story line, I was not sure as it never seemed to come up in the script but none – theless! We were going to be filmed at different locations starting at Liverpool Street train station, bouncing around a few other places like Covent Garden and such like and ending up at the London Eye where I was going to be cornered in one of the pods and forced to hand the disk over at gun point. It was to be done in a Laurel and Hardy slapstick comedy type manner whereby the villains would have all sorts of mishaps in their endeavours to apprehend me. The baddies were going to be played by four members on the board of directors of BUPA and they were, by all accounts, well known people within the organization. The idea for all this was apparently it was going to be used at the opening ceremony of a big BUPA conference being held in Prague a couple of months later to introduce some new policies and services to their customers. They had hired none other than Jonathan Ross to host the whole event and after our little production had been shown as the opening, Mr. Ross was going to walk out on stage with what was supposed to be exactly the same disk that I was to be carrying in the film, pop it into a laptop and project its contents on to a large screen to reveal the new policies to the audience.

The date of the job came around and off I went to London to meet everyone. The first shoot was going to be at Liverpool Street Station at seven a.m. and that is where I first met everyone. I got off at Fenchurch Street, and as it was only ten minutes away I decided to walk to Liverpool Street rather than mess about jumping on the tube train for a couple of stops. About half way there, as I was walking along Hounsditch towards Bishopsgate, I realized, (and I don't know why it hadn't occurred to me before), that I hadn't actually been told whereabouts at the station we were to meet. Liverpool Street Station is a big place and as I had never actually met any of these folks before, I was a little concerned that I would miss them. I needn't have worried though because when I arrived, it was very obvious. I walked through the south entrance which leads onto a first floor causeway with plenty of shops around. That then leads to some stairs taking you down to the next level where the train platforms are. It turned out that the production company, Flying Colours, with their lovely big BUPA budget, had hired that whole top floor area! They had cordoned it off (much to the annoyance of the rush hour commuters, bearing in mind it is seven a.m.) and had put up a tower of lights and several camera platforms a couple of hours earlier.

It all looked very industrious with crew members scurrying about everywhere. I've no idea how they managed to get permission to do all this but they had. Must have greased the right palms was my reckoning. I was to meet a chap called Peter Bird who was one of the producers but not having met him before, I wandered up to the nearest cameraman and asked to be pointed in his direction. "Oi, oi, it's Tom, the main man" was his response then he shouted, "Peter! Tom's arrived" beckoning a chap over. So I met Peter and I liked him instantly as he held out my favourite drink ever, a nice cup of tea – yum! We discussed what was wanted from me for that day and I was sent to the makeup truck, a big Chrysler van, which was parked in Primrose Street just behind the station. After a bit of gel in the hair, make-up on the face and donning the already- supplied outfit I was to wear, I was ready. As I walked out on to the set, I started to notice that the whole scene was starting to draw a few curious bystanders but before we had even started, it turned into a small crowd that were gathering at the edges of cordon barriers. Very quickly, this morphed into a rather large crowd; everyone wants to know what everyone else is curious about, it's human nature after all. Some folk had started jostling for a front row position. With all the cameras, lights and busy crew members running to and fro, they must have assumed some major film shoot was going down. It certainly looked like it. Of course, not too long previously, there had been a big scene in the Mission Impossible film that had been shot at Liverpool Street Station. In fact, it was right on the spot that we were now occupying, so with all this stuff going on and a guy all dressed up looking just like Tom Cruise himself, even dressed in the same outfit as worn in the film, wandering about the set; who could blame them? As I looked over at this crazy scene of people, I realised they were all looking at me. I heard someone shout, "Tom, Tom, can I have your autograph?" quickly followed by one or two others. Now being the kind of guy who doesn't like to miss an opportunity to have a bit of fun, I started playing up to the crowd and giving them a wave. I casually walked over to the front row of people who were holding out bits of paper and pens and with the best Hollywood smile I could manage, started signing autographs. They didn't seem to twig I was not the real article, (getting caught up in the moment I guess), and I was very careful not to actually say anything to give the game away. I didn't actually sign as Tom Cruise; just wrote things like 'all my love, Tom' and 'to whoever, love Tom' and such like. I was getting carried away in the moment when one of the crew came over, Peter, and, not wanting to ruin things with these poor deluded people, boldly stated, "Come along Tom, time to do some work." so waving back to the crowd once again I accompanied him over to where I was needed ready for the first take of the day. On the short few yards walk back to where I should have been, he said quietly in my ear " Word to the wise Gary, don't do that again, it could turn ugly." I wasn't sure what he meant at the time but I sure was going to know the next day..... Apart from a couple of false starts, mainly due to a few technical problems with the lighting, nothing particularly untoward happened at this first shoot. It all went to plan; me running up and down the stairs being chased by the bad guys, all tripping over one another in the usual slapstick manner that was the order of the day. We did every shot of each scene three or four times as is quite common when filming apparently. But not knowing too much about the behind the scenes of the film business, I asked why this was and was told that they repeated each shoot several times so the guys in editing had lots of film to play around with; to mix and match and add the best bits together. 'It is better to have it and not need it than to need it and not have it' was their watch word and after hearing them say those very wise words, it became one of my favourite sayings too. At the end of this shoot the bad guys managed to capture me by me accidently tripping over and then the baddies all falling over each other, and me, in what looked like a big rugby scrum. "Cut" came the shout after the third or fourth shot of this and that was the end of the first scene of the promo. This was music to my ears as I was feeling a little bruised and battered by now, having had the odd accidental boot from one or two of the others guys whilst they were piling on top of me. The whole shoot took about six hours all in all, right from setting up all the equipment to packing it all away again and being ready to move on to the next location so we were packed up and gone from that locale by eleven that morning. The actual filming part only took about two hours and in the final cut it wasn't even five minutes long.

The next location was a flat in Fulham which was going to be the scene where they search me for the sacred disk. The flat itself was actually owned by one of the cast, a member of the board of directors as you may remember from earlier. But once we arrived there, the producers and the director decided that, despite previous decisions regarding this location, lighting and shot angle problems, it would probably look better in the final cut if we did what the script wanted us to do here at the next location. So whilst the powers that be discussed script alterations and logistics to compensate for a location change, which held no interest for the rest of us, we decided to put the kettle on and have a nice cup of tea. Time was pressing by now and we needed to move on, (tea not withstanding of course), so after this we hauled ourselves back into the waiting vans and headed off to our next place of calling; it was lovely.

After about a forty five minute drive, we pulled up outside the Conrad hotel in one of the poshest parts of London, Chelsea, down by the water front. I think it is called Wyndham Grand now. Now to a working class lad like me this was all rather awe inspiring. If you have ever been there you will know what I mean. Flying Colours had hired the diplomatic suite for the day and a pretty penny it must have cost too. It was absolutely lovely but we were there to work, not to admire the view and so the crew got busy. It took them about an hour to set everything up ready for the shoot and in the meantime it was off to make up for a touch up for the cast members. It didn't take long. We were ready before the film set was which gave us just enough time to have, (you guessed it), a nice cup of tea, albeit a posh one this time. With the set ready, they put me into position which involved me being tied to a chair whilst the hapless baddies interrogated me as to the whereabouts of the computer disc. Part of this interrogation was for them to search me which they did by running their hands inside my shirt and tickling me. As I said, there were four of the bad 'guys'; two men and two women, and it befell to the women to do the searching of my person. On cue, the chair I was in tipped back and we all fell onto the floor in a pre-arranged and well-rehearsed tangled mess. I should imagine it looked quite funny in the completed article but alas I never did get to see it. As the script demanded, they did the searching with zealousness and kind of pseudo sexual grimaces on their faces mouthing words like "Phwoar" as the camera did close up shots of them. It reminded me of Benny Hill and looked like something out of a 'Carry On' film which, of course, being a spoof, was exactly what was required. Well done, ladies. One of them was a very large lady and a very nice person to whom I had gotten on with well, being a fellow tea drinker and all. The other femme fatelle was very fit for a slightly older lady so I quite enjoyed this scene if truth be told. The final shot was of all four of them going out onto the balcony to discuss what to do next, as they had had no luck in finding what they were after, and leaving me spread-eagled upon the floor. At this point I had managed to loosen my bonds and whilst they were not looking, make a dash for the door to hasten my escape. The final shot was of me disappearing down the corridor, hands flailing in the air all the way. We did a few takes of these various shots for the editing boys to work with later on and then called it a day to which, after being de-makeuped and another cup of tea, I headed off to catch the train home. The whole day had lasted about fourteen hours in all and I was knackered. I made my way to Fulham Broadway tube station, got the train to Tower Hill, walked over to Fenchurch Street and got the next train home. Funny how you remember little details like that. Feeling rather exhausted after a long days graft as soon as I got on the train I fell asleep and completely missed my stop at the other end!

Filming the different scenes that the story line requires doesn't necessarily have to be done in chorological order. They are usually done in order of convenience as was the case today. So although the next day's first location was the shoot at the London Eye which was going to be the final scene, we also had to fit in a mid-film chase scene at Covent Garden's later that on that day. So we did have a lot to fit in. However, the good news for me was that I didn't have to be there until twelve o'clock mid-day so I didn't have to get up too early. This was nice because I was still feeling rather knackered and having missed my train stop the night before it had made me rather late home. I had a nice lay in and a catch up on my sleep. In fact, I managed to sleep right through my alarm clock. However, as luck would have it, my kids had no school that day and knowing that dad was supposed to be 'lookaliking' this day and therefore should be up and about by now, woke me up with a cup of tea they made especially for me and a jump all over daddy in bed! After having done the usual morning ablutions and a nice hearty breakfast whilst chatting to the kids what I was getting up to, I set off raring to go and looking forward to what the day might bring. I got a lift down to the train station and headed off to London once again. Arriving at Fenchurch Street, I decided to take the river boat today instead of the usual boring tube train as the boat stopped right outside the London Eye; it was a nice sunny day which I wanted to enjoy. A good day for an outside film shoot. I walked down to the riverside jetty and as luck would have it, there was the Thames clipper already in dock. After boarding, I sat on the top deck admiring the view from the river as we cruised along the Embankment. I remember it well because, with the sun on my face, the breeze in my hair and slurping a nice cup of tea I had bought upon boarding, it was one of those 'life doesn't get better than this' moments, which I'm sure we have all had at one time. Lord knows life can drag us down enough from time to time, but not today. It was a good day and, thinking how lucky I was to be doing something like this, I felt happy. Alighting at the London Eye jetty, I strolled over to the Eye itself where the crew were waiting and said my hellos to everybody. Everyone seemed to be in good spirits ready for filming the final scene for this BUPA spoof. The first shoot of this particular scene involved me being chased across the pavement area in front of the giant wheel and into one of the pods. Whilst they were setting up the shot, the other members of the cast and I were ushered once again in to the makeup van. Flying Colours had hired the whole of the Eye for the next three or four hours and some of the surrounding areas as well and as with yesterday's Liverpool Street shoot, they had got permission to cordon off the area to keep spectators at bay. I have since been to the London Eye taking my daughter Mollie as part of a day trip up to London and just to get a ride in one of the pods is expensive enough as a tourist but to hire the whole thing for a few hours? How much must have that cost? Even with their lavished BUPA account, it must have put a dent in the budget – but that was not for me to worry about; I was just enjoying being the star of the show for a day. As Andy Warhol said, "Everyone has their fifteen minutes of fame". It was time to start filming and I was called on to the set. The makeup van was quite close to one of the makeshift barriers that had been erected and all this filming activity, as before, had drawn a rather large crowd. Being as this was one of London's major tourist attractions, the crowd consisted not of curious commuters passing on their way to work as at Liverpool Street but American and Japanese holiday makers who not only had all the time in the world on their hands but wanted a piece of the action as well. As I stepped out of the van I heard one of them shout "Hey, you all" in a broad southern American drawl "It's Tom Cruise" so I gave the crowd a wave as well as one of my well-practised Hollywood smiles. With that, what seemed like the whole of the Japanese contingent burst forward straight through the barriers as if they weren't there and totally surrounded me. Swamped me they did, thrusting paper and pen in my face shouting "Aww Tom Cruise Tom Cruise, we want your autograph, autograph please" It just seemed to erupt into utter chaos with all these people with silly hats on, (you know the type only the tourist seem to wear), jumping up at me, cameras flashing, people pulling at my clothes, lots of pushing and shoving. Suddenly I felt out of control of the situation and quite out of my depth. What started as a little play with the crowd was turning onto something quite scary. It seemed to go on for ages, although I was told afterward that the whole silly scene only lasted a couple of minutes, and for the first time in my life, I felt claustrophobic. Something akin to panic was starting to take hold of me and I just had to get out of there as quick as I could and by any means possible. I started to lose it and was just about to start flailing about when I felt a strong grip on my arm and with a sharp pull to my right, I was clear of the crowd. It turned out there had been three or four policemen standing nearby watching the whole malarkey and one of them had dived in when they saw things getting out of hand and pulled me out of there; just in the nick of time, if you'll pardon the pun! The other boys in blue started calming the crowd down and ushering them back to behind the now re-erected barriers in the inimitable style that only the police seem to be able to do god, bless them. What's the saying? 'Where's a policeman when you need one?' Well, there was more than one when I needed them that day, thank god. Cheers, boys. Not for the first time in my lookalike career, or the last for that matter, I had had a close escape.

What never ceases to amaze me is that I am just a lookalike and not a replica of my character and neither are most of the lookalikes that I know. How can people really mistake us for the real thing? I mean come on, the whole lookalike business is only supposed to be a tongue in cheek kind of thing. For a start, I am good few inches taller than Tom himself, probably my biggest flaw as a lookalike, but whenever I have found myself in these mad situations, people never seem to realise it; a kind of 'mass suggestion' type of thing. What looked like a large film set and someone shouting "It's Tom Cruise"- so that's what they saw. Then there is the outbreak of psychopathy that seems to go along with it all in a large crowd situation; they all wanted a piece of someone, in this case Tom Cruise, and were going to get it whether it was to the detriment of that person or not. Another part of human nature I suppose; people see what they expect to see at the time and today they expected Mr Tom Cruise. Scary stuff I can tell you. If that's what famous stars have to put up with on a daily basis, no wonder they go a bit bananas sometimes.

I felt a bit shaken up so accompanied by a member of staff, I went to the cafe next door the Eye, and as I sat down she offered me a cigarette to help calm me. But as I had given up smoking a few years earlier, I'm glad to say, I settled for a nice cup of tea instead which certainly did the trick. Peter came in and sat down beside me and said in a rather condescending tone "For fucks sake Tom, I warned you before about doing that sort of thing didn't I? Perhaps you'll listen to me the next time, and now we've lost about half hour shoot time so get yourself together and let's crack on, shall we? With an unexpected reassuring pat on my back he added, "Mind you, we managed to film all that. Got some good shots we did, might come in handy in the final print so not all's lost!" and with that and a smile he walked off. As he was sidling away, I poked my tongue out at his back and said sarcastically "Gee, glad to be of service" at which point the crew girl and me burst out laughing. Another case of all's well that ends well. So back to make up for a little touch up as I was rather dishevelled, the crowed having pulled me about a bit and all, and I was ready to go once again. The scene started with me being chased across the paved area in front of the Eye, the part where the people would normally be queuing. The baddies in hot pursuit once again, all falling over each other, and we were all heading in the general direction of one of the pods that was available at the bottom of the slowly- turning wheel. Then up the ramp where I darted into the pod, leaving the inept and mystified bad guys scratching their heads as to where I had gone. Like it wasn't obvious but it was all part of the comedy! Meantime all the gathered spectators who were now obligingly standing behind the barriers, were cheering me on excitedly. "Awe Tom run away run away" came the Japanese accented cries; I have to give it to those guys; they did this with the absolute zealous enthusiasm as they do with everything in life. We did this take three or four times as usual and with the final wrap in the bag, we broke for lunch and back into the cafe for sandwiches and yet another nice cup of tea. To the annoyance of the film crew, we only took a fifteen minute break, barely enough time to finish, as we were running a little bit behind schedule due to my little escapade earlier. But they forgave me; after all it was a rather amusing distraction for them so they delighted in telling me all afternoon. Yes guys I get it, I was there! And so on to the final shoot for this scene, and what was to be the final scene in the promo. This involved being inside one of the pods where I was going to be cornered and the baddies would finally get their hands on the disc. We all piled in, us five actors (if you could call us that!), two sets of cameras with the associated crew, the sound guys and the director as well as one of the producers. Now I'm not sure how many people these London Eye pods are supposed to hold; they are quite big so I would imagine quite a few but with us lot and all the equipment, it was a bit of a squash. Everyone was jostling for their positions and it took a little while to get things sorted, by which time our pod had done a full revolution; not good apparently because they wanted a nice view of London in the back drop so round we went again. It was show time! "Quiet on set, please" shouted the director and after a couple of moments, "Action!" I stood at one end of the pod, camera pointed right at me, with an exaggerated look of horror upon my face whilst the other four approached me in a slow and menacing manner. Comedy style of course; they looked like something out of Scooby Doo with Shaggy and Scooby creeping about in their inimitable style. Before they got too close, I threw the disk up in the air at them and they jumped up and tried to grab it all at once, all bumping onto each other and ending up in a heap on the floor, disc still bouncing in the air as many hands tried to grab a hold of it. At this point they all struggled to their feet, brushing themselves off, wondering who the hell had the disc and looking at each other rather perplexedly; none of them so it seemed. With a camera shot back to me, I stood there rolling my head back laughing like the bad guys do in those James Bond movies and holding the disc once again high in my hand. "Is that the best you can do? Ha ha" I cried. At which point I threw the disc at them for a second time and they all ended up on the floor once again but this time it ended with an arm held high with the disc in it. They all got up, with their backs towards me, all looking at the disk and gibbering excitedly. But when they turned around to face me, I was gone, disappeared without a trace. But they had their disc now and the scene ended with them all jumping up in the air with a rousing chorus of "Hooray!" This was going to be a freeze frame shot right at the end apparently. A good ending I thought. The only trouble was we had to do it over and over and over again so many times in fact that the pod had done another full revolution. The biggest problem we were having was the fact that where there was so much gear about we, as the actors, were always bumping into some piece of equipment or another, or a member of the crew, or there was a piece of said equipment that kept getting into shot. It all got very frustrating for everyone, so much so that when the pod reached the end of the second rotation, the director very nearly threw half the stuff, and staff, out of the slowly opening door. He didn't of course but he did order a lot of it, and them, off sharpish, mumbling something about, 'Why this hadn't been all sorted out in logistics beforehand was beyond him' and 'Did he have to think of everything around here?' in a rather irritated manner. Luckily, the doors do remain open for a few minutes to allow tourists to get off and on so there was time to sort out the essentials, even if a little hurriedly. So off we went again third time lucky, or in our case third circuit lucky, and managed to do the three or four necessary takes without further mishap.

Now I need to talk about tea at this juncture and, boy, do I like my tea in case you hadn't guessed, often having something like ten cups a day. The only other person I know who can drink more tea than me is another sister of mine, Kay. If tea were beer she would drink me under the table! Now in my adult life I have not always been the best of sleepers, having suffered bouts of insomnia from time to time and tea contains a fair bit of caffeine so I tend to drink de-caff tea wherever possible. Now another thing about tea, is that it is diuretic and de-caff even more so, so I'm told; in other words it makes you want to pee a lot. The reason for this little digresses is that the Eye pod takes something like thirty minutes to do a full revolution. So given how much tea I had drunk that day so far, we were on our third trip around without getting off and my bladder was a tad full, to say the least. I was bursting! And we had only just passed the halfway mark. Doh! Luckily, or unluckily for me as I had nothing else to concentrate on, we had finished filming by now and whilst the crew were packing the gear away and the rest enjoying the view, all I could think about was the bloody toilet; and you will probably know from experience you always want to go more when you can't. It was only about ten minutes till landing but it was like ten hours for me. At first I was just doing the obligatory wriggle in my seat routine which in no time at all turned into the full blown hop from side to side dance. "Hey, Tom can you keep still? You're gonna shake the whole damn pod loose at this rate, mate" came an amused cry from one of the staff as they all turned to look at me. I would have been embarrassed but I was too full to care by now. "Can't you make this thing go any faster!" came my anguished cry as they all started sniggering. Here's the thing though; as with laughing or yawning, needing the loo when it is not available is infectious and as we came in to land there was four of five of us all jiggering about in unison by the door, faces all of a grimace. We were looking like something out of a seventies disco film by that time, "*Ah ah ah ah staying alive, staying alive.*" By this point as I started to feel like I was going to explode. The doors started to move at last and squeezing out of the half opened doors, we all made an Olympic dash to the toilets accompanied by another rousing chorus from the Japanese audience of, "Aww, here comes Tom again. GO TOM GO!" closely followed by, "Oh. Where'd he go?" as I disappeared inside the cafe and to the nearest place for relief. Eat your heart out Husain Bolt; I'm sure we did that hundred meter dash in eight seconds flat! A little later as we were all piled in to vans once again, someone quipped, "Who needs steroids when you've got tea" to which we all laughed as we headed off to the final destination and the last shoot of the day.

The producers were getting a little worried about the time of day as this *was* November and the nights were starting to draw in. It was all a question of continuity because, as I explained before, although this was the last shoot to be done it was not, however, going to be the last scene in the film. They didn't want the mid-scene to look later in the day than the nice bright sunny day we had at the London Eye. So we made haste to our destination which was Covent Garden. This is one of my favourite places in London; very lively and vibrant with St Paul's church on the west side, the market in the middle with the little archway cafes down the steps plus all the street entertainers touting themselves around the outside streets that encircle it. We went to the east side, on the corner of Russell Street where there is a line of marble pillars that support the building overhang above. The ground floor is a recessed pavement area and just right for our purposes as this area is in shadow thus making it darker than the open places. Therefore it is a little more conducive to us should the light start to fade as it is supposed to be in shadow anyway. So they started speedily setting up the cameras and stuff whilst us five cast members where hanging around. We had a little wander and started watching one of the street entertainers who was holding out dried spaghetti with one hand and cracking a rather dangerous looking whip with the other. He started to slash little lengths off the spaghetti with the whip to the applause of the audience that had started gathering round. Then, as he was opening another pack of dried spaghetti, he started talking about what his finale was going to be; something he called 'The Sandwich of Death'. It all sounded very intriguing and we were quite enthralled. Next he placed the spaghetti in his mouth, all the while cracking his whip ominously, and then using the whip, proceeded to lop lengths off it getting ever closer to his face. The audience gasped as did we. Very entertaining, I must say. The finale was approaching. "Ladies and gentlemen, the moment you have all been waiting for; please be silent as I need to concentrate for the very dangerous "SANDWICH OF DEATH!" The crowd fell silent, holding our breath and with the tension of anticipation in the air there came a sudden tap on my shoulder that made me jump. "Come on guys, time to start filming" said Peter in a rather deflatatory tone of voice. "Oh no, bummer" we moaned as we wandered off back to the set. We never did get to find out what the 'Sandwich of Death' was and I still find myself wondering about it to this day. So the filming began. It started with shots of me running down the pavement looking over my shoulder and then disappearing around the corner into Russell Street and, with the usual three or four shots in the bag, that was me all done. I wanted to watch them filming the 'baddies chasing me' shot as they were going to be doing it on skateboards. They had been practising all day the day before and me along with them when I got the chance, as none of them had ever really used a skateboard before. But one of them, the larger lady that I previously mentioned, June, had learned to do a complete three hundred and sixty degree board jump on hers and being proud that she had managed it, reckoned she was going to do it the next day on this chase scene. I wanted to see as I had previously made a secret five pound bet with one of the crew, a guy by the name of Jim; he bet that she couldn't do it, me being the one who thought she would. They took a few minutes to prepare for the shot so I took the opportunity to nip around the corner in the hope of seeing the street entertainer again and maybe witness the 'Sandwich of Death' but alas, he had packed up and gone and the crowd had dispersed. It was a bit of a long shot that he'd still be there but I had to try anyway; after all, who would want to miss something with such an intriguing name as that? I got back just in time to see take two of the skateboard chase. I asked someone if June, had managed her three sixty trick without any mishap and was told so far so good – so I was still on for my fiver. Take two. They came scooting around from the top of the pavement, whizzed past the camera and around into Russell Street just as I had done earlier only on foot. A good shot, I thought and again, no mishaps. As usual, the shenanigans were pulling in curious spectators and as before, a crowd began to develop. This time however, there had been no barriers erected or any visible means to keep them at bay but somehow they managed to keep a nice respectable distance from our proceedings; not too far away that they could not see what was happening but not to close as to impede our efforts. A shout from the crowd "Hey Tom, any chance I could have my picture taken with you?" Looking up, I spied a very pretty young lady jumping up and down near the front. Who was I to deny such an attractive damsel? So with yet another one of my well-honed Hollywood grins, I started to smooch over to her. I hadn't taken two steps when a sudden tug on my arm arrested my progress. "Oh no you don't!" Peter said in one of his rather menacing tones, (you could tell he was used to dealing with wayward actors). "You actor guys never learn, do you? You want a repeat of what happen earlier? Well do you?" I looked at him incredulously "Don't talk to me like that, pal!" came my angered response. How dare he? Who did he think he was? Very quickly followed by the thought ,'I tell you who he is Gary, he's the guy paying your fee, and he's right; you nearly got ripped to pieces a bit earlier on for doing exactly what you're about to do right now, der!' So he was right; I hadn't learnt, had I? Of course, these thoughts go through your head very quickly and he was only looking out for me and the film shoot; we couldn't afford another half hour delay with a repeat of what happened earlier; it was getting a bit late in the day and the light was starting to fade. So I followed up with, "Sorry, Peter. Yeah, you're right mate, my apologies" With another reassuring pat on the back from him he replied, "No worries, Bud" and all was well between us.

Looking around, I had started to notice that we were drawing more of a crowd than the street artists and it was starting to look like we were drawing their trade away. Not good if you rely on only passing the hat around for tips for your living and I have to say the thought did crossed my mind to pass our hat around see if I couldn't get enough for a few beers in the pub afterward. But there was nothing I could do about their plight so I turned my attention to the next, and as it turned out, the final take of the skateboard chase.

"All quiet please, ready for take three" and with that a hush fell over the crew and audience alike. I waited with bated breath, rubbing my hands together, looking over at Jim who was looking back at me with the same expectant look on his face. I silently mouthed the words, "Show me the money", a reference to the film 'Jerry Maguire'. Jim, upon seeing this had to stifle a fit of the giggles which I could see he was struggling and that set me off too. Luckily, our silence prevailed. Now who would win the much coveted fiver? I know it was only five quid but it wasn't about the money. We had, on and off since making the bet, been jibing each other so now it was the principle of the thing, I just had to beat Jim. "Cameras rolling and action" came the cry and right on cue, our four baddies came a wheeling down the pavement. Now being the very large lady that June was and thus giving her a little more kinetic energy than the others, she started to pull ahead, scooting herself along with her free foot, building up speed ready to try her three-sixty flip over trick. She jumped up into the air, clipping the side of the skateboard with her foot as she went so as to flip it over and at that point, everything seemed to go into slow motion. The board flew off at a tangent, spinning all the way, and right through one of the plate glass windows that align the adjacent shop front wall. The window just exploded! Luckily, most of the glass flew inward and rained down on the display there, missing everyone completely but, wow what a noise! It sounded like a bomb had gone off; it was so loud; it certainly made us and the crowd flinch. Meantime poor old June went sailing through the air, arms and legs a flailing, screaming all the way to land with a cringing 'whump!' squarely on her behind. But as luck would have it, and with a large helping of all that padding to cushion the blow, she hurt nothing more than her pride. Getting off lightly. The only thing red about her was her rather embarrassed face. Some of the crew rushed forward and making sure she was alright and helped her to her feet. How she never got hurt I don't know but I was glad she wasn't. She was a very nice lady after all. Once the whole episode was over, the watching audience, who had started whooping and cheering, let out a rapturous round of applause to which the good hearted June, seeing the funny side of it in her usual jovial manor, took a well- deserved bow. As the applause subsided, I overheard the director say to one of the camera men, "Don't suppose you managed to get that, did you?" "Sure did" he replied, "every last inch of it. It couldn't have looked better you'd scripted it with a stunt man". "Cool" came the director's mercenary reply, "Think we'll use that shot then." Followed by "It's a wrap everybody. Well done, let's call it a day". Just in time really as the light had just started to fade and with a back drop of a dispersing crowed, everyone started to pack all the gear away. That was the end of the BUPA shoot for me so I started wandering back to the van to get changed into my normal clothes again when I noticed a bloke in blue stripy leotard type trousers standing a little way away watching the proceedings. I noticed him because he was the same guy who had a little while earlier been performing the whip cracking stunt. His trousers being the big giveaway. I walked over to him. I just had to know what the "Sandwich of Death" was. I asked him and he raised one eye brow, bit like Mister Spock does in Star Trek, and said in a slow, theatrical kind of voice "That's for me to know and you to find out, mate" and with a slow nod of the head and keeping the theatrical tone up added, "I'll be back here again this time tomorrow" With that, he took a slow turn and sidled away. A strange character indeed!

Anyway, whilst I was inside the makeup van getting changed and getting ready to go home, I heard a commotion outside. Sounded like two men arguing so stepping outside I could see a suited man gesticulating at Peter, getting all irate about his broken window and Peter, with a repeating lowering gesture of his hands, was trying to calm him down. Peter was the liaison guy after all so I would guess the job of sorting out the broken window out would fall to him. Having said my goodbyes to nearly everyone except Peter, I shouted over, "See ya Pete, I'm off now". "See you later, Tom. Thanks mate. I'll send you a copy of the promo soon as it's done" and I let him get back to his row. Bet that was going to be a big expensive insurance claim; still I should imagine they were well covered.

Planning the best route home I decided it would be quicker if I walked to Tottenham Court Road tube station rather than get on at Covent Garden only to have to do a one stop change at Tottenham Court road anyway. So, with thoughts of what a good couple of days I had just had and can't wait for a beer with the lads tonight tell them all about it, I set off for home. I had only managed about two steps when a wry faced Jim stepped out in front of me and with a hearty laugh, stuck his hand out and said "Oi Tom, five pounds please".

I never did get to see the full length finished product. I did try several times having speaking on the phone to various members of the Flying Colours outfit at their offices and although every time they promised faithfully to send me a copy on DVD, I never did get one. In the end, I just gave up trying. A shame really as I would have loved to have seen it. Judging by all the mishaps that in the end worked out well, I bet it was very funny to watch and would have been a nice thing to add to my lookalike portfolio. Never mind; it wasn't the first time I had not seen the end result of my lookalike efforts and it wasn't to be the last. Just one of those things I suppose; what might be important to someone is not to someone else. To the guys at Flying Colours, it was just another job that had been and gone along with the endless others they must have done. As with my lookalike jobs really; the amount of jobs I have done and the amount of people I have met along the way who have been thrilled to have their photo taken with a real life genuine lookalike. But for me, although every person is important to me, it was the just the next gig before the next one and the one after that and having done so many, you just can't remember every single one. Having said that, I would not have missed a single job given my time again.

There was a short cut down version of the promo film used as an advert on the telly a few months later. It was only a few tens of seconds long as these TV adverts are. Ran for a couple of months and in one of the shots, it showed the skateboard accident in all its glory, and thus showing the need and benefit of private medical insurance. Plus one or two shots of me running about. I had no idea they were going to use it for this, maybe it was a bit of an afterthought, but it came as a bit of a surprise as one day sitting down with my family to watch a film on the telly, suddenly there was my ugly mug looking back at us.

CHAPTER 8

ANOTHER MISSION

Whilst we are on the subject of Mission Impossible, almost exactly three years to the day from the BUPA job, November 2003, I was contracted to do another secret agent gig dressed as Tom in his Ethan Hunt character once again. This time it was a mortgage company called Mortgage Solutions. Primarily a nationwide Mortgage advice company that dealt with not just mortgages but practically every aspect of money products. These guys were good and a recognised force within this industry. One of the new services they were about to launch was something called M2I. This new branch of their business, as I found out, was a sort of legal accreditation, training, advice and support network for independent financial advisors and all the little financial advice 'one man bands' that were out there at the time. Apparently, up until now there was no legislation, regulation or any type of control over this area of the industry and any one could set them selves up in business whether they knew anything about money matters or not. So for obvious reasons, there were a few cowboys out there and it was time for some regulation to come into play. Fair enough I hear you say, when it comes to money matters we all want to know we are getting sound advice, don't we? So as from 2003 the Financial Services Authority, FSA for short, decided it was time for a change and the whole industry had to be regulated. This all sounds good for the general public and anyway, as I say, who wants bum advice? So legislation was going to be passed and any and all financial advisors had to be registered, accredited and have all the legal certification to allow them to practice their profession in place by the time this happened. All good so far. Now at that time, it did not seem that there was anything in place to help the financial guys get on board with all this. Hence the Mortgage Solutions Company, taking full advantage of this situation, decided to set up this M2I branch of their operation. They advertised their services, canvassed all these money advisors and set up seminars and show cases at six major and strategical places across the country using top class venues. All, bar two, were being held the much coveted Marriot hotels; a nationwide chain of large and very up market places with some of the best conference facilities available. They could, if they got this right, gain a huge amount of business. So this was one of those no expense spared, push the boat out type affairs, I only know this stuff because I got to know some of the guys involved and, being the inquisitive kind of guy that I am, got chatting with them. They told me what was what, although oddly enough it never crossed my mind to ask what the actual M2I stood for; 'Money 2 Invest' would be my guess. So M2I, having the obvious connotations to MI2, the Mission Impossible 2 film, decided to employ a Tom Cruise lookalike as Ethan Hunt, i.e. me, to help things along and take a little bit of the edge off the serious side of things. So with all this in place, the scene was set once again for another mission for little old me.

I got the usual call from Helena at the Susan Scott agency.

As I explained earlier, this particular agent got me a lot of my work back then and Helena had become my main contact with them. I liked Helena. All we lookalikes did. Having met her a few times at the office and gigs, I had got to know her a little. She was a nice girl and had a pleasant, and very calming, manner about her. In my earlier days, my first few gigs before I found my feet as a lookalike, she would often give me some help, advice and the right encouragement to help me along my way for which

I thank her. The other lookalikes I know and have worked with along the way all have nice things to say about her as well. She left the agency rather suddenly and unexpectedly for some reason later on through my lookalike career and she dropped off the radar. We never knew why, and all we lookalikes missed her at the time. My opinion is, reading between the lines, that she had had a row with Susan the business owner over something, money probably 'cos that's what I and one or two of the other lookalikes had rowed with Susan about. As I explained earlier, although never unpleasant, Susan could be hardnosed at times and quite unyielding which, whist good for business and making you glad she was on your side being the agent and all, was rather tough for her staff. Although Helena was there for a long time, longest of all in fact, the agency did seem to have a high turnover of staff compared to the other lookalike agencies. We later heard through the grapevine that she got married and raised a family but having lost touch with her after she left, we never really knew what happened to her. So, wherever you are Helena, I hope all is well for you.

So back to the story; Helena rang me as usual, checking my availability and willingness. Of course I was available; who would want to miss another adventure after all? She told me about this job which was actually six jobs rolled into one. I was, of course, to be in my Mission Impossible guise with full regalia of the black combat outfit of the type I described earlier and to include the props that went with it i.e. mock gun and holster, sun glasses, ear phones with mouth piece and a black briefcase to boot. I was to be bounced to these six different locations across the map in a 'meet and greet, mix and mingle' type gig starting at the Marriott Hotel at Grosvenor square in London and ending up finishing at the Marriott in Newcastle, visiting the Birmingham, Bristol, Manchester and Glasgow Marriott's along the way. This was to be done over the course of about a month in November which worked out to one every few days. The timing was good what with Christmas looming in the next few weeks; it is an expensive time of year after all. I had some other lookalike gigs booked to fit in between these ones from other agents, as well as my usual bread and butter band gigs around the pubs and social clubs. But upon checking my diary, and as would luck would have it, it all seemed to work out nicely so it was all systems go.

Helena emailed over to me all the details and the itinerary and I noticed that the Mortgage Solution had asked for me to contact them directly in order for them to make my travel and accommodation arrangements. This was rather unusual as for the most part I didn't usually meet or talk to the clients until I had actually turned up at the job. Also, I would be the one having to make my own arrangements for anything outside the job itself and then claim back the expenses afterwards in the usual manner of keeping all the necessary receipts, submitting them through my agent to the client who would then forward the money back to the agent along with the agreed fee for the job who would then forward all the money, less their commission of course, on to me. As you can imagine, from time to time this led to confusion, receipts getting lost, or the wrong expense amount being paid and all the usual expected mishaps. It didn't happen very often I hasten to add, clients were usually quite good and prompt at this sort of thing and more often than not it was the agent cocking things up. But when it did it go wrong, it was always a nightmare trying to get it sorted out. More often than not, if the error was under thirty quid or so I would just give up trying after a couple of attempts; it just was not worth all the hassle. So it was refreshing, not to say a relief, when I saw that the client was going to take the time and trouble to deal with all the logistics and expense stuff of my arrangements directly and not leave it down to me to sort it out. Can you imagine the grief of all that too-ing and fro-ing if this little lot got cocked up? It was bad enough on one job if things went wrong but on six...

So having been given their administration department contact number and speaking to a very nice lady, we set about discussing my travel and accommodation needs. She basically let me call the shots; telling her what I would need for each job, her taking down the information and then just leaving it to her to book everything.

With the London job, I was just going to get the train there and back. Some of the others I thought best if I drove to them. I was going to fly to the Glasgow job but for Newcastle I decided I would get the train. I didn't have to; they offered to fly me there as well but it had been a very long time since I had done a nice long train journey and I quite fancied it, to be honest. It is a novelty if it is only once in a while and besides, I like looking out the window at all the scenery and the various towns along the way. It wasn't going to take too much longer than flying, by the time I had checked in and hung around for the flight to take off and then hanging around again to collect my suitcase at the other end. Airports are boring, trains aren't.

She was going to book me into Travel Lodge hotels, the nearest ones to each particular job as possible. Using all the charm I could muster, and bearing in mind I used to be a salesman – and a good one at that, I did try and talk her into letting me stay at the Marriot hotels themselves but alas, even my best closing techniques couldn't persuade this tough customer. This nut was not for cracking but, hey, you can't blame a guy for trying can you? "I deal with your type all day long, love. I can see right through you but I take my hat off to you; it was a good effort. Maybe you should consider coming to work for us, I'll put the word in for you if you like" was her jovial response. "No thanks I'd rather be a lookalike it's much more fun" I retorted and with that we both had a little chuckle. The only things that were not covered were any taxi fares i.e. going to and from the jobs to the hotels and my petrol expenses as we didn't know how much they were going to be until I had done them. So she very kindly made arrangements for me to give the relevant receipts to my liaison guy, a chap by the name of Andy Puffin. On the day of each job and he would give me the cash back there and then. All sounded great to me; no waiting for an expense cheque to arrive through the post, no scrolling through the internet looking at hotels and flights to book and train timetables. All I had to do was tell her what I wanted and she organised the lot for me. A couple of days later I got everything I needed through the post and with that, I sat back and looked forward to the first gig at Grosvenor square in London the following week.

So the following week came around and, as it was an early start, I packed everything I needed into a little suitcase, outfit, props and even a tub of gel for my hair having had my hair cut specifically for this job a couple of days earlier. I am lucky really I have a good head of hair but it is quite thick and doesn't really lie like Tom had it in the Mission Impossible films so gel aplenty needed to be applied to my bonce to get it styled right for looking the part. So much so, that when it dried, it was like a solid lump of cardboard glued to my scalp; you could practically knock it with your knuckles and get a tapping sound out of it! Hell or high water weren't going to shift that little lot once it had been fashioned, I can tell you. Another thing about my hair was that around this time, although I have never lost any and still haven't being as it is so thick (lucky me), I was over forty years old by now and just starting to go a little grey around the edges. This meant that I had to start to dye it; something I wasn't very keen on. I have never liked the vanity thing in men. It is ok in women but when men do it, somehow, it just comes across as vain to me.

Humour one of my little digressions here: I have a friend, naming no names, who hasn't aged so well. He's thinning on top with lots of grey so he dyes it. He smokes like a trouper so he has his yellowing teeth whitened on a regular basis. All this other stuff he does to try and make himself look younger but he just looks stupid. He can't pass a mirror, or shop window for that matter, without checking himself out, always glancing in whatever reflective surface is available. It's cringe worthy. I'm sure we all know someone like that. He reminds me of the character 'Cat' in the comedy syfy show Red Dwarf, of which I am a great fan. Anyway having to dye my hair reminded me of all that but the lure of keeping on with all this fun lookalike stuff was far greater than not wanting to feel vain so the dyeing of the hair prevailed.

I got the usual train into London that bright and early morning. I made my way by tube to Marble Arch station where after alighting, and being a little on the early side, I took a leisurely stroll along Park Lane running beside Hyde Park and enjoyed the view. It just happened to be one of those cold but sunny mornings and the park looked lovely. I like to people watch from time to time and enjoyed watching all the London work force folk scurrying past me getting to the office on time. Glad I didn't have to do all that anymore; all that nine to five stuff just 'not my bag man'.

I never really thought much about London when I used to work there years before in my younger days, just a place I had to travel to work to I suppose. But thereafter visiting it from time to time, I have learned to appreciate the capital a lot more and have come to really like the place.

I turned into Upper Brook Street and wandered down to Grosvenor Square past the American Embassy to my right and round the bend to the Marriott Hotel. I noticed that there were a couple of army soldiers parading up and down outside the American embassy, looking rather menacing. As I understand it, anything inside the boundaries of the embassy was considered American soil and so, as far as I know, they are allowed to have these soldiers about. But, they still looked menacing to me and they were keeping a beady eye on any passers-by. Not surprising really when you consider that the 9/11 attack on the World Trade Centres in New York had only been about two short years before. In fact, the whole of the western world was on high alert at that time and there had been another series of threats recently. Paranoia was rampant in every major city back then and everyone was suspicious of everything. I noticed that they were paying particular attention to me as I walked by; I couldn't figure it out at first, what they looking at? Then it dawned on me; is it any wonder with all that suspicion about and here was a guy leisurely strolling passed them, looking like he was casing the joint and pulling a smallish black suit case behind him? So not wanting to get shot or anything, I quickly averted my gaze and hurried on past.

It had been arranged that I was to meet my liaison chap Andy Puffin at ten o'clock outside the main entrance of the Marriott. The whole day's event was supposed to kick off at eleven so I would have plenty of time to be briefed, get changed and sort out the concrete hair do. I had also been told that Mortgage Solutions had hired the whole of one side of the entrance foyer as well as their executive conference hall. But when I arrived; no Andy. I asked the very well-attired door man, (nice hat, dude, by the way) if I could go in which was fine with him and he opened the door for me. But as I stepped through, nothing! Strange, I thought. So I got my paper work out and check the details but, no, I had got it right. Not knowing what to do, I wandered over to the reception desk and asked the young lady if she knew anything about it but she just said as far as she knew, they were supposed to have been there at eight o'clock that morning. I gave the agent a ring, explaining what had happened but they didn't know anything about it either. Oh well, I was under contract so if they didn't show up I was still going to get paid. So what the heck, time for a chill.

I wandered into the restaurant area next door and over to the bar which was in the process of getting ready to open at eleven for the day business. I asked the girl behind the bar if I could have a coffee. After staring at me for a little bit she said, "You're the Tom Cruise guy I've got coming here today aren't you?" "Yeah that's me, love. I'm supposed to be doing a job here but I don't know where everyone is. Any chance of that coffee while I'm waiting" I said then added, "I bet it don't come cheap in a place like this though!" "Don't worry about the money, honey, I'm an absolute Tom Cruise fan. This one's on the house. In fact our speciality here is brandy coffee. Wanna try one?" said she with an absolutely delighted look on her face. Bit early in the morning for alcohol I thought, but what the hell, it's only the one. "Don't suppose you could make it de-caff could ya?" "Yeah 'course I could, anything for you, Tom. In fact, I think I'll join you if you don't mind. I'm not actually on duty today, I only come in to see the Tom Cruise lookalike but I didn't think I was actually going to get to talk to him. By the way, did I mention I was an absolute Tom Cruise fan?" she added, "I met him once you know, only briefly mind, got me picture took with him, 'ere look" and with that, before getting the coffees, she got her camera phone out, (they've all got cameras on them these days but back then they were still a bit of a novelty), she showed me some photos and proceeded to tell me her Tom Cruise story, bless her. It passed the time and I did get a free brandy coffee out of it so who was I to deny her her little tale?

Mmm, brandy. It is my second favourite drink in all the world (my first favourite being of course, tea in case I hadn't mentioned!) Now I like a drink or two just like the next man but the usual going down the pub for a couple of beers with the misses or your mates is usually enough for me. However, when it comes to brandy, even if it is in coffee, after I've had a couple I get a taste for it; you know the feeling. It has a tendency to lower my barriers and so I often end up getting rather inebriated. For that reason, I try to avoid it unless it's for a special occasion and I certainly wouldn't drink it during the day let along whilst I was working on a job. How unprofessional would that be? But here I was doing exactly that. But, hey one wouldn't hurt; it's only a liquor coffee after all.

After finishing our drinks, it dawned on me that I still had the telephone number of the woman in the administration department at Mortgage Solutions written down on my paper work. Not having my mobile on me, (still not being to bothered about carry one around with me very much at that stage), I asked the young lady if I could borrow hers to see if I could find out what was going on. She very kindly let me so I rang the office and was told that things had been set back and kick off wasn't until one o'clock now. They should be arriving there shortly and she didn't know why I hadn't been told so many apologies. Andy Puffin should be there any moment to meet me. "Oh well," said brandy coffee girl, "let's have another shall we?" and with that she shouted, "Dave, couple more please". At that moment a rather breathless and dishevelled looking fellow came running in and coming over to our table said breathlessly "Gary, I presume?" "Yeah that's me" I said "Andy I presume?" And we shook hands followed by me saying "and this young lady is...." not knowing her name. "Oh hi Lisa or should I say. Brandy Girl, ha ha" Andy said to which she replied "Hey, it's 'The Puffer' how you doing?" A little perplexed, I said "Take it you two already know each other then?" "Yeah" Andy said breathing normally by now "we met when the firm booked this place. Lisa kindly showed me around and we had a couple of brandy coffees as I remember" to which Lisa responded, "We sure did and the rest. Hey Dave, make that three please, mate" "Watch her, Tom, she likes a tipple or two" Puffer said, letting out another little laugh as they did the kiss on the cheek thing "damn well nearly got me pissed, she did". "Didn't see you complaining" she smiled as they launched into a little banter between them. I have never got the pretend kissy kissy thing on the cheek; all seems rather false to me. Why dont woman shake hands like us blokes do? Still anyway... "Sorry about the mix up, Tom I got here as fast as I could. Didn't want you buggering off or anything." "No worries, Andy. I rang your office just before you came in and they explained what happened" came my reply "and anyway, what's with the 'Puffer' thing?" I added thinking that it might just have been because he was out of breath just now. "Oh that's my nickname. Please feel free to use it. I prefer it to being called Andy, everyone's called Andy, but whatever you do, don't call me Puff alright, or I'll slug you one" He added with a some-what menacing tone. "What, as in Puff the magic dragon?" I couldn't resist saying. "No, that's not what I mean" but I knew exactly what he meant. And that is how I was introduced to The Puffer.

A "Puff" by the way, for the uninitiated, was a very old deroga-tory slang word used to describe someone who is gay. These days there are not many people who can't accept the gay community but years ago it was a different world. Check out the song 'Jilted John' and you will hear this reference.

Puffer, after giving me my brief, explained that the rest of the crew would be along shortly and, being well-practised in this sort of seminar thing, they could have the whole thing set up in an hour and a half. At this point, as there was not anything for us to do right now, how about yet another round of brandy coffees which, at Lisa's behest, actually turned into three large brandies. I looked at Lisa and said, "You missed out the coffee part, didn't you?" at which point Puffer said, looking at me with a sly little grin on his face, "Naw you're all right, Tom".

I liked these two or their propensity for brandy at any rate and having already had a couple in my coffees, without realising it, my barriers were now down.

We sat there chatting for about an hour or so whilst I watched the crew transform their hired half of the entrance lobby into a Mortgage Solutions reception area and it was looking good. As well as their company regalia, there was a few interspersed posters of Mission Impossible placards which tied up nicely with the MI2 to M2I twist that were doing. They regaled the entire conference room with the company logos in the form of banners and had erected a low level stage at the front with a projection screen higher up behind it. Everything was set ready to go and it was now time for me to get changed into costume ready for the 'meet and greet'. So I stood to my feet. Wow, I was pissed! I had felt fine all the time I was sitting down, you don't realise it do you? But once I had stood up that's when it hit me and I had to grab a hold of the side of the table for a moment till I gathered myself. "Feeling a little woozy there are we, Tom?" Lisa said with a laugh but not wanting to show I had had one too many, especially in front of Puffer who was effectively my boss for the duration of these jobs, I gave a little cough and said "Nah, I'm fine". But I wasn't. At that moment Puffer stood up himself and did the 'grab hold of the table thing' as well. He must have felt the same as me which somehow made me feel a bit better; we had both kind of accidently got drunk together. Looking over at me he said, "See what I mean about her? She did this to me last time" and they both let out a well- meaning laugh.

I went off to the changing rooms, probably staggered more like (I couldn't believe I had let myself get into this state) but after splashing some cold water in my face and a few deep breaths, my head started to clear a bit; enough for me to be able to get ready anyway. Once attired, I stepped forth ready to do battle, so to speak. It was now one o'clock and the first of the guests started to arrive. I did my usual stand at the entrance of the conference room thing, handing out glasses of champagne that were being handed to me from the girl behind and shaking hands with what seemed like a constant stream of grey suited old men. All the while I was saying one of my favourite Lookalike lines that I had invented for just such an occasion "Hi! Tom's the name, Spying's the game!" in my usual loud caricature of an American accent voice, followed by, "If you would like to follow one of the girls, they will take to your seat". None of them chuckled; in fact no one even cracked a smile which was unusual as normally you would at the very least get some kind if interaction with the folk and I was kind of thinking 'I don't think these guys get the senti-ment here'. I realised that at most 'Meet and Greets' there was always some kind of party thing going on but this was turning into a rather sombre do. I overheard one or two of them saying to each other things like, "Bloody legislation. Now we got to waste a day away having to do this kind of thing instead of being in the office getting on with it!" and other such like comments. Clearly they felt like it was some kind of necessary chore so the last thing they wanted was a lookalike all up in their face trying to make a joke of it all. In a way I could see their point of view.

I went over and spoke to Puffer, who had already drawn the same conclusion as me. So, picking up a couple of glasses of cham-pagne, handing one to me and having a few slurps between us, we formulated a plan to try and liven things up. Bearing in mind our previous consumption of a not too small amount of brandy on top of our now second glass of champers each, we decided that, as their morose attitude seemed to have started when they first started talking to each other (misery loves company and all that), it might be better if I were to greet them right on the steps of the main entrance. They seemed to be coming in one by one and therefore not having a chance to converse with one another yet, we might catch them in better spirits there. But alas, this didn't seem to be working either. However, feeling 'four sheets to the wind' by now, I couldn't have cared less. I was in full swing at this point and as usual, enjoying every moment of it. So was Puffer as he had decided to stand a few feet out in front of me on the pavement, introducing the delegates to Tom before they got to me, just to try and help them to get in to the 'swing of it' as it were. Although we were drunk, we had managed to maintain our composure and at least a reasonable degree of professionalism so far.

The tide of financial advisors was starting to thin by now and most of those who were going to attend had already arrived. Most, but not quite all. Me and Puffer had a little chat whilst consuming another glass of the good ol' champers; which actually was the straw that broke the camel's back for us because we went from holding our own to proper drunk. So, deciding to have a laugh, we formulated a, "what seemed a good idea at the time", type plan; a *good idea* when you've had one too many, that is! I was to go out on the pavement down the side of the hotel, where the clients had been walking down from the tube station and, drawing my fake pistol from its holder, see if I could chase the last guy down the road and in to the hotel. As I say it seemed such a good idea at the time in our less than compos mentis state. It just didn't occur to us that it might scare the shit out of someone let alone actually be illegal; holding a gun out in public even if it was fake. What were we thinking? But of course we weren't thinking! But the biggest mistake, that hadn't even entered our stupid sozzled heads, was the fact that I was going to be running off in the direction of the, "on very high alert with soldiers posted outside it", American Embassy, waving a gun in the air! Bang, bye bye Tom!

So with the pair of us giggling away and drawing gun from holster, off I went. I only managed to get ten to fifteen yards or so when – thump! I was completely knocked off my feet. Having the wind knocked out of me, I realised that I had been rugby tackled to the ground by the hotel doorman. Thank God, I hasten to add with the benefit of hind sight. "What the hell do you think you're doing, you stupid prat?" he bellowed at me as he picked himself up and dusted himself off. It turned out as he was standing by the entrance where we were when we hatched our little plan, he had overheard everything we had said. Thinking we were just mucking about, he hadn't said anything, just ignored us. But when he saw me start to move and getting my gun out, he thought it best to arrest the situation as quickly as possible before anything untoward happened. He chased me down the road and, being a rugby player in his spare time, did the first thing that came to mind to stop a moving target – and down I went.

I came to my senses very quickly and sitting rather indignantly on my arse on the pavement, hands splayed out behind me, I looked up at him and with wide and rapidly blinking eyes said, "I'm really sorry, mate, and thanks. What the hell was I thinking?" He straightened his jacket, breathed a sigh and shaking his head slowly he said, "Silly sods" and stepped back to his holding position by the hotel entrance. He was a pretty cool cucumber, if you ask me.

Luckily for us, no one had noticed our little escapade except for what looked like two couples who were out for a stroll on the other side of the road and they, after laughing their heads off, gave us a whistle and a clap and shouted, "Encore!" Even luckier for us, no one from inside the hotel had spotted our antics either as it was the wrong angle. Most importantly, any staff from Mortgage Solutions would not have been able to see what transpired as they were all standing by the conference room door ushering the last of the financial guys into the seminar. So we had got away with that by the skin of our teeth.

I got changed as I had finished my part of the event, (to the client's satisfaction, I feel it necessary to add, given our more than slightly inebriated state.) Puffer, who was also not needed on this occasion, decided he was starving, such are the benefits of alcohol. Ever been down the kebab shop after a night at the pub? Well, it was one of those situations. So we headed off to the hotel restaurant and knowing this was going to be on the Puffer's company hospitality credit card, we had a nice big slap up meal. We were joined by Lisa once again who had been hanging around so she could catch up with us later on. With a little persuasion from her, not to mention having got the taste for it from earlier on, the brandies flowed once again whilst we relayed our story of what happened outside the hotel. She found it all rather hilarious and the three of us chatted away like we were old friends until about four o'clock in the afternoon.

By the time we decided to call it a day, we were so pissed that we were slurring our words. God knows how I was going to get home in my state but I had to try so after asking Puffer if he wouldn't mind hanging onto my suit case and get it to the next gig in a few days, I bid my goodbyes and staggered off. At least I had the presence of mind to know that there would be a fair chance of me losing my case on the train or something. The journey home was a bit of a blur. I managed to stumble to the tube station, I think it was Marble Arch but I'm not sure, and somehow made my way to Fenchurch Street. Probably more by luck than judgment. Not being able to read the platform signs because of my now blurred vision, I got on to what I hoped was the right train and immediately fell into a drunken stupor. I've no idea how I managed to actually make it home from this point – my next memory was standing in the road outside my house beside a taxi fumbling with my wallet, dropping it at least once or twice, handing over a couple of notes to the driver and saying, "Keep the change mate". I could not work out what I actually paid him but I remember he seemed more than pleased! And for my next trick, make my way to the front door. That must have taken about ten minutes of more. My neighbour, Jamie, later mentioned that I looked like some kind of cowboy who had just got off his horse after a long, long ride as apparently I was doing the wide leg stagger.

The next obstacle to negotiate on my drunken assault course was the dreaded front door. No way did I have the where-with-all for managing the door key thing; it just wasn't going to happen. So I banged on the door nice and loud, if a little relentlessly, and as it was opened, I fell through. The only other thing I can recall from that oh-so-memorable trip home was looking at the clock as I fell into bed still in my clothes, after negotiating the stairs straight from the front door. It said eleven o'clock. The next morning I had such a hangover like you wouldn't believe and I vowed there and then that I was never going to drink again-Ever! Ever! Ever! Well... until the next time, ha ha!

Here's the thing though, the trip home would have taken at most about two hours or so and as I left the hotel at four, I should have been home for around six-ish. Where had I been? Who knew? Certainly not I. I had managed to lose about five hours and to this day, I still have absolutely no idea where they went!

The next job in this series of gigs was in Birmingham at the Hilton Metropole hotel three or four days later. It was to be the same scenario as the Grosvenor gig with me doing the 'meet and greet' at the entrance. But this time, Puffer wanted me to do a little 'mix and mingle' at the reception where, as before, their clients would be offered glass of champagne and have a chance to meet each other; have a little chat and compare notes. Then they would go into the conference room where they would have all explained to them and be pitched for their business. Their business was to get the necessary accreditation they needed, with the help of Mortgage Solutions of course, and to join the company's ever growing financial advisors after sales club, M2I. This way they would get all the backup they needed in the form of on tap legal advice and all the latest developments in the financial world as well as the latest products etc. All rather dull and mundane; for me anyway. All right, I suppose if that sort of thing floats your boat, and you would have to if you were in that line of work; after all, we've all got to earn a living one way or another so I'm not knocking it but I find it hard to get to excited about such stuff it just doesn't sound like fun to me. I like a bit of fun, that's why I was playing guitar and singing in a band and did lookalike work; singing for my supper is where I'm at. So from my point of view they may, or may not, have earned a better living than me but I felt I was having a more joyous life and you only live once.

Having said all that, I'm not knocking the financial industry. After all, money makes the world go round as the saying goes and besides, I probably would not have had been a lookalike at all as most of our gigs are corporate functions of one kind or another after all. Plus, of course, I would not have been able to buy my house without a mortgage, so good on ya, boys.

So off I trundled to Birmingham to put my best foot forward once again. This particular gig, whilst fun, was not particularly noteworthy. It was quite 'bog standard' for a lookalike job but nothing wrong with 'bog standard'; it was the lookalike's bread and butter after all. It was an early-ish start and I did not want to get up at silly o'clock to get there in time, and then be knackered whilst I was working when I was supposed to be all smiles bright and lively (not to mention having to sit in rush hour traffic on the M6 and the M25).

It's hideous! If you have ever had to stand still for hours on end in the morning traffic on the M25, you will know it is best to avoid it all costs. I feel sorry for people who have to that every day, poor sods!

So I drove up the evening before to arrive at the Travel Lodge that had been booked for me. I met up with me old mucker, Puffer, in a pub just around the corner from my hotel in time to have an evening meal and a couple of beers together (even though in the not too distant past I swore I would never drink again!) We had a bit of a catch up and spoke about the events of the previous gig. I asked him if anyone had said anything about our escapades and being a little drunk on the job but he quelled my anxieties by saying, "Hey, I'm the one who organised this particular branch of the operation so I can do what I like. Don't you worry about it." Cool, I thought, but we did promise not to drink on the job again.

I liked the Puffer; we got on well, we were on the same wave length, he liked having a laugh and liked a brandy, (all though, just for the record, none consumed that night), so he was all good in my book. We bid our good nights and parted company till the morrow. Then back to the hotel and off to bed for an early night.

The next morning after checking out and then making my way to Hilton Metropole hotel, I met up with all the crew. Like the last time, they had hired at least half the entrance foyer as the reception area and hotel's best and largest suite to put the conference in; transforming the look of both with the same regalia that they had used before. We discussed the up and coming day's events and who was going to be doing what. I got changed, having picked up my suit case form one of the staff who kindly fetched it along for me, then it was all systems go. I did the 'meet and greet' and 'mix and mingle' with my usual enthusiasm, (and lack of folly this time around I hasten to add), and all went well. Then thinking my job was done, Puffer sidled up to me and said that the guy who did the initial opening introductions at the actual seminar hadn't turned up. Apparently, he had contracted laryngitis, (not good when you a speaker), so would I mind doing the opening speech for them? That was ok with me but what the hell do I say? I knew nothing about this line of business but once again the Puffer way laid my fears. "I'll knock a little something up for you to read out Tom" he said and that's what he did. It was a cut down version of what laryngitis man was going to be saying being only three or four minutes long and any way there was a bottle of brandy in it for my good self apparently! Gee I wonder who thought of that bribe then? So who was I to say no?

When everybody was seated and the intro music finished, I walked up on to the make shift stage, approached the microphone and reading from the script, I delivered the introduction speech.

I had no idea what I was on about; all this product talk about money was just gobbledygook to me, but I read it with true professionalism, (with a bottle of Courvoisier riding on it who wouldn't?), and then introduced the main compare and handed over to him for the rest of the proceedings. "Well done, mate" Puffer said "that went well". "Did it sound ok? Didn't have a clue what I was talking about" was my response. "Well you would not have known it all sounded very well delivered. May be you should have a professional vocation as a speaker" he said with a little pseudo wink and a nod but all I could think of was that nice bottle of plonk I was promised so with a held out hand I responded with, "Bottle of brandy please".

It was time to make tracks homeward so once again after getting changed back into my civvies, repacking the costume and props in to my suitcase and then bidding adieu to all concerned, I made my way out to the car, pulled out of the car park and hit the road home.

The next couple of Mortgage Solution gigs after that were pretty much the same as the Birmingham job. The venues were in the Marriott hotel in Bristol and the Radisson SAS Hotel up in sunny Manchester. Both were fun to do but fairly straight forward and not particularly taxing for an experienced lookalike as I was by now. I drove to both jobs and stayed in the nearest Travel Lodges to the venues, did my 'meet and greet, mix and mingles' as was my remit but on these occasions. I was now also doing the introduction speech at the beginning of both of the seminars. Laryngitis Man had still not recovered and given my Oscar winning performance the last time (ha ha), not to mention my very reasonable recompense of one bottle of brandy per show, how could I resist? Actually I would have just done it for nothing as it was helping then out and I was getting well paid anyway. However, as the said recompense was offered before I had said anything, I thought it would have been rude to refuse! Five bottles of brandies I earned myself in the end. As I didn't really drink much at home, it took me a very long time to work my way through them; three got drunk over the course of time, one went out as a Christmas present one year and I still have one bottle left in the cupboard in doors. Actually, as I've just reminded myself about it, I think I'll have a wee tot right now, just to help me along with my writings you understand.

The only thing that was different was at the Bristol gig where ol' Puffer introduced me to a member of their staff, an Indian lady by the name of Anusha. The name Anusha, she later told me, meant 'A Beautiful Morning Star' in Indian and I remember thinking, what a cool name to call your daughter. Must have been a bit of a mouthful at times though; can you imagine calling your kid down for breakfast "Hey, A Beautiful Morning Star, it's breakfast time"? How long would it take until it got abbreviated to something like "Oi, Booty"! My mates call me Gal (pronounced 'Gauw') all the time; yuck eh? In our country, British names don't tend to mean anything, (well some do if you back far enough), but on the whole they are just words used as names. My own daughter's name is Mollie, which as far as I know does not stand for anything in particular, just a nice name. However she is *my* 'Beautiful Morning Star'.

Anusha had very dark skin and long black hair but spoke with a very loud and broad Scottish accent which seemed a kind of contradiction that I found amusing. She had been tasked with the job of keeping a journal of events for Mortgage Solutions; what, why and how these M2I events where doing. All part of the company keeping abreast of the effectiveness of how their sales strategies were working, so she told me, and also it allowed the company to tweak things along the way if necessary. It turned out she had a particular fascination with the world of lookalikes and she asked me that at some point, if I did not mind, could she do an interview with me which I agreed to. After that, I noticed her about all over the place; talking in her loud Gaelic voice, taking notes about this and that, whereas I had never noticed her before. It's funny isn't it; once you are aware of someone or something, you wonder how you could have ever missed it, like when you get a new car you see that make and model everywhere afterwards. She did do her interview with me but it was not until a later date.

The Glasgow job was pretty much along the same lines as the previous two with the exception that this time, I flew there. I drove to Stanstead airport and got an internal flight up to the Glasgow airport which took only about an hour and I slept all the way. Having then taken a taxi to the Travel Lodge, once again I was settled in my room by the end of the afternoon. This time I had no Puffer to keep me company and I was bored.

Now, being in the middle of Glasgow city and my first time in Scotland, I decided to out to explore. I stepped out of the hotel and walking around the corner, I found myself at one end of a shopping precinct. It was just after eight o'clock in the evening by now so most of the shops were shutting up for the day. After walking to the other end of the precinct and out onto a street, I heard the sound of music coming from a bar at the other end of the road. Cool, I thought, I'll go and have a beer and watch a band playing. After I arrived and ordered a pint of the local brew, I found myself a seat in the corner and watched this absolutely wonderful acoustic band. They really grabbed my attention as one of the members was playing an instrument called a mandola and, as a mandolin player myself, it fascinated me.

Let me explain; I am a musician and I play a few instruments such as guitar, piano, harmonica and the mandolin so I appreciate a good muso when I see one. With the violin, the next size up is the viola which plays in a slightly lower register. So it is with the mandolin; the next size up is the mandola, and as a mandolin player, I could see the guy playing it was mustard; it sounded excellent. The rest of the band consisted of a chap on the drums, another chap playing an upright double bass and the main singer strumming on an acoustic guitar (an Ovation Balladeer no less, the same guitar as the one I have at home). The singing was also a delight to listen to as their harmonies were spot on; upper thirds, lower fifths and such like so the four of them together sounded like a choir.

They played a selection of songs ranging from popular classics over the years to acoustic versions of rock songs to traditional Scottish folk music. The guy on the mandola was quite an old dude; he had a mop of unkempt greying hair and a straggly grey beard. He looked like a tramp but with the voice on an angel! Looks wise he reminded me of that old American Blues player with the three stringed guitar, 'Sea Sick Steve' he calls himself if you know who I mean. I remember them doing a particularly good rendition of the old Simon and Garfunkel song 'Bridge over Troubled Water' and one of my favourite of theirs 'Sound of Silence'. I was so impressed that I phoned up my mate from the band that I was playing in at the time, and said, "Listen to this" then held the phone up in the air for him to hear.

After about half an hour or so of listening to this wonderful ear candy, I was so enthralled that I didn't notice some guy sideling up to my table and plonking himself down beside me. My first awareness of him was when I felt a hand on my knee! It made me jump, and when I realised it was a fella, I jumped even further. This had never happened to me before and so, not expecting anything like this out of the blue, I was a bit stunned. Not really taking in the situation, I looked over to him with complete surprise on my face as I rather...forcibly pushed his hand off my knee. Seemingly unperturbed, this guy leaned over to me and said in a Scandinavian accent, "Hey, you wanna go somewhere and have some fun?" Now the more homophobic amongst us probably would have slugged him one right in the mouth but luckily for him I suppose, I don't have anything against gay people. I'm not homophobic myself but neither am I gay, so keeping a cool head I said back to him, "No thanks mate, my bread's not buttered that side". Realising his mistake, he stood up and putting his hands out in front of himself, he started to back away, saying "Oh sorry, I'm really sorry." With a frightened look on his face, disappeared up the other side of the bar. Still feeling a bit perturbed and realising my pint was empty, I walked over to the bar and ordered another. I said to the barman, "Did you see that?" "Yeah I did" he said. "What's his problem?" I said to which he responded with a laugh, "What's your problem, more like". I didn't get what was he on about then he added, "Look around you, mate" as he poured my next brew. So I did. There was not a single female in the joint and then it dawned on me, I was in a gay bar! I had been so captivated by the music I was hearing I hadn't even noticed when I walked in and besides, it did look like an ordinary pub to me. "Not from around here are you, Bud?" said the barman to me, "this is the hang out for the local gay community, on a Thursday night at any rate; tonight is the best business of the week." Luckily for me, I have a good sense of humour and was amused by the whole situation I had accidently put myself in. The beer had been poured and the night was starting to come to an end so I stayed a little longer listening to the bands encore and finished my drink. I managed to have a little chat with the mandola guy and we talked about the benefits and deficits of guitar verses mandolin; acoustically speaking, they are a good two instruments to blend together especially as the mandola is in a similar frequency range as the guitar. If you are interested in that sort of thing that is, as I am, of course. I did ask if the band were gay being as they were playing in a gay joint. They said they weren't but they do play a lot of gay places because as one of them put it, "They pay more than the Hetties." I gathered from that that 'Hettie' meant heterosexual. At the end of the night I made my way back to the hotel and got my head down for the night, ready for the day's work tomorrow.

The next day we had another early start to the day and I did more of the usual 'Meet and Great, Mix and Mingle', still enjoying myself as ever. One thing I had noticed was that the further north we migrated with each event, the more 'up for it' the clientele became. By the time we reached Scotland, the reception turned into something more like a party. They seemed a little less inhibited somehow than at the other places we had been to so far but it didn't take long for me to realise why.

Now the Scottish have a reputation for liking a drink or two don't they, or as they like to say 'a wee dram' and these guys, right from the start, were really knocking back the free champagne. They were getting louder and louder and laughing lots... and taking absolutely no notice of me whatsoever, but it was all good natured. They hustled and bustled in to the conference room, still loudly conversing as they all took their seats. However, as I took to the stage and approached the microphone to start speaking, a complete and instantaneous hush befell the place. It was so sudden that it was spooky. After delivering my speech, I had done my bit for this event and made my way to the changing rooms to change into my civvies once again. On the way I bumped into Anusha, busily writing her notes. Remembering that she had said she wanted to do a little interview with me, after saying our hellos, I asked did she want to talk to me now? However she said she would have a chat a little later. I told her about my little saga last night at the gay bar which made her laugh but I did say to keep it quiet from The Puffer "cos we know how he likes to take the piss". She said she would but of course she didn't. Within about ten minutes of me coming out of the changing room the Puffer came up to me and said, "Ooh ooh, nice boy" in a mocking effeminate voice, "What's your name then? Must be Tomalisious" to which everyone in ear shot, who had obviously been told, started laughing. Talk about a rumour spreading like wild fire; this lot where gossip central and for the rest of the day at least, Tomalisious was my new name.

As it had been a long day on this event and my flight home wasn't until tomorrow so I retired back to my hotel. I met up with the Puffer and one or two of the others for a bite to eat and a beer and discussed the day's event. Everything was going really well; they had got lots of clients on board and they were more than happy with me. I was in my room by 8.30 and deciding on a night in, I plonked myself on the bed to watch a bit of telly. At about nine o'clock, my phone rang. It was Anusha, ringing from her hotel phone in her room. She wanted to have that chat/interview thing with me so I said come over and we'll have a beer but she declined saying the she doesn't drink and, as she was a bit knackered, she couldn't be arsed. We ended up chatting for ages; not just about lookalike stuff but just about everything under the sun and by the time I put the phone down, it was a quarter to twelve. We had been on the phone for nearly three hours! She told me at the next gig in Newcastle that that phone call had cost her over two hundred quid! Bet she'd wished she'd had a beer instead it would have been a lot cheaper.

CHAPTER 9

THE LAST M2I

The final one in these series of seminars was to be at the Marriott hotel up in Newcastle. This one was a slightly different arrangement in the fact that rather than being more of a lunchtime thing, they were doing it in the early evening instead. It was a bit of an early start so I timed it all so that I could arrive at the Travel Lodge around four in the afternoon; it had been booked for me to stay overnight after the 'show' this time. So I got the nine o'clock train to Fenchurch Street then the tube train round to Kings Cross train station and caught the eleven o'clock express train to Newcastle Central station. The journey there took about four hours and the train was half empty so I put my feet up and prepared for a nice relaxing trip. We stopped off at one or two places along the way, none of which I can remember, and the first half of the journey was pretty uneventful so looking out the window I enjoyed the view of the passing English country-side. Somewhere about two hours in, half way along the trip, (it was about ten minutes since the train had last stopped and quite a few people had got on here) I noticed a man, who was sitting with his wife and kids opposite me, kept peering over the top of his laptop every so often and taking a look at me. I thought to myself, 'Oi oi, another gay guy wanting to try his luck' and let out a little unintentional laugh. His kids were looking at me as well and whilst nudging each other giggling were whispering into each other's ears, as children do, whilst their mother was telling them off in a hushed voice saying, "Don't so be rude" and "Stop staring", like I couldn't hear what she was saying. They were only young; a brother and a sister, and looked about eight years old to me. This went on for about five minutes until the father leaned over to them and said rather curtly, "Stop that!" and gave them both a gentle tap on the leg. After another couple of minutes, with the kids starting to play up again, the chap leaned over towards me and said, "Excuse me, sorry to interrupt you but I know you, don't I?" He was ever so polite and spoke with a public school boy type accent. "I don't think so, fella. I've not seen you before" I replied. "Yes I'm sure I do you know" he insisted. I responded with a polite "To be honest I get that all the time" and with not wanting to give away who I supposedly looked like I added "I've just got one of those faces". He wouldn't give up though he said, "What do you mean?" So I said, "Well, to be honest, I work as a lookalike" and with that he snapped his fingers and said, "That's it! I saw you on the television last night. You were the Tom Cruise chappy on 'Your Face or Mine'."

Now I have to go off story for a little while here. A few months earlier, I was offered a job by one of my agents to appear on a popular T.V. program at the time called 'Your Face or Mine' that used to be shown on Channel 4 one evening every week. It was very popular at the time and attracted a great many viewers; one of those sorts of programs that the 'girls in the office' would be discussing on the Monday morning tea break type thing. It was one of these types of pseudo agony aunt programs whereby people would apply and the 'lucky' invited guests would appear on the show, discuss their relationship problems and then the show's host would get the programs resident councillor to sort them out and send then on their way. It was a little bit along the lines of the Jeremy Kyle show, as we touched upon before, but not quite so low life. Not so flamboyant and in your face. The guests were real and from relatively normal walks of life, (well how 'normal' must you be to want to air your personnel problems to the nation?) and reasonably well behaved. I say "reasonably" because it did have its little moments of flare up. The point is they were not all these fat scuzzies on the social 'effing and blinding' at each other; these guys had jobs and lives and stuff so it tended to be a little more tame and relatable. I think that is what made it popular, people could actually identify with the guests a bit more. However, it would nearly always be a love triangle type of theme whereby one half of a couple being torn between two people and having to choose which one they preferred, hence 'Your Face or Mine'. Plus they always had a mystery guest walk on, usually the other person in the love triangle. Matters of the heart; never fails to entertain and get the tongues wagging. This time however, the episode involved a couple who were on the verge of splitting up because of this girl's obsession with Tom Cruise and her fella could not handle it any more. So this is where I came in. I was to be the mystery guest that night and after this couple had had their counselling session, I was to walk on, unbeknownst to either of them, plonk myself down beside her fella and then she would have to choose between us. Great stuff, if not a little cheesy, and as it was a piece of primetime T.V., I was quite happy to do it. Not only is it good for the ego, (and let's face it we all have one to some degree or another) it was an excellent way of raising my profile and therefore a great advertisement for me as a lookalike.

Every time I did something on the telly, the amount of lookalike jobs used to at least double for a few weeks. Sometimes more if it was a primetime T.V. slot like this one. The other thing that always happened, which I found a bit annoying, was my phone wouldn't stop ringing for a few days. People and past acquaintances that I hadn't heard from for like, ever. The type of 'friends', and I use the turn loosely, that never bothered with you. We all know the type, we have all had them; you make the effort and make the effort and it's never reciprocated until in the end you just think, "Sod them" and give up. Or you are of no use to them until they need you for something, or of course, they see you on the telly then suddenly they all want to know you and start chasing you up pretending you're their best mate. Call me cynical but do you really want people like that in your life? They are never

there for you when *you* need someone. If you take it to the
extreme, look at how many hanger-ons and sycophants famous
people, especially celebrities, have to put up with, especially on
their way up – but when they are on their way down where have
all the bestest buddies gone? It must drive them mad; I know it
would me. Just having these fair-weather friends appear every
time my ugly mug appeared on the box or a magazine was annoying enough. Which reminds me; I must quickly tell you about
'Stalks', 'cos we like 'Stalks' (so if I may digress from this digression for a moment!)

From the very first time that I did a high profile job as a lookalike,
which was a T.V. programme, a bunch of us lookalikes did for
the UK living channel (my very first T.V appearance) I started to
get mysterious phone calls from a secret admirer. It came on my
mobile mostly, but sometimes my on land line as well so it was
obviously someone who knew me well enough to have both my
telephone numbers. It came in the form of the number being with-
held (of course) and when I answered it, whoever it was would
just be silent. I could hear them breathing quietly then after about
five or ten seconds, they would hang up. This would happen
about once or twice a day. Pretty bog standard stalker type stuff.
Now these sorts of calls are usually designed to upset the recipi-
ent, even though the perpetrator must be a rather sad individual
to want to do something like that in the first place, but because
of this sense of humour that I am lucky to possess, I found it
all rather amusing. I had my very own friendly neighbourhood
stalker! Why even bother to answer it you may well say; well,
because I liked it and as I say, found it funny. When he rang, well I
call him he but it was more probably a she; can't really see a bloke
having a Tom Cruise lookalike obsession, can you? Anyway when
he rang, I would be like, "Hey stalker how you doing?" and in no
time at all 'stalker' quickly morphed into 'Stalks'. So then he had
a character and when he rang it would be, "Hey 'Stalks' me
old mucker. How you doing?" quickly followed by, "So what you
been up to then?" or something along those lines I'd manage to
get in before he hung up. Great fun! I would tell people about him

like he was a mate or something and it got to a point where they would actually ask me if I'd heard from 'Stalks' recently. I would get most upset if he didn't ring for a while, saying with a sad face, "Oh, I haven't heard from 'Stalks' today." I need not have worried because although it happened on and off all the time, it would defiantly increase in frequency after a T'V appearance or something; so then I would know all was well between 'Stalks' and me. So, never 'diss' the Stalkster; he's my mate! I haven't heard from 'Stalks' in a long while and I miss him so, "Hey 'Stalks', if you're out there, hope you're ok mate, give us a ring".

So... back to the original digression; you know the one about the T.V. program 'Your Face or Mine'. The recording for this program was to take place at the London Television Studios, Upper Ground Street in London. You would recognise it if you saw it; it is their big, white, square building on the south bank of the Thames opposite Victoria Embankment. Recording of the program was an evening shoot, which was a little unusual as nearly every piece of pre-recorded filming work I had done before was shot during the day. It was to take place on Wednesday, February 12, 2003 in front of a live audience. I was to be at the main reception at 5.30pm where I would be met by a member of the production team. It was a casual Tom persona, not specifically any one of his characters, so I used the generic outfit I explained about earlier; wearing the suit jacket and trousers over the tee-shirt look and of course, plenty of gel in my hair. So hitching my usual ride on the Fenchurch Street train line, I headed into London once again. It was in the middle of the evening rush hour and folks were heading on home but I was heading into the city instead of out of it so the crowd were heading in the opposite direction to me. Although I couldn't quite put my finger on it, for some reason there was something rather gratifying about watching them fussing and rushing past. Going in the opposite direction whilst I was just strolling along with all the time in the world. I think that it probably stemmed back from when I used to work in London and did the stressful rush hour thing myself every day but luckily now I didn't have to. After taking the tube around to

Temple station, I took a stroll along Waterloo Bridge and headed along a road called Upper Ground. On into the reception of the London Television Studio's building where I announced myself to the guy at the reception desk. After a quick call, I was met by a young lady and was shown up a few floors to where the studios were. I was lead into the dressing room where I got changed. Now, as you probably know, most television shows are pre-recorded and the recording of some of them takes place months in advance of when they are due to be aired; this one wasn't due to be shown until the November. They looked after me well, supplying me with something to eat and drink but, as is very common with these types of things, there was a lot of hanging around. To pass the time until I was needed and to relieve the boredom, I thought I'd have a little explore. So I wandered out for a nose behind the set where they were filming. I kept myself quiet and well out of sight because, as I said earlier, I was supposed to be the mystery guest and the other guests were not supposed to know who I was. From my vantage point I could see and hear the proceedings quite well and I have to say the couple, who were on set by now, were having more than a heated discussion about her fixation on Tom Cruise. The deal was that if she ended up choosing her man, she would have to give up her long standing obsession with dear old Tom once and for all. Although she was a hothead, she was also a very fine looking young woman and well above his station, I thought. Although he came across as a nice guy, he also seemed a little jealous and possessive which was not surprising given her modelish looks and obsession with someone else; even if the real article was a Hollywood mega star and therefore a bit out of her reach. Also the show would certainly never been able to afford the real Tom's exorbitant fee, let alone getting him to put his time into an English chat show such as this, especially as there would be no promotional value in it for him. Hence them engaging my lookalike services, after all it was a lot cheaper. Anyway the guy's argument was that wasn't he himself good enough for her then? I felt a bit sorry for her fella and I have to say, from what I was hearing, if I were him I would have just dumped her and moved on. Too much grief for me. However he obviously loved her and he was hanging on in there trying to sort it all out. Things got a little over-heated and the host had to send him off for a bit while they tried to calm her down after she had given him a slap across the face. All good for the ratings! He was striding angrily in my direction so I quickly ducked back into my dressing room and closed the door behind me. They had apparently told him to wait in his own dressing room which, as it turned out was next door to mine, and opening the wrong door, he walked straight into me. After him staring at me for a couple of seconds, you could see the realisation dawn on him. I was the mystery walk on guest and being a Tom Cruise lookalike, when it came time for his young lady to choose between him or me, you could see on his face that he knew who it was going to be. Bit cruel, don't you think? Making him go through all that just for her to dump him; still, it was his choice to go on the show, no one made him do it. But I don't think he realised that the production team where going to be pushing such temptation at her. I could see the look of thunder on his face as he clenched his fists. I thought this could go one way or the other; either he was going to launch himself at me with all his might or he was going to burst into tears. He was only about a twenty year old geezer and I was a forty one year old middle aged bloke. So if he did go for me, with youth on his side, I probably wouldn't stand a chance; besides, he was a good few sizes bigger than me. So as I was starting to have a quick look around the room for something to grab hold of as a weapon just in case, his shoulders slouched and he said to me in a defeated kind of way, "I know who you are. You're that Tom Cruise lookalike; I've seen you on the telly before. Oh crap, I've got no hope now" and he slumped down in the chair. It was as if the wind had been taken out of his sails. It totally disarmed me and as I sat down as well, I felt for him. We shook hands and introduced ourselves; "Pete" – "Gary". We engaged in conversation for a little while in which he told me that coming on the show has been his girlfriends' idea and although he was happy to go through the motions, he wasn't really comfortable with any of it. He did think that if he went through with it, she would appreciate him more because she was a bit of an attention seeker and a drama queen, as he put it, and she was loving all this. Things we do for love eh? Poor bloke.

I could tell he was suffering and needed to talk so I let him have an off load whilst we waited to go on set. He had just started to tell me that he was having second thoughts about something but about what, I did not get to find out at that point because at that moment a member of staff popped her head around the door saying, "Oh there you are. What you doing in here? Come on Pete, you're wanted back on set." So off he went in a kind of defeated shuffle. Back on set, he didn't give the game away but he didn't bother making much of a fuss or argument either after knowing what the outcome was going to be; it was if he had resigned himself to what he thought was the inevitable.

Now because of Pete's abject resignation to the situation, the whole show had started to lack lustre to some degree and the audience where getting restless. Time for Tom to enter the fray. Now my remit was to try and make myself a little bit dislikeable so that the audience would not want to warm to me, all for the cameras of course, and generally help inject some excitement. But I also had to try and be charming so that Pete's young lady might choose me. A bit ruthless of them, don't you think? Just for the ratings? But they were paying me to do a job and that was the job they wanted me to do. I was under contract after all, however I did feel bad about being made to do it 'cos if she chose me, Pete was walking and he did love her. It was time for me to get on stage and as the introduction music started, on I strolled giving it the well-polished Hollywood smile and the best arrogant swagger I could manage. The audience let out a gasp, 'Oh no, it's the Tom Cruise lookalike; how awful for their relationship' which was quickly followed by a round of applause and a cheer which then descended into booing. All directed at me and contrived, of course. I sat myself down opposite the young lady and next to Pete. The audience quietened and the host spoke' "It's crunch time, Honey" he said sounding a bit like an American evangelist, "time to choose. But who will it be?" as his voice raised up a notch. Another gasp from the audience. It was getting hard not to laugh at this point but poor old Pete looked like he was about to burst into tears. The host then turned to the audience and said in a booming voice with his arms out stretched "Well, ladies and gentlemen, it's your face or mine!" "Oooh" went the audience then they fell silent. She looked at me, then to Pete, then back to me again, back to Pete; you could have cut the atmosphere with a knife. "Don't know why I'm bothering" I heard Pete mumble under his breath followed by, "How did I ever let her talk me into this?" The tension mounted.

They do like to drag these things out, don't they? Bit like the Jeremy Kyle show when they announce the results of the pregnancy test; "and the father is...." then cut for a commercial break. Then the young lady said "I choose....." a bit more tension just before the moment of choice (although all I could think was, 'God, how cheesy') "I choose....." she said again. I just knew that they would be sticking a commercial break in this spot of the show when it was aired. A couple more moments of silence and in a loud tone she said, "I choose Pete!" The audience let out an enormous cheer followed by a huge round of applause. The young lady dashed out of her seat, over to Pete, and wrapping her arms around him, proceeded to snog his face off. Everyone cheered again. She then started to renounce her passion for Tom Cruise, swearing in front of a live audience that never again would she allow Tom to come between her and the love of her life. Although Pete had reciprocated in putting his arms around her and was smiling for the cameras, you could tell by his body language that he was not a happy chappy. It was almost like he was squirming under the spotlight. The host had a final little chat with the audience, giving it some old twaddle about love conquering all and with the audience giving one last round of applause, the lights went down followed by, "Cut!" The show was in the bag.

After shaking hands with everybody, I was lead back to my dressing room by the same member of the production team who had met me at the reception a few hours earlier. She was thanking me for my efforts and I had that sense of job satisfaction once again. As I had just finished changing and was about to head out of the dressing room door, I could hear raised, but muffled, voices coming from the changing room next door. It was Pete and his lady and they were having a flaming row. I was intrigued; what could they possibly be arguing about now? I thought they had sorted everything out. Gosh, I just had to know. So getting a drinking glass from the food tray that was still in my dressing room from before, I held it up against the wall and put my ear to it. This time it was Pete having a go at the girl instead of the other way around as it had been thoughout the evening's proceedings. He was dumping her! After all that, he was dumping her! How ironic, after having put himself through all the humiliation of him having to sit there while his loved one chose between him or a Tom Cruise lookalike; all to be aired in front of the whole nation. Not to mention the heartache of what he now realised was unrequited love. How dare she? Who did she think she was! Oh it was great stuff; it could not have been scripted better. Just a shame that it was not in front of the cameras. It was the best bit of the evening for me; sweet revenge on his part for making him go through all that just for her own selfish ends. I could hear her starting to cry, sobbing, "What about me? What about me?" "Yeah, what about you, eh?" he responded with a sarcastic yell. By now the whole place could hear them as Pete had opened the door ready to leave. "Me, me me; that's all it's ever been with you, hasn't it. I pity the next bloke who ends up with you. I'm off!" And with that, he stepped through the door way, slamming the door behind him. Good on you, Pete. You deserved a pat on the back for that sterling performance, mate. Nice to see you finally stood up for yourself. It was a just desserts kind of thing and a satisfying end to a satisfying evening. With that, I left my dressing room, exited the building and headed on home.

Now back to the main plot. So there I was making my way to the last Mortgage Solutions job up in Newcastle on the London to Newcastle express train, minding my own business, when I get accosted by this family who had recognised me from 'Your Face or

Mine' which, as I had just been told by the guy, had been aired the night before. I often missed myself when I appeared on the telly because, as I mentioned before, they were recorded sometime before they were due to be shown and often, I used to not know when that was going to be! Usually only finding out when some else told me about it the next day or something, not to mention all those 'I want to be your best buddy' phone calls I told you about. Not that I particularly wanted to watch myself because to me it is a bit like hearing your own voice that had been recorded and when you hear yourself back you go " do I really sound like that?" It is one of those type things when you see yourself on the telly. However, as the agent once said, it's a good idea to record stuff like that as its good for the port folio, and besides it is all memorabilia, a phase in my life and a little something to tell the grandkids.

Looking back I should have known something was afoot, after all 'Stalks' had been trying to ring me a little bit more than usual . Good old 'Stalks' reliable as ever. "You where the Tom Cruise Chappy on 'Your Face or mine' " The posh sounding bloke on the train had said quickly followed by his wife saying "oh how wonderful our own real life celebrity right here on the train with us." I was about to say "don't get to carried away, love" when their kids jumped up all excited "Can we have your autograph please, can we have your autograph?" Being a father myself, I didn't want to make these kids feel disappointed so I went along with it for a while. Soon wished I hadn't though. Their children were quite polite and nice enough kids as most kids are just rather excited, thinking they had met someone famous. Not wanting to burst their bubble, I signed a couple of scraps of paper they had pestered their mum into giving me. Digging deep into her hand bag she handed me a pen to write with and said "don't suppose you would mind doing one for me as well would you?" which I duly obliged. All this commotion was attracting the attention of the other people in the carriage and, as is common in life with the 'if you tell people you're a rock star they think you are' type syndrome, other folk started to come over for a nosey too. Now I'm not sure if half the people there thought they know who I was or not but not wanting to miss out just in case. The next thing I know the whole carriage were queuing up for an autograph and wanting to shake my hand. "This is bloody ridiculous" I was thinking "who do these people think I am? I'm just a bloke who happens to be a lookalike and got on the telly occasionally." They certainly were not thinking I was Tom Cruise, that's for sure, as I was signing my own name and they seemed quite happy with that. It seemed to me to be another one of those situations whereby one or two people recognise you so then a few others think you are someone famous and then the next thing you know everyone around you thinks you are someone famous and then, as goes with the territory, they all want a piece of you. So here I was in this very surreal situation, suddenly being a celebrity for no other reason than the people around you thought you were, which incidentally, apart from the recognition of being on the telly last night by a couple of kids, had absolutely nothing to do with Tom Cruise. It was all very bizarre to say the least. Next thing I know the word must have spread to the rest of the train as people were coming in from the other train carriages for a look as well. It was a bit of a laugh up to this point but as there was starting to become a lot of people surrounding me; I started to flash back to the London Eye incident and that claustrophobic feeling I experienced. I did not fancy getting into that situation again and besides being cooped up on a train carriage, I had no one to help pull me out of there this time and nowhere to run to either. I had to do something and quick before things got too far out of hand. Luckily, by this time the train was pulling into the another station so I stood up and said in the loudest and authoritative voice I was able "You will have to excuse me everyone but this is my stop and I need to get off so if you don't mind!" and with that I grabbed my bag from the overhead rack, pushed my way through the crowd of people and exited the train quick as I could. It was such a relief I can tell you, stepping on to the platform and away from that claustrophobic arena. I could have kissed the ground! As the train pulled away with folk waving at me out of the window, I made my way to the ticket office to find out when the next Newcastle train would be arriving. At that point, I could not have cared less how late this little escapade was going to make me. It was nice just be able to feel I could breathe again. As it happened, I did not have to wait too long there was another due along in about half an hour that had departed from somewhere else, stopping at this station and ending up at my destination, so I wasn't even going too be late for the gig that night after all. It's funny how everything more often than not seems to work out in the end, with the benefit of hindsight of course.

The next train arrived and on I got. This time it was fairly empty, thank god, but to be on the safe side I tucked myself in to an end seat as much out of the way as I could and burying my head in to a newspaper that I bought on the station platform I had just left; just for the purpose of hiding my face just in case as I did not want a repeat of what just happened. I settled myself in for what turned out to be an uneventful rest of the journey, thank God. Leaving me plenty of time to reflect upon about how in the hell I managed to get myself into such scrapes sometimes.

Arriving at Newcastle Central Railway station I got the Tyne and Wear Metro train round to the Callerton Parkway stop which was right near the hotel I was booked into. After all that additional getting on and off the mainline trains earlier on, I managed to arrive not much later than I had originally aimed for. I settled into my room and after having a quick bite to eat, I got a taxi to the Marriott hotel at Gosforth Park. Once again I made sure I got there in plenty of time to get changed and met up with the crew including my old mate, Puffer (who, thank god, had seemed to have completely forgotten about the Tomalisious thing.) This was the last M2I gig for all of us and as such, one or two of the crew had already had a beer or two, or a few, earlier on. A liquid lunch as it were and the Puffer looked very slightly the worst for wear. The reception area was done out in the Mortgage Solutions M2I regalia as before but this time there, tucked just inside the entrance, happened to be the most beautiful Steinway grand piano that I had ever seen. It was in all gloss black with the sexiest set of legs you could imagine and a set of the most 'come play with me' keys I had ever wanted to tickle. Now being a bit of a piano player myself, I recognised it as an M-170 model, or it may have had something to do with seeing the information plaque underneath the keyboard! A Rolls-Royce amongst the already Rolls- Royce of pianos, retailing at something like £60,000 I believe and well worth every penny. It was so gorgeous that it was making my mouth water. I so wanted to caress her. Now how's this for a turn of good fortune; ol' Puffer, in his slightly inebriated state and knowing I played a little, had decided that it would be a good idea that, instead me of doing a straightforward meet and greet when the punters arrive, wouldn't it be great if they had me playing that very piano thus creating a fine ambience to the proceedings whilst they drank some champagne before heading into the seminar; not to mention the novelty factor of having Tom Cruise playing the piano for them. Having had already arranged it with the hotel manager, he asked me if I would be interested? My jaw hit the floor and I was so taken aback with the opportunity to caress this most beautiful lady that all I could think to say was the most ungracious line of befitting an offer like this, "Fuck yeah. Does a Bear shit in the woods!" and with that sunk down a beer in one that the Puffer had just handed me. The guests arrived as Tom sat down at his prize piano and I started playing some classic background type tunes such as an instrumental version of that great Beatles song 'Let it be' that I had taught myself a few weeks before, a piano version of the Dave Brubeck number 'Take five', (it's a bit tricky that one 'cos not only is it in five/four timing but you have to play the lead clarinet part as well) and one of my favourite piano songs Misty. Oh, I was in hog's heaven once again as I sipped at the second pint the Puffer had given me in between ditties. By the time everyone had migrated into the seminar room me and the Puffer had downed about four pints each and, once again having been sitting down thus far, had not noticed how squiffy I was becoming until that is I stood up to go into the conference room to make my little introduction speech. "Whoa steady there Tom old bean" Puffer said grabbing my arm as I wobbled a bit when I stood up "you're as pissed as me" he added with a laugh. I must admit I did feel a little light headed and once again, with a little help from the Puffer, I had managed to drink a little too much a little too early and not for the first time on this set of jobs. Having seen the amount old Puffer could put away and his propensity for alcohol in general, I think he had a much greater tolerance to the stuff than I had, he certainly seemed a lot more functional than most on his level of consumption, that's for sure. It wouldn't surprise me if he was a borderline alcoholic and as with most alcoholics, they like people to drink lots along with them. Must be one of those psychological things, makes them feel not so bad about their bad habits if others are doing it along with them. However my little opening speech, which earned me my final bottle of brandy by the way, was so well rehearsed by now that I could recite it in my sleep so I managed it with no woes. Funny enough, I still didn't know what half of it was on about though.

I wandered back out to the reception area and up to the bar and sure enough there was Puffer knocking back the brandies. "Oi Puffer you're a bit of an alcy aren't ya" I said laughingly to which he readily agreed and with that we ordered a couple of large ones. "Got one last favour to ask of you Tom if you don't mind?" he said with a little cheeky grin on his face "would you mind playing a little bit more of that back ground music once the punters come out of the seminar please? I want to try and get them to hang around for a bit while we sign them up. I would rather get it all wrapped up tonight if possible rather than get the girls to chase the stragglers up on the phone over the next few days. Strike whilst the iron is hot and all that" How could I resist another chance to caress that gorgeous piano again? "Yeah, count me in" I said. "Cheers Gary" he added, that was the first time I had heard him, or any of the Mortgage Solutions people call me by my actual name other than the very first time we met which was over a month ago by now. "Then we are all going to have a little end of work knees up if you care to join us Tom? All drinks on me" and with that I was sold. I had done six jobs in just over a month for this lot but it felt like I had known them all for a lot longer by now. They were a good bunch and I was going to miss them. However the night was still young and with brandy in hand, I slipped back behind little Miss Steinway for a caress once again. The punters where out and back in the reception, everyone was having a laugh by now and the drinks were flowing. I lost track of time, drinking and playing and the more alcohol I consumed; the faster and louder the songs became until in the end I was bashing out such classics as 'Great Balls of Fire' and 'Tuti Fruti'. I love a bit of boogie woogie me, Jules Holland being one of my musical heroes. Everyone was singing and dancing all getting carried away. But it all came to an abrupt halt when I decided to put my foot up on the piano whilst standing up to play like Jerry Lee Lewis would at one of his legendary concerts. Sacrilege for such a beautiful piece of art work such as this instrument was. Had I been sober I would not have dreamed of doing something as derogatory as that in a million years but in my now inebriated state, I was 'into one' as it were and being egged on by a pissed and dancing audience didn't help matters. Suddenly there was an enormous and residing cry that nearly shattered the windows and certainly brought the proceeding to a sudden stop. "Get your fucking foot off that piano!" In the stunned silence we all turned to look in the direction of the call. It was the Hotel Manager, the very one who had given permission for us to use it in the first place, leaping over the counter. "How dare you treat it like that!" Well, you could have heard a pin drop. Everyone, including me, had their mouths open. The crowd who ware looking at the manager at this point all turned their heads in unison, or at least that's my memory of it anyway, and started to stare at me at which point, with drink in hand and one foot up in the air, I lost balance and fell over. Just as well really or I think I would have got a punch in the mouth. Luckily the humour of the ridiculous scene managed to diffuse the situation and every one fell about laughing, everyone except the manager (who had calmed down with a little help by means of a fifty quid bribe courtesy of the Puffer) but he forbad me to play the piano anymore. Just as well really because I was becoming too drunk to play by now and anyway was fast descending into a Les Dawson style.

By now it was past midnight and time to end this party. The place looked like a bomb had hit it. Anyone capable of standing helped anyone else who wasn't into a taxi and on their way. I barely remember much after that except staggering about saying goodbye to everyone. Puffer called me a taxi, (how he was still standing after all the drink he had consumed was beyond me he certainly could put it away that's for sure.) We shook hands and had a hug like old friends would do after having not seen each other for a long time, it kind of felt like a brothers in arms type of thing, and with that he helped me into the waiting taxi, paying the driver for me and instructing him to make sure I got inside my hotel safe and sound. I wound the window down for one final hand shake and a say of goodbyes and with that, the taxi pulled away and, sad to say, I never saw him again.

Oh no it was another morning after the night before. Not only had I woke up drunk in my hotel room I had the mother of all massive hangovers! Now I woke up on the floor under the bed wondering where the hell I was. Still wearing the clothes from the night before, and obviously having fallen off the bed sometime in the night, I was tightly wrapped in the bed sheets and looking like an Egyptian mummy. I had no recollection of the taxi trip back to the hotel, let alone how I had managed to make it to my room and that morning it took me a while to gather myself enough to know where I was. I lay there, semiconscious, for a while trying to figure out how to unwrap myself from the restraints of the sheets. Gosh, my head hurt. I managed to wriggle out of the sheets and plonk myself down on the edge of the bed. It must have been quite early in the morning because, as I hadn't drawn the curtains. I could see that the sky was starting to turn light but there was no sun up yet. Sitting there with my head in my hands, I must have dozed off again for a fair while as when I woke up and lifted my head out of my hands I had the full glare of the sun shining right into my bloodshot eyes. Ouch! My feet were wet for some reason and looking down, I could see I had a least managed to take my socks off at some point. Then I realised my back was damp, must have been where I was laying under the bed in the night. Rather perplexed, I looked down at my toes as I watched them squelching on a water logged carpet. What was going on? I could hear the sound of running water coming from somewhere and it took me a little while to realise where from. It was the bathroom; I could hear a tap running. I dashed over, pushing open the bathroom door to behold a sight of the cold tap on nearly full blast and the sink full up with overflowing water. Oh my God! Even though much of the water was trying to drain away through the plug hole and overflow, it was obviously not enough as the water was flowing over the side of the sink and on to the floor which was now covered to about a depth of an inch or so. It had then flowed onto the carpet in the bedroom over the course of the night soaking onto well over three quarters of its area which was now very sodden and squelchy. What a state. It was obvious to me that after I had staggered into my room last night I had tried to get a big glass of water and, being as drunk as I was, had left the tap running. I must have dropped the glass at some point which had hit the little stand by the bedside and smashed. There was glass all over the place. I quickly turned off the tap and grabbed as many of the towels that they supplied as possible and began the massive mop-up operation. After having spent about an hour of soaking up the water, mostly by doing the foot shuffle, especially on the carpeted area, and wringing out the towels in the bath, I decided to have a go at clearing up the glass. This proved rather difficult as it was mostly in tiny little pieces and on a wet carpet and I wasn't in the most sound of minds that morning as you can imagine. I must have dropped that glass with some force because as I said it was everywhere and after cutting my fingers once or twice, accompanied by a taking Gods name in vain a few times, I got the 'ump with it all and stopped. Looking around the room, it was still in a hell of a state and all I could think of was how much this little lot was going to cost me. I needed another plan of action and quick but what to do? Bearing in mind this hotel room had been pre-booked by the nice young lady in the accounts department of the Mortgage Solutions Company, and not my name, the only other thing I could think of was to leg it so that's what I did! However I could not find my little suit case anywhere.

I must have lost it last night in the taxi or left it at the Marriott as I did have to take it to the gig because it had my Tom Cruise clothes in it along with a change of underwear, a clean shirt and my tooth brush. All I had was the clothes I currently had on, and had spent the night in. My jacket which, thank god, still had my wallet, keys, phone and homeward bound train ticket in it. I didn't even get time to have a shower. Time was running out as I could hear the cleaning maids going into the room next door, besides there was no clean towels to use thank to my little failed clean-up operation. So after having recovered my socks and shoes and standing on the only bit of carpet that was not wet, I hopped about putting them on. I only managed to fall over the once so although I ended up with a wet arse the rest of mc was dry. But I didn't have time to worry about that as I should have checked out half an hour ago and I could hear the cleaning maids coming out of the room next door which meant this room was next! I did not want them to see me and ending up in some kind of confrontation about the state of the place, and knowing it was me. So stinking like a minger I hot footed it out if there just in the nick of time. After having dropped the door key into the reception, (to my relief there was no one there at that particular moment) so I just dropped it into the keys return box. So far so good; I had made my escape. I made my way round to the metro line and headed off to the Newcastle main line station. I made it there just in time for the eleven thirty morning train back to London so, plonking my still wet bum on the seat in the end carriage, I watched the station roll by as the train pulled away. Phew, I had got away with it and I never did hear anything more about the flooded out room.

Although not feeling so bad now, I was still hung-over somewhat a needed a nice cup of tea so I made my way to the buffet car where I ordered a tea and a sandwich. As the young lady was serving me, she nudged her mate who she was working with then leaned over to me a little and said "are you that Tom Cruise lookalike that was on 'your face or mine' a couple of night ago?" 'Oh no' I thought 'not all this again I just can't handle it, not now, not after what I've just been through', so I stepped back, screwed my face up and said with a put on angry sounding voice "No I'm bloody not and I'm sick of people keep asking me that! I don't know who he is but it's not me!" She looked at her mate and they both sarcastically went in unison "oooooooo! tetchy" and laughed. She looked back at me and said "It's not my fault you're a lookalike of a lookalike of Tom Cruise" which I thought was rather witty. With sandwich in hand and tea in the other, I made my way back to my carriage at the end, it was nice and empty which was just how I wanted it, and sitting myself down on my squelchy bum, I settled down for sustenance and a bit of contemplation. How on earth did I keep getting myself into such scrapes?

It has always been a bit of a mystery to me but ever since I was at school, I was always the one out of all my mates who managed to get himself into, (and out of usually by just by the skin of my teeth,) dodgy situations. It always seemed to happen to me and it did not help that I have always been a bit accident prone to boot. My mates back then used to say that it was like they had their own Frank as in Frank Spencer from that old seventies T.V. comedy show 'Some Mothers Do Have 'Em', and I have to say it has been a bit of a running theme throughout my life. So throw working as a Tom Cruise Lookalike into the mix and there was a bit of a recipe for disaster but it has led to some interesting and amusing situations for me to talk about. Whilst contemplating all this I finished my sandwich and then fell asleep and slept all of the way back to London. Arriving at Kings Cross I woke up feeling nice and refreshed and my hangover finally gone, but I did promise myself that I would never drink again; once again!

I got home early evening and after having my dinner and playing with the kids for a while I gave me old mate Keith a ring and, after meeting up, I told him all about my latest adventure over a pint down the pub!

CHAPTER 10

NOT ALWAYS ALONE

So far I talked a lot about jobs that I have done for the most part on my own as a lookalike but this was not always the case. I would say probably about half of all the jobs that I did were done with a least one other lookalike and often with several of them, all of us working at the same gig. In my time there were lookalikes for anyone and everyone ranging from the sublime to the ridiculous as they say. There were the "long termers"; the lookalikes who looked like someone who had been famous for a long time such as the Hollywood heavies for example, like Mel Gibson, Bruce Willis, Jack Nicolson, Liz Hurly, Sean Connery, Anthony Hopkins, George Cloony, Leonardo DiCaprio and of course Tom Cruise. However that was just one sub section of the long termers. I mention them because of course that was lot I was involved with and I did get to know some of those guys quite well, but you get the idea; basically anyone who was famous for a long time from whatever category in life. Our type, and if you were lucky enough to be one of the long termers, usually got a fair bit of work, depending on how popular their particular character was, sustained over a long period of time. I clipped very lucky there as Tom Cruise has been one of the most popular actors to have come out of Hollywood and has stood the test of time, so far still going strong. Then there were the "mid termers" such as say, politicians who had been voted in for a term in office. A good example of this would be Tony Blair, as I remember in my earlier lookalike days back in the nineties, when he was the Prime Minister, this was a very popular lookalike to have at a party or opening a super market but these days as he's not really in the public eye so there would not be much call for his lookalikes anymore. Or there are the sports stars like footballers or may be cricketers and such like, who were about for a little while before they drop off the scene or basically anyone who was famous for, let's say, one to five years. This group would work to a similar level as us long termers but, for obvious reasons only be around for a year or Two. Another thing with this group was that there were often several lookalikes for the same person. There was in all lookalike groups but with this lot, it was particularly prevalent. Therefore any gigs would often not go to the same person all the time but be divvied up between them, usually to who was ever in favour to whatever agent was offering the work at the time. I saw a lot of those guys come and go during my time. Then there were the short termers. The lookalikes who happened to lookalike someone who had become famous for a short period of time, usually only for a period of months or sometimes even just weeks. Although there were lots of categories with in this little lot, a couple of example groups that come to mind would be someone like the Olympic athletes; intensely popular for a short period of time whilst they were in the limelight but afterward generally everyone would forget about them. Another group that was a very annoying lot, in my opinion anyway, of celebrities who were made famous by being on some reality show or another, the obvious one being Big Brother. This lot were only famous for being famous and most of them had no particular skills or special talent to help sustain their popularity and so after they were off the telly for any length of time they were soon forgotten about as the general public moved on to the next batch of wannabes that were coming through. These poor old lookalikes, whilst often more talented that the people they actually looked like, would may be do a job or two then never work lookaliking again. Still they can't really grumble at least they had a little bash at it even if it was fleeting, their fifteen minutes of fame and a story or two to tell their mates down the pub at the end of the day so good luck to them that's what I say. However their characters were never going to get themselves into the hall of fame or Madam Tussauds, you know the famous wax works by Bakers Street along Marylebone Road up in London, which leads me into my next story.

Back in '99, the famous television magazine 'TV Times' announced that they had decided to sponsor something called 'The Madame Tussauds Celebrity Lookalikes Star Search' which was to be held at , yeah you got it, Madame Tussauds, on March 10th of that year. They made a big fuss and a splash about it, advertising heavily in the news papers and on the telly and everywhere else for that matter and it was to be shown apparently on both the BBC as well as Channel 4. It wouldn't have been the first time us looka-likes had been shown on both of those channels during my looka-like career, (he says with mixed feelings.) Anyway the idea was that there was to be a nationwide search for people who looked like famous people, and it encouraged folk from all walks of life who had ever been told they looked like someone to just have a go. There was to be local heats all over the country and all were welcome. It was rather like the 'Britain's Got Talent' show type thing where by only the ones with real talent (or the complete no hopers who would make total prats of themselves) managed to get through and everyone else in between got thrown to the wayside. It was all good for the viewing figures as you can imagine and after all that's what it's all about, is it not? And so it was with the lookalike competition.

Can you imagine how much gossip and laughter the 'non-looka-likes' would get? Laugh at the loonies, as the Victorians would have said. Everyone loves to judge from the comfort of their own armchair don't they and, if I'm honest, I'm no exception to the rule either. Can you imagine us registered lookalikes watching something like that? We would be the worst critics of all and it would be hypocritical of me to say otherwise, I can assure you.

Now the powers that be decided to invite along a whole bunch of us lookalikes, (for our usual fee of course as negotiated by the agent with their usual fifteen percent,) with characters famous enough to have a waxworks figure at Madam Tussauds which, luckily for me, included Tom Cruise. This was to help along with the flow of the show and the general ambiance for the programme as it where. If you are doing a show about lookalikes, it's good to have a few lookalikes about the place and all that. The lookalikes that the show wanted to use had been tracked down by the programmes production team and our invites where duly sent out to us. This is a direct quote form part of the letter that I received....

'TV TIMES INVITES YOU TO THE CELEBRITY LOOKALIKES 'STAR SEARCH' AWARDS MADAME TUSSAUD'S – Wednesday March 10

You may have seen in 'TV Times' or on TV, the announcement of the Madame Tussaud's Celebrity Lookalikes' Star Search. In case you missed it, a photocopy is enclosed.

The winners will be announced at a star studded awards ceremony at Madame Tussaud's on Wednesday March 10. As you can imagine, with the event being sponsored by TV Times, ourselves and Madame Tussaud's this will be a spectacular party, which is expected to be televised by the BBC and Channel 4.

Unfortunately, since you're already registered as a Lookalike, you can't enter the competition, but you could be invited to the big awards party where you'll not only rub shoulders with lots of real celebrities but will also have the opportunity to 'strut your stuff' on TV and in front of the executives who book Lookalikes all over the world.

Madame Tussaud's is part of the same group as 'Rock Circus', 'Alton Towers', 'Thorpe Park', 'Warwick Castle' and 'Leeds Castle' which are some of the biggest bookers of Lookalikes in the country. Bookers from all of these venues as well as from EuroDisney are expected to attend.

The party will also host the casting directors of many of the largest advertising and PR agencies in the country including Saatchi &Saatchi, J. Walter Thompson and Leo Burnett. Casting agents from many film and TV production companies will also be invited, all looking for new Lookalike talent!

The number of Lookalikes and guests we are able to invite to Madame Tussauds is strictly limited, which is why we are writing to you today. If you would like to attend the party, please complete the enclosed form and return it to us as soon as possible so that we can calculate the likely numbers.

Please return the form no later than February 28. Invitations will be allocated in the order we receive the forms, so the sooner you return your form the more likely you are to receive an invitation.

See you at the Lookalikes event of the year!

Ron Mowlam.

Chief Executive.

Now although I had no doubt this was a good opportunity to tout our wares as lookalikes to some new clientele, it was also an opportunity to get our mugs on the telly, which was always good for business, (not to mention expediting a few more calls from my old mate 'Stalks' whom I hadn't heard from for a little while. Don't forget 'Stalks' frequency of phone calls was my gauge as to how much my profile was raised and therefore meaning extra work for me. In other words I had learned that it was a direct ratio, the more calls I got from 'Stalks' the more work I was in for.) Now I don't want to sound too ungrateful here but, despite all this 'what a wonderful opportunity this is for you' stuff, my own personal cynicism made me view this as a rather shallow attempt to get as many lookalikes, the ones who had their originals in Madam Tussauds at any rate, on board as possible for their own benefit, and why not?

The reason I inserted an extract of the invitation in at this point is because what do you think? It came across to me as one of those double glazing companies trying to gain your business; you know the double glazing leaflet that comes through your letter box that says things like 'you have been specially selected for our last minute offer. Fifty percent off for a limited time only just for you, apply quickly or you will miss out' and all that. Now given how my sense of humour works, all things cheesy are funny and this certainly came across as cheesy to me, so, oh my word how could I possibly resist such an offer? Ha ha.

However, it was also a great opportunity to get together with a few of my old lookalike mates and have a party up. Lets 'av it! I was beaten to the punch however, as before I knew it, one of the guys rang me first. "You up for it, Gal?" the Mel Gibson lookalike said to me over the phone. "Cool. I'll give the guys a ring". The guys included some of the girls as well, you know some of the long term lookalikes that we had worked with over the course of time. As I say we had all got to know each other quite well and we could be a bit of a crew on multi lookalike events such as this was going to be. We all put our names forward, (well we could not miss this tongue in cheek once in a life time offer now could we?) and the stage was set. I told the agent that they could count me in and got my brief, via email, explaining all a couple of days later. My remit was to get to the event nice and early with the rest of the lookalikes because, as with most events that involved the public, i.e. the invited members of the public who had successfully applied to go on the show and members of the audience, we were going to do the 'Meet and Greet' thing as they arrived whilst being filmed by the production company.

A good old honest to goodness 'Meet and Greet' gig, a least that is what I thought at this point, and with some of the other looka-likes as well. That is what I liked doing the most; getting to mix and mingle with normal ordinary folk and all having a laugh. That is what it's all about in the end, at least for me at any rate. I was looking forward to it.

When I arrived at Madame Tussauds that day, I met up with the others at the entrance and after having a cup of tea and a catch up with everyone, we were led to the changing rooms. Instead of me wearing the cloths that I had brought along with me to change into, (the usual generic look,) I was given an outfit to wear. It was similar to the suit jacket and tee-shirt that I had originally intended to avail myself of except they were of a different style and colour to mine. Mine was a white tee-shirt with a dark blue single breasted jacket over the top and this new outfit was of a dark coloured tee-shirt with and even darker suit jacket over the top. Still, no one had told me why I was expected to wear this and when I asked the person handing it to me, they did not seem to know either. What the hell? I had been asked to do stranger things and anyway they were the ones paying our fees at the end of the day so I was up for whatever they had up their sleeve for me. Still, all a bit odd though I thought, considering none of the other lookalikes had been handed anything different to wear. They were all dressing in the clothes befitting their particular characters that they had fetched with them. If you have ever been to Madame Tussauds you will probably remember that once you have got passed the ticket office and entrance area you then enter the walk through main area which is basically a kind of path way that you follow round the whole exhibition so as you don't miss any of the exhibits. Well, that was how it was set up back then at any rate; don't know how the current layout is, haven't been there recently, but I would presume it still follows the same format. Now, also back then, not too far from the main entrance there stood the waxworks figure of Tom Cruise himself. However, he was not there that day just an empty plinth with his name plate affixed to the bottom. You can guess what was going to happen, cant you. One of the day's events organisers sidled over to me and said "'ere Tom, you up for a laugh? How good are you a being a statue?" "What? What you on about?" came my perplexed reply. Now you have to bear in mind that up to this point I had not seen the empty Tom plinth and neither had I been told what the last minute change of costume was all about. "Do we really have to spell it out for you?" the guy said to me "Yeah, yeah you do, I don't have a Scooby what you're on about" I said still perplexed. With a look of indignation on his face he said "We thought it would be a good idea if we got you to stand on the Tom Cruise plinth because after your compatriots have met all the audience as they come in, you know, relaxed them and kind of thing, got them in to the mood and the swing of things as it were, the audience will undoubtedly go around having their photographs taken with all the different waxworks on their way through to the auditorium 'cos that's what the public always do" I was told. "Yeah so?" came my reply. Call me thick but I still did not get what the bloke was on about at this point. "Well, how about you stand on the Tom Cruise plinth which is quite near the start of the walk through and as the audience come up to you, (and don't forget they are going to think you are a waxworks statue, long as you can stand still enough that is,) when they go to have their photo taken with you, you suddenly you step off the plinth and may be say something like 'Hi, how you doing?' Watch then shit themselves! How funny would that be? You up for it Tom or what?" Took me a second or two to process what he was talking about but when it did finally sink in, it was like one of those ideas that you wished you had thought of first. What brilliant idea and what a laugh. I was well up for it and I came out with the immortal line once again "yeah! Does a bear shit in the woods!" and with that the deal was sealed. So with everyone in place and all the other lookalikes standing briefed with what was going to happen and standing at the entrance ready to meet everyone as they entered the complex, the cameras in place and me back a ways standing on my plinth, it was all actions go.

The doors opened and the first of the public audience started to make their way in. These were going to be the opening shots for the show apparently. There was an air of excitement as the folk looked forward with anticipation to what lay ahead for them that afternoon. After all, they were going to be on the telly. Everyone was enjoying shaking hands with the lookalikes too. Now as expected and as the cameras rolled recording every little move made for editing later on, the folk made their way through and ,also as expected, were having their photographs taken with all the waxworks along the way.

Now there was I standing on the Tom Cruise plinth trying to stand as still as I possibly could. If you have ever tried to do something like that it is actually much harder than it looks. The worst thing is trying to keep your eyes open without blinking and of course the more you think about it the harder it becomes. With a little practice I realised that if you look towards the ground, so your eyes didn't dry out, and took shallow breathes you could manage it, at least for a little while anyway, so that's what I did. I became a statue. As it was the ladies that preferred having their photos taken with Tom, (well more so than the male contingent at any rate,) the ladies would, at least at first, walk by giving me a good looking at, and as they did so, I would make a very, almost imperceptible, movement. This would facilitate a double take from the first of the parade walking by in their little groups. I could hear some of them saying to each other "'ere did you see that? Did he move?" quickly followed by "Spooky" as they quickly moved on. I must admit it was one of those hard-not-to-laugh situations I can tell you but I didn't. I did this a few times as people went by; just a little movement you understand, just a little shift in balance on my feet maybe or a small arm movement or something. Not enough to give the game away but just enough to creep them out a bit but not quite know why. After doing this a few times, I started to get the knack of it and it was fun.

This had gone on for about five or ten minutes when the moment I had been waiting for arrived. I had the first bunch of people wanting to have their photos taken with the Tom Cruise waxworks, aka me. The folk were getting more bunched up than before, this must have been the main flow of people making their way through, I decided that it would be a good idea if I just let the first lot of photographers take their shots with me without giving the game away thus lulling the next lot into a false sense of security and there for expediting a greater sense of shock when I made my move, which is exactly what I did. So, whilst not moving a muscle, a couple of girls stood either side of me with their arms around my shoulders whilst one of their partners took a couple of shots. There were lots of other people having their photos taken with some of the other waxworks figures up and down the way so why should this one be any different? After reviewing their pics' on the digital camera for a couple of moments; they started to move on. No sooner had they done so than next lot of photographers stepped up. This was what looked like a couple of young woman and their mother. The girls stepped up to me whilst the mum took the photo. I had, at this point, folded my arms behind my back and the two girls linked their arms through mine and just as the photo flash went off I, as quickly as I could manage, unclenched my hands and wrapping my own arms around these two poor unsuspecting ladies, I said in my loudest voice, with that awful fake American accent I did, "Hi ladies how's you all doing!" and moving forward at the same time so as to make all three of us step off the plinth together. Well, you can imagine the result cant you? These two girls let out the most unearthly piercing scream you can possible imagine, right into my lugholes I must add, and pushed themselves away from me as fast as they could. They screamed so loudly that I made my ears ring for a minute or two afterwards; instant tinnitus! The mum stood aghast for a moment. There was silence for just a moment, (well, at least for everyone else that is, my ears were ringing like a son of a bitch,) as everyone close by froze for a second. Obviously waiting for their brains to assimilate what had just occurred. The mum was the first to get what had just happened and as she cracked a smile and threw her head back she let out this most wonderful belly laugh and in no time at all everyone around was laughing along too. Most were laughing at the gag but you could hear that one or two were doing that nervous type laugh, just relieved I suppose. After all it must have been quite scary if you hadn't been expecting it. Well, as the scene calmed down, I got a unexpected round of applause, from those closest to the event to have witnessed it at any rate, and with that I took a bow. All a good natured bit of fun so far. As this bunch moved on I stepped back on to the plinth to await my next unsuspecting victims as they wandered through.

The next couple times went just as well as the first with everyone jumping out of their skins and having a good laugh about it.

"Scarier than the London Dungeons" I heard one of them say. This was loads of fun and I was, once again, thoroughly enjoying myself. Then came the sucker punch. When people get unexpectedly scared, as we all do from time to time, we tend to have the 'fight or flight' reaction. It is a throw back from the caveman days that would have saved our bacon in dodgy situations back then, and this reaction still prevails today as I was about to find out. After the last lot of 'Scaredys' had been and gone a couple and a male friend walked over to where I was standing, still on the Tom Cruise plinth and as still as ever, the girl said to their mate "hey Steve, can you take a picture of me and Dave standing next to Tom here?" "Sure thing Lynn" he replied "you two get over there by him and I'll get a good shot for you" and so they did. They both got on to the plinth with me and with Dave leaning his arm on my shoulder and Lynn doing the same on the other side, Steve lined up his shot. I sprang into action. With a large jerking movement I stepped off the platform extending my right hand towards Steve the photographer and with a big grin shouted "Toms the name...." but I didn't get time to finish my sentence when, with an abject look of instantaneous fear in his now very wide eyes, Steve leapt forward and sucker punched me right in the side of the head! Crack it went. It was a good round house, I'll give him that, and it knocked me right on my arse. There was no screaming involved this time around just a stunned silence as people stared at me prostate on the floor. A moment later Stevie boy let out a wounded cry "ow! My bloody hand" and with that the tension drained out of the air.

Now if you have ever been in a fight you will know never to punch someone in the skull; it is as hard as a bowling ball and far more of a match then the delicate bones in your hand as Steve, bless him, had just found out to his detriment.

People were just staring at all this by this point. The joke had gone wrong. Dave and Lynn, with one or two others rushed over and helped me to my feet asking if I was ok which, apart from another ringing in my ears, I was. I was without injury; just a dent in my pride that was all which is more than can be said for poor old Steve's hand. He was holding it at the wrist by now and a couple of those knuckles didn't look good. That crack I heard was most probably a bone or two breaking in his hand. I looked over at him and realising that he had meant no malice, just a defence reaction, I felt I owed him an apology. "Sorry mate" I said "I really didn't mean to frighten you like that it was supposed to just make you jump that's all" By now he had the other two fussing around him and I am glad to say he took it well "I'm sorry too mate. I wasn't expecting anything like that to happen. I just saw what looked like this inanimate object come to life and come at me!" he said with a painful looking grimace on his face. That hand must be hurting I thought. "You just came at me and I thought you were going to attack me so I just lashed out, I didn't think about it". By now a couple of the event organizers had come through to see what was going on. Someone said from behind "think you should go a see a first aider mate, that don't look good" "Think you're right" he acknowledged and after we nodded a good bye to each other his two friends helped him back to the entrance. I felt quite bad about all that and the organizers checked I was all right. I didn't seem to have been injured at all in that little fracas so, after brushing myself down and straighten myself up, I stood back on to the plinth once again.

I felt a little nervous about doing the next one so I tamed it down a little and got back into the 'scare the shit out of people' game. After a couple more that went without incident, the passing crowed began to thin out as we started heading into the last of the audience that were making their through. However it was not the last incident. There was, towards the end, a couple of middle aged women making their way through when one said to the other "Take my picture with ol' Tom there for me, will ya?" "Course" said the other getting her camera out of her bag. The first lady got up and put her arm around my waist at which point she real-ised that I was a real person but I winked at her and said very quietly "Shhhh don't say anything" She got the joke immediately and started playing along. Her mate, meantime, had not noticed

YOUR FACE OR MINE?

any of this, fumbling around in her bag as she was trying to find her camera. So as she got into position to take the photo I did the usual, but the tamed down version of, stepping off the plinth and saying "Hi Tom's the name and....." but once again I did not get the chance to finish my sentence. This poor lady screamed like her very soul depended on it! She screamed and screamed and screamed barely having time to draw breath in between. She was absolutely hysterical; I've never seen anyone go like that before. Once again, the rest of us just stood and stared for a moment, trying to take it all in. Me and her mate moved towards her as the organizers appeared once again. I was starting to explain that it was all right; I am a real person and it was just a bit of harmless fun. Harmless my foot! Not only had it earned me a punch in the head, this poor devil seemed absolutely inconsolable. No one could get near her she had her arms up with fists clenched and eyes screwed tightly shut still screaming. Eventually, after what seemed ages but was actually only a minute or two, this poor hysterical lady started sobbing as someone put a blanket around her shoulders and she was led away. Oh my god, how awful did I feel at that moment? When I was first asked to do this it seemed like a very good idea but by now I beginning to wish they had asked one of the other lookalikes to do it. At that point instead of getting back on the plinth I decided that I was done with this particular practical joke. Fun that it had been, this last prank had nearly cost someone their sanity and although I am always up for a laugh and a joke, I do have a heart and this last one had overstepped that mark for me, (besides as most of the audience had gone through by now there was hardly anyone left to scare.)

I walked back to where the other lookalikes were at the entrance and saw that the production crew were busying themselves wrapping up the filming of the 'Meet and Greet'. One of them glanced over to me and said "What you doing back here Tom? Aren't you supposed to be around the corner, scaring the shit out of everybody?" "Been there done that" came my somewhat despondent response. "What do you mean? You can't have finished already" he said, looking somewhat perplexed "Well, yeah, there's no one left to jump out on they've all gone in" I replied. There was a short but pregnant pause, it was as if I could see the cogs turning from behind his eyes whilst he tried to assimilate what I had just told him. Slapping himself on the forehead with the palm of his hand, he came out with "Oh bollocks", (one of my favourite expletives as well by the way just thought I would mention that, anyway back to what he was saying) "Oh bollocks, how could I have made such a stupid over sight. I wanted to get some film of that. Bollocks!" Shrugging my shoulders I replied "Dunno mate but after what just happened in there, I don't think I'll wanna be doing that anymore" and headed off to the shop canteen for a nice cup of nerve-calming tea!

Us lookalikes had a ten minute break before we were required again back in the auditorium where they were filming next. When we arrived the public had been ushered into their seats and the lookalikes, as instructed, spread ourselves out and sat in amongst them so that when the cameras panned across the audience, there would be a few famous faces amongst the crowd. All good for the viewing figures of course and, once again, that's what we were there for. As luck would have it, I just happened to sit just in front of the bloke who lumped me one. I felt a tap on the shoulder turned around and there he was grinning at me. "How is the head Tom?" he said. I put my hand up to where he had hit me and felt a nice big lump coming up so I turned to him and said "A bit lumpy" and we laughed. Then enquiring after his wellbeing I said "How's the hand?" "Broken!" he said as he lifted his now heavily bandaged hand up for me to inspect and we laughed again. "Bloody hurts though, they do think I might have broken something. I'm supposed to go to hospital but I didn't want to miss this lot so I elected to stay. I'll go to A&E when we get home" "Good luck to ya" I replied and turned back to face the action.

The action consisted of all the runners-up who had managed to get through to these finals, being called up on stage, one by one, and to parade themselves in front of the judges and the audience, not to mention the cameras. Then they were questioned about any funny instances that may have happened to them that related to them looking like someone famous.

Now something to bear in mind here is that, like I touched on at the beginning of these tales, just because you were lucky enough, (or unlucky enough depending on your point of view) sometimes, to happen to look like a famous person, doesn't necessarily mean you will be good at it. I was fortunate enough to already be in the entertainment industry before I became a lookalike, treating it like doing a gig but without my guitar like I said before. So the confidence to act in front of an audience was already within me and as such, I managed to take to it quite well, probably why I was nearly all ways the one who ended up doing such stunts as the one earlier on that evening. But this was not the case with a lot of the guys. Most had regular jobs, working in an office or as a plumber or secretary or some such thing and therefore not very used to performing in front of people and a lot of the new guys fell by the wayside early on, especially the shy ones. So, as you can imagine, this lookalike game was really not for the faint hearted.

Now most of the shy ones in this competition would have been weeded out of the running in the regional heats, or so you would have thought. Unfortunately for the some of the poor devils who had found themselves up on the finalist stage tonight, had not. With hindsight, this had obviously been done deliberately because those judges hounded the shy ones, and the not very lookalikes that were deliberately allowed through, relentlessly; showing them up, making one girl run off stage crying. All in the name of entertainment and of course, those very revered viewing figures. There were originally about twenty five contestants but in a very short space of time, this had been whittled down to about ten through this very humiliating experience. The audience were told when to laugh and clap, as is very common with these types of pre-recorded shows, but I found the whole thing rather distasteful and the judges quite brutal.

Ha, the 'judges', I had never heard of any of them. Apparently a couple were supposed to be high up in the entertainment industry and the others some kind of celebrities, so we were led to believe at any rate, but for all I knew they could have been members of the public selected at random. Our distaste for their treatment of some of the qualifiers, (that is me and a few of the other lookalikes,) must have been quite apparent because during one of the pauses in filming, a member of the production team made their way over to the Brad Pitt lookalike, who was sitting at the end of the row in front of me which was only a few seats away so I could hear what was said, and stated in no uncertain terms that if he, and some of us other lookalikes for that matter, did not start joining in with rest of the audience we would be chucked off the set. Oh and while we were at it, start doing smiles instead of scowls every time one of the judges cracked one of their rather unfunny jokes even if it was at one or two of the contestant's expense. Have you ever watched 'Slum Dog Millionaire'? You know the way that host treats the main character at the beginning of the proceedings? Well, it reminded me of that. Now I had got to know this particular Brad Pitt lookalike, (and there were quite a few of this particular character around back then,) quite well over the course of time, having worked with him on more than one occasion and, whilst he was a nice bloke, he could be quite feisty at times especially when someone was having a go at him. Anyway he responded by standing up and in a rather loud tone said "Don't you threaten me pal or I'll lump you one mate. And anyway 'Joke's'? I'll tell you what the real joke is here, shall I? Making them poor bastards suffer up there while you want us to laugh at them. Tell you what pal, shove it up your arse!". 'Good for you' I thought and let out a cheer which was quickly followed by a few other folk doing the same. We gave him a round of applause and with that, he shoved past the bloke and stormed off and I don't blame him. It was one of those things that you wished you had thought of saying first but knowing how cutthroat the lookalike industry could be and that once word had got back to the agent, he would probably never work as a lookalike again and so the mercenary side of me started to kick in. I was having far too much fun as a lookalike to jeopardise it all by standing on principal here so once old Brad had gone out of the door, I settled back down into my seat and decided I was going to enjoy the rest of the evening come what may.

After a couple of hours of stop-starting up on stage, (you know to get the look right for the cameras,) events started to draw to a close. Some bloke who had dressed up as 'Dame Edna Everage' won it that night and his prize was a rather crappy looking statue type thing and an interview that was going to be published in the T.V times as well as a contract to work as a lookalike. A bit unfair I thought because anyone could dress up as a 'Dame Edna Everage' character and get away with it; it was after all only a mimic of someone else's alter ego. However the guy did pull it off well and was brimming with confidence, unlike the rest of them, so I'm sure this particular lookalike agency could make some money out of him as well as it being good T.V viewing. Gosh, how cynical am I. Being in this business for long enough does make you that way; it does have a tendency to chew you up and spit you out if you're not tenacious enough.

By now the whole afternoons events, which had run into the evening at this point, were drawing to a close. There was still the 'mix and mingle' part of the job left for us lookalikes to do at the after show party where we had the opportunity chat with everyone and there were a few talent scouts there having a 'noss' at us lookalikes. As you never knew who you might be talking to, not to mention they were going to be filming it all as well, we were all on our best behaviour and being as charming as we knew how; shaking hands and 'putting on the ritz' for the cameras. The whole thing only lasted about an hour or so and we were wrapped up by about eight o'clock that evening. Incidentally, I still did not see anyone I recognised as being famous but what the hell, it was a bit of fun.

The members of the audience were starting to disperse by now, having made sure every last one of them had had their photographs taken with each and every one of us lookalikes, (well minus the Brad Pitt guy 'cos he was long gone,) and with all the judges 'cos they thought they were famous. It's that old adage again that I mentioned before; if tell people you're a rock star they think that you are. At this point I was approached by one of the production guys, the same one as it happens who had slapped himself on the head for not thinking to film my antics when I was scaring the shit out of people earlier on that day, even though it was his idea in the first place! Anyway he said to me "Tom, old chap, would you mind if we borrowed you for a moment?" Well, me and a few of the other lookalikes, now that the night was over, had arranged to go down the pub for a beer or two before we went home and were putting our coats on as we spoke. "What you after?" I said "It is beer o'clock you know". "Yeah, well I wouldn't ask normally but as you know I kind of messed up earlier and was wondering if you wouldn't mind if maybe we could try and retake one or two of those shots again, you know if you wouldn't mind that is?" He sounded a bit desperate and he was looking down at the ground, running his hand through his thinning hair all the time he was speaking to me. I could smell an earner coming on! "OK" I said and with my mercenary head still in play I added "What's in it for me?" "How about I bung you fifty quid for ten minutes of your time?" "As long as you don't want me too snog some gay bloke" I said jokingly remembering when I got caught out in that gay bar up in Scotland that time. "I'm in". "What? What you got against gays then!" he said a bit curtly. "I'm gay, is that a problem for you then?" 'Oh crap' I thought 'I've upset him now, he's bloody well gay but more to the point there goes my fifty quid!' "No sorry mate. I didn't mean it like that" I said back pedalling as fast as I could as I watched my 'nifty' slipping away. "It's just that, well I'm straight and I had a bit of a bad experience a while ago and well you know…" I realised that I was just digging myself in even deeper "You know what just forget it, each to their own, what you want me to do then?" I said letting out a big puff of breath thinking I had blown it. "Ha! Fuck off. I'm just pulling your leg, Tom. I'm not gay, just winding you up you silly sod. Should have seen your face!" and with that I let out one of those nervous laughs of relief.

What he wanted me to do was to re-enact the events of earlier on. Trouble was that by now the members of the public had buggered off home so his idea was to stage a set up with a few members of the production team. So back we went into the 'Corridor of Doom' as it were, once again. So the cameras were set and there I was back on that Tom Cruise plinth once again. "And action" came the call and without further ado we attempted to reconstruct the events of earlier on. However because of the fabrication of what was supposed to be a spontaneous event. The whole thing did not quite have the same flavour as before and we kept falling flat. This was mostly due to the over acted reactions of the supposed innocent passers-by as I stepped off the plinth. It didn't help that I could not stop giggling at their over dramatic attempts at pretending to be frightened. What kept coming to mind was that it all looked a little bit like the damsels in distress in one of those nineteen fifties classic science fiction movies, of which I happen to be a great fan by the way. So we took a few shots of not very convincing frames of film and called it a day. So with fifty 'sponnies in my grubby', everyone concerned decided to call it a day and with that it was a wrap. So with this little bit of extra cash earned I ventured down the pub where the rest of the lookalike crew were currently residing and as it just so happened to be my birthday the next day, I bought everyone a round whilst we swapped stories of the day's events.

CHAPTER 11

A FUNNY ODD
SPINOFF OR TWO

As it happened, doing that 'mix and mingle' at the after
show party on the Madame Tussards job turned out to be
quite beneficial for some of us lookalikes; we managed to
get some extra work that we would not have otherwise have got
the opportunity to do which was good. Sometimes together and
sometimes individually but somehow always through the agents,
(well, we would not want then missing out on their fifteen percent
now would we. Ha ha.) I shouldn't knock them really. After all, if
it wasn't for them none of us would be doing anything like this in
the first place. As with a lot of things in life, one thing can lead to
another which in turn leads to something else and so on and so
forth and so it was for us lot. One of the spinoffs was some of us
ended up doing some modelling work. Mind you, if it wasn't for
the Tom Cruise connection, I can't imagine anyone wanting to
stare at my ugly mug for any length of time, (well may be with the
exception of my wife Teresa but that's usually only because
I've done something wrong that I'm about to be made aware of.
'Men, we don't know what we've done!') Anyway back to what
I was saying, the modelling work was mostly for clothes cata-
logues and women's magazines. You can imagine the type of
thing, can't you; Tom Cruise wears the latest leather jacket as
I stand there with a nice pair of aviator shades on, my concrete

hairdo and one hand on my hip with the other pointing towards the horizon at some unseen thing. Or may be Tom wears the latest designer suit, (nice suits they were as well,) all topped off with a grubby white tee-shirt worn underneath, Tom style of course. I did a few jobs like this but I did not find them every exciting. There was a lot of hanging around to be done interspersed with makeup people fussing around you getting you ready for the next shot or hold ups 'cos the lighting wasn't quite right. All a bit mundane and boring and not particularly well paid either; not like when you get the chance to 'mix and mingle' and stuff, so it was not long before I got a bit fed up with it all. Having had a little taster of all that, it certainly isn't the glamorous world we are led to believe it is and the next time some airhead bimbo, man or woman, tell you they are a model for a living, impressed would not be my reaction. I think I would feel sorry for them.

One time during this period I did a photo shoot for a new after-shave that was going to be released, a sort of 'Hey if it's good enough for Tom its good enough for you' the promo caption read. Of course, they did not have the endorsement of Tom Cruise himself so they were careful not to use his name as such; just an implication of him hence Tom instead of Tom Cruise and the use of a lookalike (namely me) but it was very heavily implied none the less. Poetic licence I think they call it.

I did enjoy this particular shoot because it involved me dressed as a Top Gun Tom sitting on a backwards chair holding out a bottle of this stuff with the label pointing at the camera. What's so interesting about that then? You may ask. Well granted it does sound a bit like the other normal mag shots but this time I had five scantily clad young and very beautiful looking female models surrounding me! Lovely especially if you were turning into a middle age craggy like me. I was getting to be around the fortyish mark about then and although I looked quite good for my age back then, (even if I do say so myself!) I remember thinking that it was a bit of a stretch trying to get someone of my more mature years to look like a young twenty something, as was Tom's age when he made Top Gun. They managed it though, professionals that they are, with a little help from good lighting and a touch of airbrushing no doubt. So back to the women. We spent all day trying to get the perfect shot and I must say, it was rather a pleasure watching these pretty young things running around all day. They were a nice bunch, got on well together, not like sometimes when you put a bunch of young lovelies together, all fighting for the spot light. Plenty of two faced back-stabbing goes on there I can tell you. I even saw a cat fight break out on a shoot once. Both girls had scratched each other's faces so bad they were no longer of use to the photographer and they got sent home. Still, it was fun to watch. So there we were, trying to get the perfect shot, and as the day wore on the girls gradually wore less and less, obviously not changing in front of us men of course. They started out in what looked like evening dresses and over the course of time, like a very slow striptease, they ended up in a two piece swimming costume which, and well I never, ended up being what they wore in the picture that was finally chosen for the promo. There were two of them sitting on the floor looking longingly up at me, (ha if only), there was one of them standing behind me looking sternly down and the other two standing either side of me with their arms wrapped around me looking like they were both about to give me a kiss. And there I was, with a big cheeky grin on my face, holding out this bottle of aftershave. At the time of course, I did not know what was going to be the shot that they would use; that was decided by the powers that be at a later date.

How I got to see it was when I was shopping for a pair of nice range jeans that they sold in the department store in nearby Basildon with a mate of mine. The same mate coincidently, Tim, who had sent my photos off to the lookalike agents and got me into this malarkey in the first place. Anyway we had just stepped off the escalators heading for the jean department when Tim who had decided to head off to the perfume counter to get his girlfriend a birthday present shouted over "Oi Gal there's a picture of you over here. Come and have a look" I wandered over and sure enough there I was with my cheeky little grin, looking an airbrushed twenty years younger by the way, with the five scantily dressed young ladies draped all around me. I must admit I felt quite proud of myself just then, allowing myself little bit of job satisfaction you know, with the nice young lady behind the counter saying politely "Aww, we've got a star here have we?" as she nudged her mate to have a look. Then Tim, yob that he was, came out with the usual young man classic line of "So which one did you shag then, Gal?" Oh god how embarrassing and right in front of these two nice young ladies as well. I replied "behave Tim I'm a married man" Although I wasn't actually married at the time, I had been living with my family for many a year in a town Called Benfleet and had three children whom I absolutely adored, Ben, Samuel and my daughter Mollie and those kids meant everything to me. (As I said earlier, I loved being a dad; it's the best, and hardest, job in the world as I'm sure you fathers out there will concur.) So anyway I made my way to the jean section and bought myself a rather expensive pair and on my way out I gathered up Tim who was still chatting to the nice young lady behind the perfume counter. He was a one for the ladies was Tim and on the way back to the car he said "Well, that worked out well Gal" "Oh yeah? What did?" I replied. "You being on that promo stand. It gave me the perfect opener so I asked the girl out. Meeting up with her Wednesday. It's well cool having a lookalike mate, good for me with the ladies, hope you don't mind". Well, what could I say? He wasn't the first friend to take advantage of who his mate looked like back then and he wasn't the last either. Now one last thing about this gig.

As I sit here writing this I can't remember for the life of me what the aftershave was called and I can't reference it as I've can't find any information in my records of the details of this job. Funny how I remember the details of those models though, must be a bloke thing ha ha, But I do remember of what the aftershave smelled like. I was given a bottle when I was doing the shoot and when I tried it on it smelled quite similar to an old discontinued line called 'Blue Stratos'. Don't know if you're old enough to remember it but, to me at any rate, it was one of the best smells in the world. A very popular brand back in the seventies and one of the first aftershaves I ever wore as a teenager as I was back then. The smell I found quite intoxicating and as I had not smelled anything remotely like it since my youth, it instantly brought back memories of lost loves and old mates whom I hadn't seen for many a year and a whole bucket load of very pleasant memories. I wore this new stuff until the bottle had run out but unfortunately, by the time I had gotten around to buying some more they had discontinued the line.

Sometime later there was another spinoff that occurred. I had received a letter through the post inviting me to attend a television show. This was an annual T.V show called 'Stars and their Doubles' I don't know if you remember it but I had watched this show before, so was aware of its high profile nature and there for its potential to once again raise my lookalike status and thus gain some extra work for me. Well come on, I did still have my family to support after all and I hadn't heard from old 'Stalks' for a bit. It was one of those London Weekend Television shows and somehow I had made it through the preliminary auditions and had been invited to take part in the show. Funny how I have no recollection of doing any auditions; bit strange don't you think? I later found out that it had been one of those boring modelling jobs I had done that had bought me to the attention of the show's producers. Oh well, I guess they had their uses after all. So the letter read:

Dear Gary and Guest

First of all let us congratulate you on passing the preliminary auditions. This is to confirm that we would very much like you to take part in the show by being a member of our specially selected and filmed 'celebrity' audience. The 'celebrity' audience is very much in keeping with the traditional LWT Audience With series. As you can imagine your appearance on the show is vitally important in contributing to the overall ambience of this gala awards evening.

And so it went on. 'Hey don't miss this once in a life time opportunity for your very own half priced double glazing offer especially just for you bla bla bla… Well you get my point. Once again, it was pitched to me as the usual cheesy once in a lifetime offer kind of thing and how could I possibly resist? They certainly knew how to play this ex-salesman kinda boy. This show was going to be made by Granada Entertainment, as I'm sure we've all heard of. They are a production company that do a hell of a lot of work for London Weekend Television and this particular show was being pitched to the public as *'Stars and their doubles 2002' A tribute to the U.K.'s best 'lookalikes'*. It was hosted by none other than Des O'Connor, who incidentally turned out to be a really nice bloke as I found out at the after show party. Now my first wife was not interested in coming along so I asked my mate Glen if he was interested. He was working as a George Micheal sound alike back then and, (as with me i.e. helping me to get some extra lookalike work,) I thought that it might help him gain favour where he otherwise might not have. We made our way to Manchester and, booking ourselves into a local Travel Lodge, settled onto our rooms in plenty of time to be at the Granada studios at Quay street in Manchester city by 6.30 that evening. We were advised to, quote *'arrive dressed and made up as much as your lookalike character as possible. The show will start at 7.30 pm with a party afterwards beginning at 10.00'* unquote. Now Glen, bless his cotton socks, didn't look much like George Micheal, not being of Greek descent and all, but tell you what though he was one of the best sound-alikes I have ever heard; better than my crappy American accent at any rate, (lucky it was not my voice they were after eh?) Anyway the point being he managed to make a living at it and I hoped all this would help him. It was said that my guest would have to be seated in a separate area to us lookalikes in with the general audience, i.e. the general public who had been lucky enough to be invited to partake in the show. Us lookalikes however, were ushered into the VIP seat right at the front of the stage where the cameras could get a good look at us all. I managed to seat myself down right in the middle of all me old muckers 'The Hollywood Heavies'. We all busied ourselves with what turned into a rather loud and animated catch up with each other and were told by some of the production crew to "shut up you lot" just before the start of the show. Old Des O'Connor was a good egg; the usual well-rehearsed and professional host, telling his scripted but unfunny jokes that we were all told to laugh at on cue. I have to say that, in my opinion having talked to him at the after show party, that if he had been left to his own devices he probably would have been a much more endearing and funny host than his script allowed him to be on the night.

The actual show was ok; there was plenty of film on the large screen of one or two lookalikes, going around fooling the general public, all pre-recorded filming of course, I especially remember the Prince William lookalike being particularly featured as he went around mingling with the general public, having a laugh. Towards the end of the evening it was award ceremony time and of course the already 'pre-decided' won everything except the 'surprise member of the lookalike audience trophy' that is. Now the guy who was supposed to have been awarded runner up was that Brad Pitt lookalike at the Madam Tussards do, who buggered off. Apparently he had been invited but, lordy lordy, he hadn't bothered to turn up. So they, at the very last minute I might add, asked me if I could do an eleventh hour stand in for him. Although this was an unpaid job, I did realise it's potential to raise my profile so without further ado I agreed. "And the best runner up lookalike is......." No one ever gets to pronounce my surname right so after poor old Des struggling with it for a moment of two he decided to just call me Tom. Up I got to a very well timed round of applause from everybody and made my way to the stage. Des came over and presented me with the prize. It was a solid glass version of what the British BAFTA awards looked like, obviously a lot cheaper but very heavy. I was supposed to make some kind of a speech at this point but being as this was a last minute unexpected substitution I had nothing planned. Unlike what is usually the case for me as I'm good at busking, being the muso and all, nothing was coming to mind. All I could think of was how hot it was under the glare of the stage lights. However, as it turned out, no speech was the least of my worries, because as I approached the microphone with award weighing heavy in my sweaty little grubby, I dropped it! I don't know how; it just sort of slipped through my damp fingers. SMASH it went, all over the stage floor to a resounding sound of silence from a very stunned audience and everyone else concerned for that matter. The silence was deafening as they say and with all eyes on me, (and all cameras for that matter), with a very wide and silly grin on my face, I slowly side stepped my way off the stage. It was another one of those 'Laurel and Hardy' moments and I felt very glad to be back into the anonymity of my eighth row seat as I waited for the floor to open and swallow me up. No such luck though as all the cameras decided to zoom in on me as I sat down. Right in my face they were and at that moment I so wished I had had my guitar to hide behind. That's the problem with doing a gig without your guitar; it sometimes leaves you naked.

Still, the after show party went without a hitch despite me having to endure a load of jibes and piss take from my fellow lookalike compatriots. Still, all's well that ends well and after a few drinks and chatting with everybody including dear old Des O'Connor himself, we all had a good night in the end. Me old mate Glen had a good time not to mention a little looksee into the lookalike world and with that we made our way back to the hotel for a good night kip for the long drive home the next day. I did not see the show when it was finally aired on the telly but Glen did and apparently they had completely edited out my part of going up on the stage and having that little accident. Can't say as I blame them and I was glad too as it would not have made a very good addition to my lookalike resume now would it?

Back in late '03 Sky decided to run a promotional champagne to advertise their movie channel 'Sky Movies'. They had decided that it would be good idea to use the Tom Cruise film *Minority Report* as their advertising vehicle as it was one of the more recent Hollywood box office hits. It had very recently done the rounds at the cinemas and Sky were the first to get their hands on it. They wanted it to be in the form of a Billboard posters that they were then going to have put up all around the U.K. As per normal they employed the services of one of their production companies to facilitate this who, in turn and having seen me in the aftershave advertisement, wanted to use me for the poster's photo. They got in touch with the agent and hired my services. Game on.

The job was for me to meet up with their photography crew one cold autumn Friday at Wandsworth Park children's playground which was at the corner of Putney Bridge Road and Fawe Park Road SW15, at 11am. My two contacts were a guy called Mike whom I met on the actual shoot and a lady called Tracey who tended to be the behind the scenes organiser. She was my first point if contact who explained what they required of me; to fetch a costume as much like the outfit that Tom Cruise wears in the film. Don't know if you have ever seen Minority Report but I went to see it at the cinema when it was doing the rounds and although I thought the plot was a little thin, I thoroughly enjoyed it. I like a good dose of science fiction, Star Trek being my personal favourite. Anyway it is about a futuristic cop, played by Tom, whose police department has a technologically advanced machine that has the ability to be able to predict who will commit a crime in their future instantly turning innocent people into wanted villains. All that techno stuff and what does it do? Burns the culprits name onto a wooden ball....mmmm ok then. Well, apart from that bit, it is a good film. Tom flies about all over the place catching these 'gonna-be' baddies using the futuristic cars that the film depicts. If I remember rightly, these cars run on rails and can go up and down the sides of buildings and allsorts. Now there is one particular shot in the film where Tom, whose name has been put in the frame by one of these wooden balls thus turning him instantly from cop to hunted criminal, is being pursued by his now ex-mates the cops. In this shot, he is about to jump off of one of these cars on to another that's passing the other way in the hope of avoiding his pursuers. So the original promo stills shot that was used to promote the film in the first place was of this photo of him crouching down ready to leap off. So this was the picture that Sky wanted us to recreate only this time it was to be a jovial shot of me, dressed as Tom in the film of course, on a day out in the park

with his son. I was standing on one end of a seesaw in the crouching pose of Tom doing the cat leap as my son is suspended in
mid-air on the other side of the seesaw with a terrified look on his
face as his dad's about to jump off leaving the poor little sod to go
crashing to the ground. Of course, the words 'Sky movie channel'
and 'Movies to match your mood' were to be splashed all over the
place. Now in the final picture that would be used for the poster
there was also going to be a super imposed think bubble coming
out the top of my head with the real Tom doing his leap and a
caption saying "Think I'm in a Minority Report kind of mood
tonight". Hopefully I have managed to set the scene. The Friday
came around and I left home that morning making my way by
train to the East Putney tube station. I had a little stroll along a
street called Oakhill Road and at the bottom of the road there is a
little café so without further ado I popped in and got myself a nice
cup of takeaway tea. After this I made my way to the park where I
met up with this chap Mike and the rest of the crew for the days
photo session. They had hired a child model to act the part of my
son, the little boy who was going to be sitting up the other end of
the seesaw; a nice young lad who was only about ten years of
age so his mum was there with him. The morning went without
mishap, (well save for a minor problem which I'll come to in a
moment,) and they must have taken dozens and dozens of photos
until they decided they had got the look. I did not mind having
gotten used to this sort of thing by now and besides I was getting
nearly double money for standing around smiling! Another good
thing was the young lad's mother turned out to be a fellow avid
tea drinker and after me telling her about the cafe just around the
corner she volunteered to keep us in supply of the lovely brown
nectar by going back and forth to the café whenever any of us got
the craving. Or to quote a line from Top Gun "I feel the need, the
need for TEA!" ha ha. The only problem we had was, despite the
fact that I must have been twice the weight of the boy, for some
reason we could never get the seesaw to stay down on my side.
It would always balance back up again and of course, as sods
law would have it, it would always move just as the photographer
was taking his shot. We tried for ages to get it to work but it just

wouldn't have it no matter what we did. Then, during one of our many tea breaks the boy's mother said "why don't I just push it up from the other side? You know out of shot or something?" It seemed so obvious once she had said it that it was surprising no one had thought of it before. Anyway that's exactly what we did and after a little while they managed to get the shot they wanted. However the problem they had at first was that no matter how hard they tried they kept getting the mums bottom in the shot, not that she was a large lady or anything, it was just that the width of the slide was not enough to hide a human being. "Oh no whatever was to be done?" I hear you cry sarcastically. Well here's the genius; as no one else seemed to be able to solve the problem, (all talking about techy solutions, airbrushing and high tech camera info that I didn't understand,) mum came out with, in a very condescending tone of voice I might add, "why don't you move the camera two feet to the left so the centre piece covers my arse boys". Well that cracked me up. I must have laughed a little too hard as I fell of the slide, well it was a bit slippery, and straight into the camera man. Luckily Mike managed to grab that very expense looking piece of equipment just as it started to fall off its stand so no damage done there. However the camera guy, having been knocked by me on my way down and bearing in mind it was well muddy that day, he started doing the backwards run trying to keep his balance, you know like they do in the cartoons, but to no avail and with legs flailing he went splat right on his back. He was covered in mud all up his back. I managed to land in the mud but on my arse so the only muddy bit on me was my bum. Anyway after another cup of tea and a wipe down we managed to get the right shot in the end. In the poster the angle of the camera is such that you can't see mum crouching down holding up the slide or my muddy arse. With all the high-tech stuff around these days we sometimes forget that the best solutions are the simplest ones. Incidentally, here is my favourite classic example of exactly that: The Americans with their very expensive and high tech space program, spent millions of dollars developing a pen that could write in space. What was the Russians solution to the problem? A pencil!

A few weeks later I took my two boys for a trip up London for a day out. Instead of Benfleet station we took a train from Basildon and all along the platform there were the Sky posters up on all the walls. I was not expecting that, being more interested in looking at the time table I did not notice at first. It was only when I felt a tugging on my sleeve from Ben and Samuel saying all excitedly "Dad dad. You're on the walls!" that I bothered to look up to see me grinning back at us whilst standing on a slide looking like I wanted to watch The Minority Report. They were everywhere. I don't just mean on that train platform but on every train platform that we passed through and all over the underground trains and platforms and posters on walls; everywhere you looked. I have to say it was rather a surreal experience seeing yourself splattered all over the place like that. Sky had really gone to town on this advertisement that's for sure. Apparently they were all up and down the country I was told by different people that I knew who lived all about and of course the inevitable surge in 'friend' phone calls that was associated with this type of thing. Incidentally, it wasn't just me that the 'friend' phone calls happened to. Other lookalikes mentioned about it when ever anything similar happened to them. It was nice to hear from me old mate 'Stalks' though; that one kept him going for a good couple of weeks.

The billboard posters were up for a week or so and that day when me and my boys returned back to Basildon station they took a photo or two of their dad standing beside one of these Sky billboards to show their mates. We did ask at the ticket office if they wouldn't mind keeping one for us when they were finished with them but when we went back a week or so later we were told that the company who had put them up there had come along at took them all away again so we never did get one for posterity's sake in the end.

CHAPTER 12

SOME UNSAVOURY OFFERS

I got offered a couple of film parts as a result of all this previous work but neither worked out though, however, they were interesting diversions from everyday life none the less. The first one was an offer to go and do a porn film (of all things would you believe,) out in Los Angeles in America. The fact that it started with an email direct from their production company to me told me that this had not come through one of the lookalike agencies but more likely to have been a result of them having gotten hold of one of my lookalike business cards or having looked on my website which at the time was www.tomcruiselookalike.net

Now a little bit about my old website here just to digress a moment. Back in the day i.e. the mid nineties', which, as I spoke about earlier on, was around about the time I started doing all this lookalike stuff, also around this time I was doing a computer course. Now back then computers and the internet were not the massive things they are today but rather more in the embryonic stages of what they would very quickly become. Makes you wonder how we ever got by without it all sometimes. My daughter Mollie who's now sixteen as I write this simply can't imagine a world without internet bless her cotton socks. Unless she is plugged in to Facebook and Tumblr, Youtube etc. 24/7 her world doesn't exist as any modern parent will agree. She does make me laugh, even if she is up in her bedroom when she's at my house at weekends and stuff rather than pop down to speak to me she will message me instead 'is dinner ready dad I'm starving'. Sound familiar, mum and dad? Anyway I was doing this computer course and I met this bloke, by the name of Peter, who was an absolute techno geek and offered to make me up a website. These days, of course, practically anyone can do it as it is made easy enough and every does. But back then it was beyond the reach of a simple layman like myself. I could barely work windows 95, as it was back then, let alone write code. Don't forget there are umpteen websites and computer programs that will make you up your very own site but around that time, apart from an early version of Dreamweaver which I knew nothing about, there was practically nothing. For the most part you had to write the HTML code yourself. He helped me design it adding text and pictures of me as Tom and a résumé of my lookalike work up to that date. Because it was all a bit novel and fresh back then, it made me sound quite professional that I even had my own website. I went round his house once or twice and his whole lounge was covered in servers. Don't know how his wife put up with it but she did. I have to say Pete was way ahead of the curve back then and what he didn't know probably wasn't worth knowing. So I had my web site up and running and all through my lookalike career he kept it live and updated for me. It made life much easier than sending photos and résumés off all the time; it was just a case of log on to the site and down load what you want and of course a link to my email. The websites down now as I haven't need it for a while but I still see Pete every once in a while.

So there I was sitting at home late one evening I decided to check my emails, bearing in mind this is now a few years later when all this was common place by now, when up pops something from a company in Los Angeles. Upon reading it I had to look at it twice to make sure I had read it right. At first I just ignored it thinking that it was probably a prank but they persisted sending me another email asking me to reconsider. According to them, I was the nearest looking lookalike they could find and would I be interested in starring in their porn film? I really did not want to do something like that for of a few reasons. For a start, apart from having a family, how do I know they are who they say they are? And besides, once it's out there it's out there and there is no retracting it. Perhaps some of the younger lads would be saying thing like "Go on just do it are you mad? I would" but think about it for a moment. Anything could happen. How would you like your private parts splashed all over the internet for anyone to see? Also how would you feel if one day one of your kids came across it? Or even, God forbid, your mother in-law! Ahh, what a horrible thought! I just felt at the time that it would all come back one day and bite me in the arse. There is also of course that I like to do that sort of thing in private, thank you very much and I'm not sure if I could perform with a bunch of blokes with cameras and lighting shoved in me bollocks, no matter how fit the birds were. Well you get my point anyway; it wasn't for me. Did not stop them trying though. The next email they explained more about what they wanted. Here's a quote from it;

Ok Gary here's the deal. The story line is of Tom Cruise having been booted out of the Hollywood Scene for certain indiscretions involving drink, drugs and women, and now no one will employ him in the film industry anymore. So, down on his luck and being broke he turns to the only part of the film industry that will have him. Porn. Upon which he comes across one of the sex industries production companies and embarks on a very successful career as a porn star. Of course there won't be much about the plot it will be more about the intercourse but, hey, people don't watch porn for the story line do they? Now here's what's in it for you; we will pay you five thousand dollars for one week's work. We will give you two days off for rest and recuperation, (and believe me you will need it!) and not forgetting of course having sex with lots of babes, all tested as clean by the way. Incidentally, if you're worried about your size we can computer enhance anything. So what do you say Gary?

Kind regards etc etc.

It did sound tempting didn't it and maybe someone else would have done it but it wasn't for me, it really wasn't. Gregarious and outgoing that I am, that was something I did not want to do. My word it's enough to make your willy shrink, ha ha! However the persistent little buggers would not let it go. They came back with another email offering me seven thousand dollars to do it this time and if I was worried about performing in front of several other people there was always Viagra. Gosh they seemed to have thought of everything! However their pre-emptions did lead me to believe they had offered this to at least one other which led to further apprehension on my part. My final response was to thank them for their very kind offer but I did not want to lose my family and although it was a lot of money, no amount of money was worth the price of losing them, and so I declined. Their final email said that they had not realised I was a family man and understood where I was coming from. They thanked me for my time and wished me luck for the future. Here's the Ironic part though. Sometime later my first wife up and left me for someone else anyway! So you've got to see the funny side of that. May be I should have done it after all, as my mates are *very* fond of letting me know.

Actually, whist we are on the subject of unsavoury offers, that last account of events reminds me. Although this did not come about as a result of Madame Tussards or photo shoots type thing, I do think it is worthy of a little mention at this point.

I was on a lookalike job doing a Hollywood themed night at a big corporate function up London one time with a whole bunch of us 'Hollywood heavies'. There must have been fifteen or twenty of us, all the usual crew 'meeting and greeting, mix and mingling'. This was one of those occasions where I was working with a Nicole Kidman lookalike, back in the day when they were a couple that is. Now I don't know why but although there were one or two Nicole lookalikes about at the time, they never really managed to get one who was quite right. Either their body shape was wrong, bearing in mind the real Nicole is very tall and skinny, or the hair was not quite right, I don't know but there was always something. So the agents were always trying out new girls and every few Tom and Nicole jobs I would do I would meet a new one. Having said all that, none of us lookalikes were exact duplicates anyway just close proximities, so who am I to judge? The biggest problem was, and this is part of me not being an exact match to my character as well, is that as I mentioned before, I am taller than Tom. Now when you saw Tom and Nicole together she was always a head taller than him but being 5' 11" it was hard to find a girl taller than me so as a couple we never quite looked right. The best Nicole lookalike I had the pleasure of working with was a girl by the name of Rachel. She looked a lot like her a lot in the face, which of course was the most important thing of being a lookalike, and had the long sort of curly blond slightly ginger hairdo that the real Nicole sported in those days. Now although her body shape was a bit out, one of the best things was that Rachel was tall. She was as tall as me standing at five feet eleven inches so with a little jiggery pokery i.e. standing in the highest high heels she could get her hands on and bunching her hair up on top, and with me wearing the flattest shoes I could find between us, we managed to give the illusion at any rate that she was taller than me, even though whenever we did a photo shoot together I would still have to bend down at the knees. Our only problem then became that we were both then much taller than our counterparts, as was occasionally pointed out, but our answer to that was "Well if you can get the real thing for the two pound fifty they are paying us what are you doing here?" which always raised a chuckle. I had been asked by the agent who had booked this particular gig that as they were sending a novice Nicole lookalike along, a girl by the name of Anna, would I mind showing her the ropes. This was her first gig and she might need a little help. We were all new to this game once so of course I didn't mind and I made sure that I went a little earlier so that I would meet her there when she arrived. So we met up and I introduced her to some of the other lookalikes and did my best to make her feel relaxed. I gave her a few pointers and explained to her that, although it was her first time and we would all help her out as much as possible, if she could manage it, try and get into the character and be a little bit of a caricature of Nicole and not just stand there being a part of the back ground. This could be a bit of a failing sometimes with the some of the less outgoing lookalikes as I said before.

After all, the client was paying us to entertain their guests at the end of the day. I could see that Anna was a little bit nervous but holding her own. I've seen some new lookalikes crack up on their first job, just not being able to act out in front of other people, and off they run never to be seen again especially if it's not just a 'meet and greet' whereby they have to get up on a stage and talk in front of an audience i.e. presenting prizes or such like. Pretty daunting for your first job and you have never done anything like that before. Some of the other lookalikes sometimes liked to tease the 'newbies' winding them up with a bit if jovial banter, nothing nasty of course. Although I have been known to partake in this practice a little myself on occasion, (undermining some cocky little upstart new to the job thinking he knows it all and we saw one or two of them from time to time I can tell you,) I did however hold the thought in my mind of the bad experience I had endured the very first time I had ever performed in front of a crowed back in my teenage days with the first ever band I was in so I never went to hard on the new guys.

I must just quickly tell you about my first ever experience of performing in front of a crowd before I continue whilst I've mentioned it so you can see where I am coming from. It was my first ever live performance with my first ever band at the tender age of sixteen. Up until I left school, the only guitar I had was an old beaten up nylon strung acoustic guitar that I learned to play on. At the age of thirteen my mum would take me and my sister to the folk guitar club on a Tuesday evening. We would learn some basic chords and play things like 'Michael, row the boat ashore' and 'Clementine' and other such simple little ditties so as we could put into practice whatever was the chord to be learned that day. I found these songs all rather boring but making music with a guitar was great and I was forever more hooked on playing the best instrument that had ever been invented, well in my opinion at any rate. It did not take me long to work out that with every new chord I leaned I could apply that to some of my favourite band and/or chart songs that were about at that time and teach myself new songs more along the lines of what I liked. Once I had learned to play, it was not long before I was having teenage delusions of grandeur about being a rock star and promised myself that as soon as I had the money I was going to get an electric guitar. A couple of years later when I left school and started work that is exactly what I did. I bought a WEM amplifier with a Selmer two by twelve speaker cabinet and a Randall Telecaster copy guitar all for seventy five quid, (two weeks wages back then,) from Rob my mate at work. He had just acquired a brand new Gibson Les Paul guitar with a full on Marshall stack including a hundred watt head, as in amplifier, and two sets of four by twelve Marshall speaker cabernets. Boy was I jealous! He was only the same age as me and we liked the same type of music, loud rock, the louder the better, so it did not take us long to strike up a friendship. I would invite myself over to his place after work sometimes just so I could hold that beautiful guitar of his in my hands, turn all the dials up to eleven and bash out a few power chords, not to mention a window or two! Kind of reminds me of the opening scene in *back to the future* where Marty blasts that guitar chord at the professor's house. Anyway Rob had just got all this new equipment and sold all his old stuff to me which was all that I could afford at the time. Even then I was over stretching myself so Rob, bless his heart, let me have a bit of a discount on our originally agreed price if I stopped going round his house and blowing out his mums windows. Seemed a good deal to me; saved me fifteen quid and saved him from yet another slap round the head off of his mum. The day I got it from him, I had to lug all that gear on to a train, on my own, so as I could get it all home which back then was my mum and dads house. After setting it all up in the backroom, or the playroom as we had come to call it, and having a good old blast, I decided it was now time to get a band together, which had been an all absorbing dream of mine for the last two or three years. This was also the start of me tormenting the neighbours for the next eight years till I eventually left home. I had a couple of mates that were also interested in getting a band going. One was a guy called Froog on account of him wearing big thick tinted glasses that earned him the name of Froggie at school which there after morphed into the less derogatory 'Froog'. I had met him originally through one of my sisters who had been dating him for a while. He was a singer and a bass player and after being chucked out of his own band, he was quite keen to form a new one. The other guy was an old school mate whom I had known for ever. We met in infants school and had remained friends ever since. His name was Andrew Boosey. Boosey by name and boosey by nature. This boy was a bit of an animal and boy, could he drink. At the age of sixteen he would spend nearly all his time down the pub, back in the day when you could get away with that sort of thing that is. He was a big lad and would get drunk then get into a fight with whoever was the biggest guy in the pub. He loved it. That was his second favourite hobby his first being the drums. All through school he had wanted to play the drums but never had the money to buy a drum kit. Like me with the guitar, he had promised himself that as soon as he left school and got a job the first thing he would do was get himself a kit. At the same time I was buying my first amp and guitar, he was getting himself his first drum kit. But Andy being Andy it had to be the biggest badest and loudest drum kit he could find. He was an animal down the pub and an animal behind the drum kit but hey, that's just what you want isn't it? After all that is the blue print for the archetypal drummer, is it not? Keith Moon of the Who comes to mind and Andy, in his own way, reminded me a lot of Moonie. He was a nutter. The three of us got together and started rehearsing at my mum's house, me and Froog writing a few songs together for the band and we decided to call ourselves 'The Metallic Acid Band' which at the time I thought was a way cool name and to be honest, I still do. So after a few rehearsals we decided we needed another guitar player. This was not only to help beef up the sound when I was zipping in to one of my relentless fifteen minute lead breaks, as kids do, but also to fill out the sound when

I was playing the harp, as by this time I was playing a bit of blues harmonica which I still love the sound of to this day. One day, Froog fetched along a guy by the name of Steve. He was nineteen at the time and we were only sixteen so it seemed to us that he was a lot older and more experienced. He certainly was the best player in the band and at the time I learned a lot of guitar technique from him. However despite his more advanced ability, he was a rather shy and retiring type of character and seemed happy to just go along with whatever the rest of us wanted. After a couple of months we had a big enough set together that we decided it was time to do our first gig. Our old school was called Gable Hall and we were still members of the youth club that the school ran in the evenings. We had a chat with the youth club organiser and asked if we could do a gig in the main hall one Friday night to which he agreed. So the Friday came around and being as it was our very first live performance, in front of an actual live audience no less, we all took the day off work and had an extra rehearsal in the playroom at my house that afternoon just to make sure we had everything together. Froog had already done a couple of gigs from before so he was not to bad but me and Andy were well nervous being as it was our first time and all. So our dads dropped us, and all of our equipment, down to the school where we promptly set up and sound checked before the big gig. Andy the drummer, in his usual brusque manner had decided to start and argument with the bloke operating the schools P.A. system. Oh what a surprise but I knew Andy very well and this was his way of reliving the tension of the nerves we were suffering. Hay, let's go and start a fight. So after sorting him out it was nearly time for us to start and all standing by our relevant instruments we were ready. "Let them 'avit" Andy shouted and that was supposed to be the cue for opening the curtains but alas no Steve! "Wait!" I shouted. I knew exactly where Steve would be and with that I dashed around behind the stage to the toilet there to find Steve throwing up his very soul with nerves. "I can't do it Gal, I really can't. You know all my guitar parts you go and do it" He was in a right old state but this was our very first ever gig and we were going to be rock stars so I was not having any of it. I made him wipe his mouth and literally dragged him by the collar to his guitar and his place on the stage. He stood there shaking but we were ready and with that I struck the first chord as the curtains split apart. We were met with the usual indifference of an apathetic teenage crowd who wanted to enjoy it but did not want to look uncool in front of their mates. But by now I didn't care; I was playing at being a rock star and enjoying every second of it. So was Andy the drummer who by now was kicking his kit all over the place. Froog was singing his little heart out when we noticed there was no Steve- again! We could hear his guitar parts all right but no sign on the stage of him. He had sort of wrapped himself inside of the stage curtain on the left thus rendering himself invisible to the audience. Our roadies at the time, Dave and Phil, decided to unwrap him and push him out on to the middle of the stage. Now you have to bear in mind that as sixteen year olds and with the angst of youth on our side, all this was terribly important to us. After all this was a first gig on the way to rock stardom. So poor old Steve, frightened to death as he was, suddenly found himself centre of attention with no sympathy from his band. Then to add insult to injury, because the audience of piss taking teenagers, (and let's face it there are none more cruel than kids,) started to let him have it, as it were. It was all too much for him and with that he fainted! And there endeth my first ever gig. Humiliated and besieged by embarrassment, it spelt the end of the band. Steve quit playing after that and we never saw him again. Me and Froog moved onto another band and Mr Boosey drifted from one band to another, getting drunk and having a fight or two. He joined a punk band which would have suited him down to the ground but after a little while I lost touch with him, him going his way and me going mine. The last I heard back then was that he had got six months in prison for steeling from of his employer. Apparently he was loading extra bags of cement on to the lorries for a back hander from the drivers. No doubt he caused no end of shit on the inside. I'm glad he was a mate of mine because you certainly did not want to get on the wrong side of him but a handy guy to have on our side in a sticky situation. Many years later our paths did cross for one final time. I was having a bit of trouble with my national insurance payments, apparently I had not been paying enough, so I was down the Basildon job centre sitting down waiting in line to see one of the advisors when this big burly bloke came up to me. He was covered in tattoos with a face full of shrapnel, i.e. piercings all over the place, and a very cropped grey hair do. "Your name Gary?" he grunted at me. My first reaction was one of horror, Christ who had I upset? "And you are?" came my rather trepid response. "It's Andy. Andy Boosey" and, as is very often the case when you have not seen some one for many a year, I suddenly recognised him. We had a hug and exchanged telephone numbers. After we were both finished at the centre we went down the pub for a catch up where he told me a very sad story. Long after we had all parted company he had met a married a girl and they had had two children, two girls. The second girl had died at only the age of two and this had devastated him as it would anyone. It was no one's fault; she had died of natural causes and nothing could have been done. Poor Andy; he had tears in his eyes as he was telling me about this awful tragedy. It split him and his wife up as they had apparently, in their grief and needing to apportion blame, started to blame each other. Here's a double whammy for poor old Andy; his wife moved away not wanting anything to do with the father of her dead child, as is common apparently when something like this happens, and as a consequence he never saw his wife or his other daughter again. I tried to keep in touch with him but after a couple of phone messages left and several texts messages he did not respond so not wanting too hassle him too much, we once again lost touch. Poor old Andy hope you're ok mate where ever you are.

Now that fateful day on our first gig all those years ago when poor old Steve, wracked with nerves, went up and fainted in front of our first ever live audience has never left my memory. We forced him onto a position that was so uncomfortable for him that he could not handle it anymore and with nowhere else to turn had simply just passed out. I have always felt rather guilty about that so that is why I am very magnanimous towards 'newbie' lookalikes such as Anna was that day.

So sitting in a dressing room, after we had all got changed in to our lookalike outfits for the evening of course, and at Anna's request I started giving her a little bit if coaching. I explained that, with me, I would talk in this over the top American accent and just try and be larger than life. But after the first meet and greet with someone, the initial novelty was over so you can just be yourself as they were not expecting the real thing anyway. It was all just a laugh so don't take everything too seriously. I explained that in her case Nicole was originally from Australia so it might be a good idea to play on that aspect for her character, mainly the accent. Now although the real Nicole is rather soft spoken I explained that she, Anna that is, should go in with a big hand shake accompanied with a nice over the top "Hi Digger how's you and your Sheila doing today?" or some other Aussie expressions and make them smile. Once you have done that, the rest of it just kind of falls into place of its own volition and once you have done it a few times, it soon becomes easy. Anna took it all in and I said I would help her out. Having done my Tom bit I would introduce her as the wife which would then be her cue; that way she didn't have to go in cold. Anna seemed ok with it all and so off we went to take up our starting positions with Tom and Nicole right at the start of the entrance where the folk would come in to be met by us first and then on to the other lookalikes waiting down the line.

As the first guests arrived I got into my usual Tom mode and stepped forth with a hand out stretched introducing myself with "Hi Tom's the name Hollywood's the game" and then after an initial quick chit chat I introduced the wife "Hey come and say hello to the misses...." at which point I was expecting Anna to step forth and give it her little bit. But instead all I got was a look of puzzlement from the two new arrivals followed by "what you talking about, Tom?" and as I turned around, no Anna! "Oops sorry" I said "must have just nipped out to the toilet to powder her nose" I said thinking on my feet as fast as I could and I quickly ushered them along to the next lookalikes. Luckily the next lookalike down the line was Greg, the Bruce Willis lookalike who,

165

standing not fifteen feet away, and realising my predicament offered to cover for me whilst I located Nicole. He and the Demmi More lookalike who he was working with that night, having seen what had happened, indicated to me Nicole's general whereabouts as they stepped forward to take our place for a moment. She was not hard to find as a few feet behind where we had been standing was a long black curtain and sure enough there she was hiding behind it. My first thought was 'Oh here we go; it's Steve all over again'. Apparently, as she was standing behind me and therefore was out of my line of sight, as the first of the evening guests had arrived and had started to make their way towards us, nerves had gotten the better of poor old Anna and she had just started stepping backwards until the curtain had enveloped her. It took me a few minutes to coax her out and back to the fore but I managed it and we took our places once again. Try as I might, I just could not get Anna to play her role, the best I could get out of her was for her to stand virtually all the way behind me and just smile as best she could and on the very odd occasion when I introduced her, she held out a rather limp hand and said "Oh hello" in a very timid voice looking down at the ground. Although it was frustrating and a little annoying I couldn't really get the 'ump with her, at least she was still there. Anyway after a short time all the guests had arrived and the 'meet and greet' part of it was over and so onto the 'mix and mingle'.

To start with as long as Anna was hanging around me, she was fine and as the night wore on her anxieties started to subside as her confidence grew. After about an hour or so she had built up enough confidence to branch out on her own and she started to wander off doing her own thing, which I have to say, given the auspicious start we had had to the evenings events was nice to see. It was also a bit of a weight off of my shoulders as well as with not having to babysit the newbie so much, I was more freed up to do my thing. However she asked would I check in on her from time to time as the night went on, to which I agreed. The first couple times I checked in on her she was fine so after about the third time I felt it ok to leave her to her own devices so that's what

I did. I happened to glance over to Anna a bit later on and she was chatting to some bloke who was holding her hand and, being as he was shorter then her, gazing up into her eyes. Everything looked fine to me so I turned back to resume my usual Tom duties. Time flies by when you're having fun and as I say I loved doing this job so I didn't actually know how much time went by but it was a while. I thought I would have a little look over to Anna to make sure she was all right and after a little searching through the crowd with my squinting eyes, I spotted her. She was still standing with the same odd looking little bloke and he was still stroking her hand, gazing into her eyes and I have to say she was looking rather uneasy so I wandered over. As I approached them I started to notice more about this bloke. He really was an odd looking fellow, looked to be quite short, five feet four may be well under her height at any rate. He looked to be about sixty with longish combed back hair that had that greyish blond 'hadn't been washed for a fortnight' look about it. He had a big red bulbous nose the kind that heavy drinkers have and a large potbelly to match, and to top it all off he had a pair of big, popping out of his head eyes. He was dressed in a rather dishevelled suit that had also become untucked and he was gripping Anna's hand tightly with one hand and stroking it with the other. He reminded me of a cartoon caricature of someone like Mr Stringfellow but without the Ritz. Because of his odd stature I remembered him from the 'meet and great' as he entered. He was with a couple of woman but they were nowhere to be seen right now. As I approached, I noticed a look of desperation in Anna's eyes and as she looked over to me she mouthed the word 'Help'. He was still stroking the back of her hand, as she was trying to pull it away from his obviously strong grip and all I could hear him saying over and over "Ow lovely lovely" like some old pervert as he smacked his lips. He was obviously the worst for wear, that's for sure. Time for some Tom intervention. 'What was the best way to handle this?' I was thinking. 'What would Tom do? He would probably steam on over there guns a blazing, kill the bad guy and save his damsel in distress' Good plan except for one thing; I might end up in prison and besides would our clients really want blood splattered all over the place? I wouldn't get paid! OK make that two things then. Besides she wasn't really my damsel was she, just a lookalike who happened to look like my lookalike's wife, OK, make that three things then. We were all just play-acting at the end of the day so why wasn't anyone else running to her rescue? There were other lookalikes nearer to them than I was who had spotted her predicament and one of them even said to me "Don't know if you have noticed Tom but your misses looks like she could do with a little help, mate". Funny how people think sometimes because she is a lookalike who happened to look like my lookalike's wife it must somehow be down to me then eh? Time for some Cruise schmooze. I slid on over and with a little trick I learned in 'Nam', (well actually it was something I remembered from a Jujitsu class from back in my youth) in one foul swoop I disengaged his hand hold and had his hand in a strong gripping hand shake as I placed myself in-between him and Anna. He looked very surprised as I started with the "Toms the name" thing finishing with "I see you have met the misses". "Oh oh sorry I didn't realise" he said most emphatically and as he went on "I was just saying hello" when I cut him off with "not really mate it's just pretend". Hang on what has all this got to do with an unsavoury offer you may ask? Well, this is where it kicked in. By this time Anna, freed from her bonds had decided to run off. I noticed his accent; it sounded maybe Mexican or something. Then he came out with something really odd, he said "Oh so she's not your wife then? That's good so... err... how much for de woman?" "What" came my dismayed reply "How much for de woman?" he insisted but I still was not getting what he meant, "What are you on about" I said with a perplexed look upon my face. "I want to spend the night with that very fine lady so how much for de woman?" I was laughing my head off at this point, the bloke was very drunk but still you have to admire his outrageous audacity. I so wished I could have thought of a witty retort right then but as I was rather gobsmacked at the absurdity of his offer, it was another one of those rare moments when I could not think of anything to say. At this point one of the two women that he had originally came with turned up and started saying something to him in what I can only presume was something like Spanish. She sounded rather angry with him and before he had a chance to say anymore, she pulled him hard by the arm turning to me and saying in a similar accent to him "Sorry so sorry" and with that led him away.

After standing there for a moment or two trying to digest the weirdness of what I had just witness I had a glance round looking for Anna but she was gone. She did seem in a bit of a state so, although weary with the babysitting role as I was, I thought I had best check she was alright. So with the help of a directional head nod from one of the other lookalikes, I headed off to the dressing rooms to find her. From behind the dressing room door I could hear sobbing so I tapped gently and after getting the ok, I popped my head round and saw poor old Anna putting her jacket on getting ready to leave. She had stopped crying by the time I entered the room but she had those 'just been crying' panda eyes and to be honest she look rather shaken. But after what she had just been through on her very first, and now last, lookalike job, I am not surprised. That must have been very unnerving for her. I asked if she was alright but she replied "That was just awful. I couldn't get away from him he just would not let go of my hand. I'm not doing this again." I felt for her. This had been her first experience as a lookalike and although she was not the most confident of people she was looking forward to becoming a lookalike and given time she would have got there I'm sure. But now this incident had undermined her and dashed her hopes for something she had really been looking forward to. I tried to offer words of comfort and explained that this was not what usually happens but she just was not having any of it and, after wiping her eyes, she said rather angrily "That was fucking bollocks. I'm never doing that again!" She looked at me and said a little more gently "Sorry Gary, it's not your fault. Thanks for your help, mate, I'll see you around" and with that she walked out the door. All I could think of was that old Queen song 'Another One Bites the Dust'. So humming away to myself I made my way back to the evenings events and carried on 'mixing and mingling'. I did keep my eye out for that weird little bloke as I wanted to give him a piece of my mind but I did not see him again either. And so endeth another lookalike before they had even got started.

It reminded me of a similar incident that had happened to me on a lookalike job I had done some time before. Back in September 2001 I had been asked to do a job for a production company called Liquid News. They were making a program for the BBC reporting on the opening night for a film called *Moulin Rouge* at the Leicester Square Odeon cinema in London. Don't know if you ever saw it; I never did myself, but it was a kind of musical thing set in the olden days in France but using some modern songs played old style befitting that period. It starred Ewan McGregor and Nicole Kidman and this was the premier, an all star packed glitzy evening type of affair. Nicole and Ewan were going to be pulling up outside in their limousines and walk the red carpet chatting to fans, signing autographs and smiling for the cameras. The BBC wanted me, dressed as Tom of course, to be sitting at a restaurant next door called Chiquita's. It is a Mexican eatery and has a first floor balcony which was the vantage point from where they were going to be filming. I was to be seated on the balcony having a meal and looking out at the proceedings as the filming was going on. Then accidently on purpose being put into shot now and again so as to make it look like they had accidently caught Tom keeping an eye on Nicole whilst reporting on the proceedings. All tongue in cheek, of course. Now the reason for all this charade was that Tom and Nicole were going through a divorce at the time with all the usual high profile acrimony being splashed all over the tabloids and news channels so, a big wig at the BBC decided that a stunt like this was appropriate.

So there I was meeting my BBC contact, a chap by the name of Stephen Rodgers inside Chiquita's. This was a couple of hours before the premier proceedings were due to kick off thus giving me plenty of time to get briefed on the evening's frolics, get changed and into character. The time came around and sitting there eating this lovely, and free, meal I watch the proceedings down below. It was a very easy job; I was not required to do anything but enjoy the food and the view and just basically let the film crew do their thing. We did try something at one point though. Nicole had arrived and was doing the rounds when I was asked to stand up and lean over the balcony whilst one of the production crew shouted "Nicole! Nicole! Up here". She must have heard because she looked up at us and we got one of those double takes, the whole thing being filmed of course, which was exactly what they wanted. The money shot so to speak. She looked none too pleased and headed off inside the cinema. The second part of the job, which was a bit of an afterthought, was for me, followed by the film crew, to wander down in to the crowd and see what kind of reaction we got. It was a mixed bag really; I kept getting glances and double takes from some of the crowd but for the most part the crowd were very much focused on the proceedings in front and did not take too much notice of us. However there was one point where, after all the celebs had gone in and the film had started, the crowd was dispersing and a few people came over asking for an autograph. This was fun for me but they kept bumping the camera man and getting in the way of the camera, blocking its view so they could not quite get the shots they wanted so after a while we abandoned the idea. Still they had got the money shot of the Nicole's double take so they were all quite happy anyway. So with job done, we made our way back into the restaurant where it was time to get changed and have a quick pint with the crew before I made tracks home.

On the way, I noticed some bloke following us. He looked like he was writing in to a pad but he was not one of the production crew which was why I had noticed him in the first place. He followed us inside and mingled himself into the back ground trying to blend in with the rest of the people in there, still keeping a beady eye on me. It was getting quite crowed by now as some of the folk from the crowd outside had made their way in for a beer and a bite. So after getting changed and standing at the bar waiting for my pint, this strange interloper sidles on over to me. I was standing on my own at that moment so I think he, upon spotting this, had taken the opportunity to approach me. 'This was going to be interesting' I thought to myself 'wonder what he wants?' He struck up a conversation with me by telling me how much of a Tom Cruise fan his wife is. "OK" I said "but I'm just a lookalike; you're telling the wrong person, mate". "Well no" he replied "I've got a little proposition for you if you're interested". Thinking this might be a private booking, maybe his wife's birthday party or something, curiosity was starting to get the better of me so I said "Go on mate, what you got in mind?" He replied with "Well, as I say, my wife is real big on Tom Cruise and it is her birthday next week and I wanted to do something really special for her so I was wondering...." then he looked me straight in the eye and bold as brass said "I will give you five hundred quid if you'll sleep with her." Well you could have knocked me over with a feather I was gobsmacked! "What? What did you just say?" came my stunned response. "Five hundred. Five hundred cash in your hand if you'll sleep with my wife" he reiterated "after all, it is her fortieth and I did promise her something special. So what do you say, Tom me old son?" He looked deadly serious about it. "The wife did it for me on my fortieth. We still watch it from time to time." At first I could not believe what I was hearing I said "watch it? What do you mean? You want to film it as well?" All sounded rather unsavoury to me but he carried on like it was a normal conversation "Yeah, if that's ok. I don't want to be there myself. We'll just set a camera up" and, still looking me straight in the eye, he held his hand out for me to shake as if to seal the deal. I looked at his hand then back to his face then beck to his hand and back to his face in quick succession a few times with my mouth wide open. Then still in his matter of fact tone, he added "Me and the wife are swingers from time to time, keeps things spiced up you know, so if you and your wife ever fancy..." he left the word hanging as he thrust his hand towards me once again. To him, it seemed just like a normal conversation but I was finding the whole idea a bit abhorrent. Each to their own I suppose but that sort of thing really does not appeal to me. "Absolutely not, mate!" was my answer "I'm really not up for that. No way" and I took an almost unconscious step back. All the reasons why

I did not want to do the porn film thing came to mind. My reaction did not seem to faze him at all as he came out with "Oh really? Ok I see, what puts you off then?" I managed to get as far as "Well for a start I'm not...." and then he cut me off in mid sentence as he came out with "I tell you what, Tom, me old son, make it a grand. A grand to sleep with the wife, can't say fairer than that now can you" He sounded like an East End market trader and was still taking all this in his stride as he put out his hand for me to shake once again. It was starting to sink in with me by now and I was starting to see the funny side of it. Got to admire this guy's balls. So with a smile now starting to spread across my face, I let out a little chuckle and said "Is this a set up? You winding me up?" expecting 'Candid Camera' or 'You've been framed'. But still with a straight face he said calmly "Nope. This is a straight up offer, a grand to shag my wife". I shook my head and said "No thanks fella but, hey, thanks for thinking of me" and with that I laughed. He just carried on looking me in the eye and with a shrug of his shoulders said "Ok bud. Suit yourself" turned around and walked out the door. At that point Stephen Rodgers, my contact man, came over and I said to him "did you see that?" and he went "see it? We managed to film most of it!" "You're having a laugh. Was it you lot? Did you set me up?" I said in dismay "No I was standing just over there" as he pointed a few feet away "and I overheard the conversation so I got Dick to roll the camera and as I say we caught most of it." Boy, was I glad my moral compass was pointing in the right direction right at that moment in time as he continued "yeah might tack that little scene on to the end. Make a good ending that would" Whether they did or not I don't know because as usual, I never got to see it when it was broadcast. Anyway happy in the knowledge that I had done the right thing regardless of whether they showed it or not, we all had a little chuckle and a pint before heading off home.

CHAPTER 13

THE FILM THAT WASN'T

S ome of us lookalikes got offered a part in a film project once that I think worthy of a mention. It all started with a letter I received from one of the agents from which I will quote a little of as it explains the situation quite well:

Dear Gary

I recently had a meeting with Paul Push, the Producer and Director, of a new British feature film called Fantasy Movies. Paul has seen pictures of you and would like to meet you and discuss the movie in more detail with a view to casting you.

Fantasy Movies is an independent British production with an international theatrical release planned for early 2003. It is a family fantasy action comedy set in London and the deep south of the U.S. and is the first ever movie starring movie star lookalikes. Other lookalikes featured in the movie range from stars of showbiz, sport, fashion and politics. A total of 90 lookalikes in the cast as well as the non-lookalike lead and supporting cast. Full details at the website.

Principal photography is due to begin July 27th 2002 around London, the south east and a couple of days in the deep south of the U.S. A seven week shoot in total. The majority of the lookalikes will only be needed for filming for one day with the exception of Naomi Campbell, Bill Clinton, Tom Cruise, DiCaprio, Gable, Mel Gibson, Whoopi, Hopkins, Madonna, Monroe, Schiffer, Schwerzenegger, Skywalker, Stallone, Liz Taylor, Tyson and Bruce Willis who will be required for up to three weeks.

Then it goes on for a while about casting and stuff which I won't bore you with and the letter finishes with:-

Paul has also given us the following statement in connection with payment which is as follows:- PAYMENT. The fee will be £350 per day and this will be paid immediately once the payment is received by the producers from the distributors for the sale of the movie. All the cast and crew will receive this kind of deferred contract from the lawyers and in addition, shares in the profits of the movie from all rights and territories will be paid to everyone for the lifetime of the movie.

It has to be your decision whether you want to participate in this project – may be the only chance you will ever get of being in a feature film and for this reason – you might be prepared to take a chance on it. It is your decision.

Just a final paragraph about the film itself:-

Fantasy movies – The first ever movie starring movie star lookalikes

A group of friends and their family are so disappointed by the new $80M Sylvester Cruisenegger movie they watch at home on video that they visualise their own 'Fantasy Movie' into reality.

Get back to me

Once again my cynicism kicked in and my first reaction to it was 'Hey don't miss this once in a lifetime half price double glazing offer just for you.....' and I was thinking of dismissing it as such especially because of the bit about the deferred payment.

In other words, we would be doing it for free until it made money upon its release if, of course, it ever did. However there was something intriguing about the whole thing, after all it was a very novel idea, and I found myself mulling it over. Also there would be a lot of lookalikes there that I knew and it would be nice to have an excuse to have a get together with some of me old muckers once again. What made me decide to do it in the end was I got a phone call from Greg, the Bruce Willis lookalike and Melita, who was the Marylyn Monroe lookalike both asking me what I thought and if I was going to have a go then they would too. So with that, I phoned the agent and told her to set it up.

Melita, (now there was a character!) The Marilyn Monroe lookalike. Also doubled up as a Madonna lookalike and did an excellent stage show as a Madonna sound alike as well. Boy, could she sing, having a very powerful but at the same time sweet kind of voice that she was able to mould into sounding like various famous singers and in this case Madonna's which I though she did particularly well. She ended up making a full time living at it. She came from up Norfolk way and was a single working mum raising two boys. I liked her. She was always a laugh and even when she was not in character i.e. just being herself, she was always a full on presence every where she went. You always knew when Melita had arrived as she whooshed in, dominated the arena, then whooshed out again. She knew how to play it and play it she did but she had this knack of tempering it all with nicety so no one ever took offence. Very clever girl. I had worked with her on and off during my whole period as a lookalike and we hit it off straight away particularly as we had the music and gigging thing in common as well as kids about the same age. She is still going strong as far as I know. I haven't seen her in a long time but last time we spoke, she had met someone really nice and was making plans to get married so good luck to you hun, hope it all worked out for you. One last thing I forgot to mention about Melita; Melita was not actually her real name more of an alter ego. Although everyone seemed to know her by that name, she kept her private life and her working life very separate and only her friends and family, of which she must have considered me one, were allowed to call her by her real name. She asked me once not to reveal it in the public arena so I won't; not that it isn't a normal name or anything it is just that that was her request. I asked her about this once and she told me that it is a psychological thing; allows her to be just her normal self in her normal life but when it comes time for work she switches into this other persona, Melita, and that allows her to be this almost over the top gregarious personality who can sing and lookalike and everything else.

Greg, the Bruce Willis lookalike was another character in his own right. He came from Kent and had a full time day job as a self employed carpenter so, unlike Melita, the lookalike thing was a part time job for him. However he claimed he earned as much out of being a lookalike as he ever did a carpenter which I can well believe as he lookaliked as much as any of us. In his carpentry job he did agency work, dropping in and out of various building site contracts which, apparently was the only way he could earn a living out of it as he kept getting sacked from the different sites he was working at for taking too much time off to go and do lookalikeing. I worked with him quite a lot as well over the course of my lookalike career. We were both part of the 'Hollywood Heavies' crew so often found ourselves working a Hollywood themed evening together doing the 'Meet and Great, Mix and Mingle'. He was another character I hit it off with straight away as we had a lot in common too. He was a fellow guitar player and gigged in a band at weekends and it wasn't unknown for us both to take our acoustic guitars along to lookalike jobs and have a strum together on occasion.

So the auditions for the film parts came around and all three of us ended up at Bodems theatre school in east Barnet near London at the same time having our auditions along with a bunch of other lookalikes from around the south east, most of which we knew to some degree or another. My audition consisted of me strutting up and down in front of a camera for a few minutes whilst they also took still shots of my face from different angles and then having a quick chat with Paul Push himself and another from the casting crew about various stuff I had done as a lookalike, paying particular attention to any filming experience that I had. Greg's audition was along the same lines but when it was Melitas turn she stole the show in her inimitable manner, bursting into one of her song and dance routines with her usual lack of restraint (bless her) and as usual, she won the hearts of everyone around her. It was a good day actually and nice to have another catch up with everyone. I managed to have a little one to one chat with Paul Push to find out a bit more about what was what with this project of his. It turned out that he had had this novel idea to use lookalikes in a film for some time now. He had been trying to get funding for it but the film industry thought that, although the script itself was good, the idea was "too out there" as he put it and did not want to take a chance on investing in such a radical idea. So he was going to finance it himself and using every penny he had and cutting the initial costs down to the bare bone he could just about do it. This was why he was asking the work force, including the actors and us lookalikes, if we would be able to work on a deferred payment contract which, luckily for him, most people had agreed to do. I admired his balls. At least he was brave enough to have a go and in my books anyone willing to go that extra mile, or in his case a hundred, for something they believed in was defiantly worth my support. Besides if it did become successful, how lovely for us guys to be in a film going on general release doing the cinema rounds on the big screen. Wow, what a great profile raiser if it did come off and 'Stalks' would be ringing my phone off the hook no less!

Now as I was one of the few aforementioned lookalikes he intended to use a lot of, I thought it best if I negotiated with him to get my expenses covered at least so, although I would not be earning initially, I would not be out of pocket either should the whole thing flop. Don't forget as Tom Cruise was featured quite a lot, I was going to be doing a lot of travelling thus racking up a lot of expenses. He was not happy about it at first but seeing my point of view, he agreed but I was not to let on to the others though. Seemed fair to me so we shook hands. I did have him over a barrel so to speak being that I was the only Tom Cruise look-alike about at the time and, as I say, featured a lot in his script, a fact of which I made him painfully aware of when negotiating the agreement with him. So with that I was on board.

I was sent the whole film script a few days later and although I had my reservations at first, they were quickly waylaid after having had a good read through and I have to say I liked it very much. It was going to be a tongue in cheek comedy. The main characters, the family and friends who watch '*the new $80M Sylvester Cruisenegger movie*' were being played by non lookalike actors and their characters have all these fantasies of different adventures with us lookalikes. It was quite fast paced and well written I thought and although I was in a lot of the scenes, us lookalike did not have to many lines to speak, which I secretly glad about given how crap I was at the America accent. Having said that it was supposed to be a comedy after all so the over the top southern drawl thing I did would have fitted in quite well. Greg and Melita got their parts as well and before we knew it it was time for the first days shooting to begin. This was done around Ealing somewhere on a film set made to look like the inside of someone's house. So I decided to drive there but wanting to arrive on set nice and early it meant I had to leave first thing in the morning, middle of the night more like, as the journey meant negotiating the dreaded M25 in the middle of rush hour. "Rush hour", my arse; they ought to rename it the "slow hours" at that time of day. Apparently it is the worst road in Europe for conges-tion but then again isn't every road in England? This country has a lot of good things going for it but the road infrastructure's not one of them. Anyway after trying to get there early I ended up being very late but I needn't have worried as just about everyone else had needed to use that road so I was on par with the rest of them.

So with great excitement at the prospect of doing something new to us, the first day began. But being as how it was all about filming and stuff, it soon degenerated into boredom. As always whenever there was filming involved, it meant a lot of hanging around while the production crew set up the shots and rehearse scenes, that did not involve us, over and over getting the lighting just right and so on and so forth. We had to be on set as the shooting schedule dictated because as and when they eventually got around to doing your scene you had to be there obviously. As I say I had done plenty of filming up to this point so I was well aware of the hanging around involved but making a feature film was a whole new ball game. When we arrived every morning we would go straight in to make up and rehearse any lines needed for the day then just wait to be called on set. However the schedule was forever being revised as it went along to accommodate the ever changing situation and for the first three days we did not get around to doing anything. As we were all made up we couldn't do anything or go anywhere, just hang around. We started to get a bit fidgety as you can imagine so we would sneak on to the set, hiding behind some of the scenery to watch the proceedings, just to help pass the time. This, as it turned out, was rather counterproductive because one or the other of us would invariably accidently get an appendage in the frame and, apart from involving us in getting a strict telling off from one or other of the production team, it also meant that they would then have to re shoot that particular scene all over again thus resulting in even more hanging around than ever. This really pissed them off as time was money and being on the tight budget that they were, they did not have a lot of either so I could understand their point of view but we were so bored we felt like we were becoming naughty school kids larking about just to entertain ourselves. The game became how long could we sneak on set for until we got a resounding "Fuck off!" This mucking about came to a head on the third day when, after sneaking in for the umpteenth time, me and Melita were hiding behind a piece of polystyrene scenery, which was one of the walls to the lounge room of the set, quietly giggling to our selves while we watch Greg sneak behind the other wall. Now what Greg did not know was that they were having trouble with that particular piece of scenery that day being as it was so flimsy it would not stand up on its own, so they had put an extra support at the bottom of it to help secure it. There was room for us to be standing up but as the Director, Paul, shouted action, Greg tripped over this extra bit of support that hadn't been there before and came crashing through the wall right on top of the actors as they were filming. Well, all hell broke loose as the place turned into chaos with half the people being knocked over like dominos rolling around on the floor and polystyrene flying around the place. Well the swearing was like something I had never heard before and Greg got booted off the set. Luckily for us, in all the ensuing carnage no one had noticed us two so we quickly back stepped off set and retreated into the dressing room bursting through the door laughing our heads off. Greg stumbled through the door a moment later looking very shame faced. He had a big red mark on the side of his face where the lead female actress had slapped him and quite hard by the look of it. Mind you he had fallen right on top of her and, with legs asplaying, she had lost all dignity so he probably deserved it. Paul came in and really tore him off a strip and Greg could not apologise enough and managed to appease him by paying for the damage he had caused, but good on him, he did not grass us up. However we did feel a bit guilty for letting Greg take all the blame so we gave him our third of the price each to help him out. Anyway that put paid to our shanagens. On the fourth and fifth day we actually got around to doing some filming and although it all went nice and smoothly, it did seem to help everyone forget the previous day's antics. So that was the end of the first week shoot.

By the second week we had changed location to a mansion house somewhere near Welwyn Garden City which was rather handy for me as it meant less of the dreaded M25 to traverse and so I didn't have to get up so early. Us Muso's just don't do early very well especially on a Monday morning after a weekend of gigging. Now it wasn't just us three, me Greg and Melita, there were other lookalikes about but we three tended to gravitate to each other mostly because of the music side of us. So that Monday morning we entertained ourselves by regaling each other with gig stories from the weekend just past which helped pass the waiting time away. We decided that tomorrow we would fetch our guitars along and have a singsong when not needed on set which is exactly what we did, well Melita did not play but the three of us sang together, me and Greg strumming and backing up Melita's lead vocal with some harmonies. We had hours to practice and we sounded quite good even if I do say so myself. This Mansion had some nice big grounds to it so after letting the crew know where we were going to be, for when they needed us, and we were told not to wander too far away. After all the grounds behind the mansion seemed rather vast. We sat out on a large blanket that Melita had fetched, under a big old oak tree to shade us from the hot sun and, with a bottle of wine to share, sat singing our little hearts out. This is one of my fondest memories of that time. We felt like a bunch of sixties hippies as we sang that old Mama's and Papa's song 'California dreaming'. Now bear in mind that the place was open to the public, except for the area that was cordoned off for the filming of course, there were quite a few people wandering about the grounds enjoying a picnic or two. Would you believe it, after a little while we started to draw a small crowd. They started to clap and sing along with us and shouting out requests so if we knew it, we would do it. Without realising it me and Greg had left one of the guitar cases open and people started chucking coins in like we were buskers so we just carried on strumming and singing for them. It must have looked weird, there was Tom Cruise, Bruce Willis and Marilyn Monroe singing for their supper looking like they hadn't a care in the world. So after a while Paul himself came out to fetch us for the next bit of filming that we were now required for and stumbled upon this bizarre scene. We watched while we sang as he stood there for a while smiling then started to frame us with his fingers like he was looking for the shot. We stopped singing and he came over saying "that looked really great guys hang on a mo" and with that he got on his phone and in no time at all, one of the camera and sound men came out and started to film us. We did a song or two then Paul said "I'm going to slot that in the film somewhere guys if you don't mind" to which we all agreed. So we packed up our stuff and headed inside for some filming. On the way we divvied up the money that had been chucked in the guitar case and we found we had made ourselves nearly twenty quid each so we high fived each other and promised ourselves that we would do the same again tomorrow. Alas a second time was not to be as one of the grounds keepers had later told Paul that it was not allowed, apart from lowering the tone of the place they were not covered on the insurance for that sort of thing: miserable old sod!

After about the third day we noticed that half the crew were not there and some of the lookalikes as well. Hey ho it was not of much interest to us but we did notice that the whole feel of the film set was a bit down. While we were waiting to go on set, which was a balcony shot we had been looking forward to, we could here Paul arguing with a member of the crew about money. It was something about not being able to do the Deep South filming in the U.S. due to miscalculating the current level of spending and we could tell by the content of the row that Paul had seriously underestimated how much money he had needed to make this film. We took it as an ominous portent. Poor bloke had remortgaged his house and spent all his savings to do this. He was already in debt up to his eyeballs and in too deep to pull the plug now but it was starting to look like the people around him were beginning to lose faith in his vision. You have to bear in mind here that nearly all of us were working on deferred payment with promises of riches once all was done and up to this point Paul had inspired everyone around him that it would all be worthwhile. So a lot of the crew had given up paid work to work on this project with him but now it was starting to look like, due to the lack of money, the vision was not going to be realised. Everyone was beginning to think that they were wasting their time and so were drifting away back to more productive things and quite frankly, who could blame them. So with half the crew and actors gone, Paul decided to try and regroup and called a meeting with all concerned. Being a Muso I was not working during the day at that time and having got all my expenses paid in the first place to me, all this was of no particular loss. But Greg, bearing in mind he was bunking off work thus getting no money, was furious about the whole thing and Melita was none too pleased either having given up a couple of daytime Madonna gigs, but we all tried to keep an open mind until we had heard what Paul had to say. What he told us was that he was in the process of securing a rather large loan to finance the short fall. He was going to rewrite the rest of the script to accommodate for the loss of personnel and if we could all be a little patient with him, things would get back on track in no time. He tried his best to convince folk to stay on board with him but alas, it was to no avail. By now the rot had set in and they were all a little to despondent with it all, thinking about what else they could have been up to and the potential loss of said earnings etc. So when Paul said he would give us all a ring when things were sorted we were all like "yeah whatever" and with a mass shrugging of shoulders we all dispersed. Us three, after hugging each, other made the usual platitudes about staying in touch instead of keep leaving it until the next time we looka-liked together and said our goodbyes. Melita was still holding out a little hope but Greg was very pissed off saying even if it did happen, which he doubted, he wanted nothing more to do with it all. He said he felt he had been very led up the garden path. I felt disappointed but as I say, there was not much of a loss to me other than my time but even then was it a loss? I had met up with a few old mates, had a good laugh and muck about, not to mention a sing along plus I'd gained a little experience in the world of acting.

I heard sometime later that the whole escapade had left Paul Push a bit of a broken man, after all he had pinned all his lifelong hopes on doing that film, and apparently after defaulting on his loans, one of his debtors had filed for bankruptcy against him. On the way home I was just saying to myself "And so ended my first and so far my last experience in the world of feature films" when my phone rang. I pulled over to answer it and it was my agent with another lookalike job for me and so as one door closed another one opened. It was on to pastures new.

CHAPTER 14

OK, HELLO.......AND ARRIVEDERCI

I could probably write as much again as I have written so far with all the different lookalike adventures I had over the years but how thick a book do I want to do? However, I must mention the photo shoot for the *O.K.* magazine.

Now I had done some gossip magazine work before from time to time over the years but one that comes to mind, because it was instrumental in helping me get established as a lookalike, was an article for *"Hello"* magazine. This was back neared the time when I first started which was not so much about Tom Cruise but more along the lines of what was it like to live with a partner who 'looked like a desirable Hollywood actor like Tom Cruise' as they put it. So they chose me and my family to interview. Now my first wife was not up for this, being the type who was not comfortable with any kind of attention, let alone attention from the media; not her fault I suppose just the way she was wired. So we phoned a friend of ours, Diane, to come and play the part of the wife to which she agreed. After she arrived, they must have taken about two hundred photos of us inside and outside the house ranging from her gazing lovingly in to my eyes in a loving embrace to us pointing accusing fingers at each other, to her throwing me out the house. Even one of Diane slapping me around the face! It was a bit of fun and although I am not a particular fan of the gossip mags, (well what bloke is?) I appreciated the free advertising factor of me as a lookalike that it afforded me. At the time I was quite new to the business so I felt it rather useful, which of course it was, in helping me get established. As I remember they ran the article and made it look like a story of a marriage on the rocks heading for divorce. Which we did several years later but it had nothing to do with me being a lookalike. But hey, you girls do love a good gossip and why not? After all, never let the truth stand in the way of a good story!

So on to "O.K." Around this time Tom Cruise, having long been divorced from Nicole Kidman with all the usual horrible tabloid exposé being long gone, Tom was now getting married to Katie Holmes. It was time for a new round of Tom Cruise Hollywood goss. Hey, let's not forget the famous scene back in 2005 of Tom jumping up and down on the couch on the Oprah Winfrey show making a fool of himself whilst professing his love for Katie. Have a look at it on YouTube; it is rather funny but in his defence, he was a bit goaded on by Oprah, still anything for the ratings eh? So with another high profile Hollywood wedding on the way and everyone jumping on the band wagon, it was time for some more of the celeb menagerie. With "O.K." being in the forefront of this type of thing it was time to employ the services of the lookalikes.

It started in the usual way by me getting a phone call from one of the agents; was I up for it? And yes I was. As ever, always up for an adventure. By now, from the "Hello" magazine job to the "O.K" magazine job, I had been working as a lookalike for about ten years. I was into my forties by now and, as I mentioned before, I was greying around the edges quite nicely. Now personally I quite like that look, kind of makes you look a little distinguished if you know what I mean. But Tom probably had dyed hair, us being roughly the same age an'all, and he was still sporting a nice head of brown locks. So bearing in mind by now I was not working with so much regularity as in my lookalike heyday, (it had been a little while since my last job,) the grey was starting to come through. This was of great delight to my new wife, Teresa, (although back then she just my girlfriend). She loves playing around with my thick mop of hair so the night before the job, armed with a bottle of hair dye and a bottle of wine, I went round to her house where she set to work on my bonce. Now one wine bottle turned into two and having had a couple of glasses myself, we got a little merry. Thinking job done, we staggered up the stairs to bed. The next morning when I got up, and looking in the mirror whilst having a shave, I realised that she had done a less than her usual perfect job. There were patches of grey all over the place! Oh bugger, what was I to do? I had to leave for the job in an hour or so no time for a re-dye. Calling Teresa down in the middle of me having a panic she said, in her usual calming 'I've got everything under control so stop worrying' kind of way she has about her "don't worry I got an idea". With that, she went to the shoe draw and pulled out a tin of boot polish, dark brown of course, and proceeded to rub it in the patches that she had missed the night before. Then, being careful of not wiping the polish away, she carefully applied the hair gel and voila! A nice head of Tom hair. She always did know how to get me out of a sticky situation, bless her. She is one of these keep calm in a crisis type, never loses her temper, (well, except with me on occasion but hey, isn't that what husbands are for?) Anyway you know the type; always cool as a cucumber which is one of the things that attracted me to her, a good personality trait but very annoying at times! Ha ha. So with hair sorted and my bag full of Tom costume, I hit the road. There were nine of us lookalikes on this job consisting of a Katie Holmes lookalike of course as well as a Posh and Becks, a Will Smith, (he was good; he did a Will Smith rap show for a living when he wasn't being a lookalike). Then there was a John Travolta, (guess him and Tom would be best mates given that they both do that scientology thing,) as well as a Brad Pitt and Angelina Jolie. To finish it off, there was a Nicole Kidman, as if she would go to her ex husbands wedding but good call for the magazine article; after all it was all tongue in cheek and a nice bit of gossip for the editor to write in to the article don't you think? And of course Tom Cruise himself, complete with boot polish in his hair. They were doing a mock up of the wedding and had hired a lovely big mansion house over Epping Forest way. This Mansion sure was a big place. It had sprawling gardens with an outdoor swimming pool and big marble statues surrounding it. Inside, it had the biggest dining room you could imagine with a huge dining table set in the middle. If you sat at one end you'd need a megaphone to speak to someone sitting at the other end, that's for sure. There were highly polished white marble floors throughout and in the hall way there was the most beautiful black marble staircase. It was actually someone's home and they hired it out for various occasions such as our one. Although it was actually in Epping, for the purposes of this article it was supposed to be somewhere in Italy. Who cared where it was? It was a perfect setting for a Hollywood type wedding and well chosen by the "O.K." team.

We all arrived at about 9.30 and met up with the photographers and lighting crew; well all of us except the Katie Holmes girl that is. So the crew got ready to set up the shots and meanwhile we all got into character and had our briefing while we waited for Katie. And we waited and waited until we realised she was a no show. Now how would that been for a bit of gossip if it had happened in real life; Katie not showing up for her own wedding? Would have suited me; I didn't really fancy her very much anyway. Not that she is unattractive or anything just not my type but hey, what do I know? I'm only a lookalike. So with the bride to be out of the picture what were we to do? So we all sat down and had a nice cup of tea. Now there was a new girl that the crew had fetched along with them and although she was a trainee at the mag they had her making the tea that day. While we were all sitting down around a table with the crew scratching their heads as to what to do, she walked in with the tray of tea and biscuits. The main woman, who had been sitting there with her head in her hands for the last five minutes, lifted her head up to thank 'Tea Girl' when she suddenly clicked her fingers at her and said "Nice hair love, looks a bit like a Katie Holmes style. You'll have to do get your kit off!" With a look of unexpected horror on the poor girls face, she was whisked away to the makeup lady in the changing room. Apparently she was only young and it was her first day on the job so she was a bit nervous and trying to fit in to please everyone. Bet she didn't expect that. They did do a good job on her but I have to say, although she was attractive in her own right, she looked nothing like Katie in the face but what could they do? Beggars can't be choosers and we were in a tight spot after all. Now the wedding dress they had fetched along with them was designed to be worn by the Katie lookalike who was rather tall by all accounts. I had not met her myself, but poor old 'Tea Girl' was only about four foot nothing and the dress was far too long on her. But as it turned out, that worked in our favour. As I say, I'm a bit tall for Tom and Katie is taller than him. So one of the crew had a good idea and grabbed a wooden box from inside their van. He put it under the wedding dress, bearing in mind it had all this extra length on it so the box was easily hidden from view, and it bought her up to about my height. For the rest of the day, poor old 'Tea Girl', everywhere she went had to stand on this box.

As usual with these things, they took loads of different shots of us all like ones of us walking in the massive door way or standing around the swimming pool. There were shots of the girls standing together and several of us boys and plenty of toasting with fake champagne that tasted foul. We were not supposed to drink it as it was just for show. However we couldn't resist seeing what it tasted like but we soon whished we hadn't. It was carbonated water with a colouring dye in it to give it the champers look and once you got its taste in your mouth it was hard to get rid of it even after several cups of tea. One particular photo I remember was a really nice shot of all the lookalikes coming down the black marble staircase with me and Katie standing at the bottom with our arms around each other. It came out well and it was used as the opening shot for the article when it came out. Out of about 300 shots they took, there were fifteen used in total along with a nice long fictitious write up. Teresa went and bought a copy when it came out and proudly went around showing all her friends, bless her.

Throughout my time as a lookalike I went all over the U.K. and visited all sorts of different places that I would not have otherwise gone to. Let's be honest why would someone go and visit some random town in, let's say, Yorkshire or Staffordshire or some-where unless you had family or friends there? Or had to work there, like me, who got to go all over the place 'cos of my looka-like work. No, you would go to a seaside town or a major city which of course I did but it was good in that respect. Because I had reason to, I got to see a good cross section of our fair country. So, in retrospect, it was good that one of the last look-alike jobs that I did was out in Italy.

It is not many lookalikes get to go abroad to work. Most other countries have their own lookalikes and not only that but a lot of lookalikes are of famous people who are only famous within that given country but not heard of outside of that realm. So by its very nature, it is not often you would get to do some work abroad. Another thing to bear in mind is that, in my experience, the English, and the U.K. in general, more than any other part of the world, seem to have a fascination with this sort of thing. I don't know why but I think it is just part of the English psyche and the British culture in general, kind of like the fascination we have with the celebrity culture. But whatever it is, we *do* seem to have that fascination so I am glad I was born in England because may be I would have never got to have done any of this fun stuff at all. Having said all of that, there is always the exception to the rule and this was one of them.

A bunch of us lookalikes, the 'Hollywood Heavies' crew that is, were asked to go out to Rome to make an advert for Italian T.V. Now the Italians, given their own psyche and culture, have quite a visual sense of humour and love a bit of slapstick. One of their slapstick film heroes is an actor and stand up comedian by the name of Massimo Baldi. This incidentally, is one of those examples of someone being very famous in their own country but virtually not heard of elsewhere. He was bringing out his latest and much awaited comedy film and was making a trailer to advertise it on Italian national T.V. Now instead of just showing clips from the film like we would do, he was making a very short advert sized mini film to promote it. The main feature film had a couple of other famous Italian actors in it and the plot of the promo was that these actors were at an award ceremony receiving an Oscar for their part in the film but poor old Massimo, who was the main star, had been forgotten about. So he had planted himself in the audience and when the presentation time came around he was going to jump up and very loudly voice his objections whilst making his way to the stage, in a very slapstick and comical manor, upon which all hell would break loose. Meantime in the ceremony audience, there were quite a few famous Hollywood actors and so this is where we lookalikes come into it. The whole thing reminded me a lot of a Leslie Nielson film, *Naked Gun two and a half* type of thing, probably why he was popular out there also. All this was right up my street given my sense of humour leans towards the cheesy and my propensity for being a little clumsy. I and one or two of the other lookalikes who came from my part of the country, (actually there was about six of us,) all met up at Stanstead airport and boarded the plane for Rome. It was about a four hour flight as I remember and we had all booked our fight tickets at the same time so that we could all sit together on the plane. This as it turned out was a mixed blessing. Somehow word must have gotten to the pilot because when he made his usual pilots announcement to the passengers, he made a point, (jokingly of course although I don't think the other passengers realised at first,) of mentioning about the six celebrities sitting at the back of the plane. As if! If we were real celebrities don't you think we would have travelled in the first class section? Anyway this was exactly what we didn't want because thereafter whenever anyone would use the toilets at the back of the plane they would invariably try and peek a look at us lot which soon turned into staring. And yep you guessed it, even though we were obviously not the real thing, everyone kept pestering us for autographs. Luckily it did not turn into the stampede like on the train going to Newcastle, which would have really worried me because unlike on the train there was nowhere to get off if we needed to should things get a little crowded! Even though they knew we were not the real thing, some of the other passengers still pestered us anyway. They were treating it like they were meeting their idols by proxy sort of thing but also one or two of them did recognise one or two of us from when we had been on the telly. I know for the real celebrities this sort of thing goes with the territory but we were only lookalikes at the end of the day and all I wanted to do was get some kip on the fight over but it wasn't to be. I, for one, was glad to get off the plane when we landed. Anyway we collected our baggage and was picked up at the airport by a prearranged taxi and taken to our hotel. That night we met up with the two representatives from the agency, Maxine and Julie. Actually they were the owners under the guise of reps for tax purposes who thought they would come along for the ride as an excuse for a short break away. They treated us lookalikes to a great big slap up meal Italian style, all on the expense account of course, after all that was tax deductible as well. The next day we were driven to the set and the day's work commenced, starting with us lot being put into make up for about two hours. The actual filming was being done in a theatre hall which held about a thousand people which meant hiring a thousand extras. Gosh, I would not have liked to pick up the bill for that little lot! Here's a weird thing though; nearly every one of them that I talked to were English who had moved out to live in Italy.

So they positioned us lookalikes along the first and second rows interspersed throughout the crowd and with the loveliest and most pretty young Italian girls, one sitting either side of us males arms intertwined, that they had bought in especially for the occasion. A little something for the Italian hot blooded males which is quite a common thing to do out there apparently. The Italians have a name for these types of girls; they call them 'Velinis'. Then whilst the action was going on the cameras would pan across the audience and every now and then pan in on one of us lookalikes with a couple of these 'Velinis' smooching all over us. The female looka-likes did not get away with it either; they would have these Italian hunks all over them as well. After the first days shoot, the two 'reps' decided it was party time and gathered up all the look-alikes for a night out on the Italian town on them. I already knew Maxine and Julie from other times I had worked for them and let me tell you, they were big time party animals and quite the double act. It was all right for those two; they didn't have to get up early for the next day's shoot. But it didn't stop the rest of us! After we ate a hearty meal in a posh restaurant, we hit a few bars then managed to find a night club that seemed to be an all-nighter. We didn't realise that at the time though; it was just the nearest one we could find that was open mid-week. So drinking and dancing like an old bunch of friends, we totally lost track of time. Luckily although having had quite a lot to drink and getting a little inebriated, I had nowhere near as much as some of the others. We *were* all being encouraged along by our hosts, Maxine and Julie, but that was ok; they were also the agents. We eventu-ally staggered out of there at about six in the morning and the sun was just starting to come up. We all got taxis back to the hotel where one or two of the less sober fell asleep. Fatal if you have to have to get up an hour or so to get to the film set on time. The rest of us, realising this, went off for some breakfast and strong black coffee. None of us were feeling to good by now but we had to wake up the others as it was time to go. So with no sleep at all, (which is better than sleeping for an hour, pissed,) we roused them from the sofas on which they had crashed which included Maxine and Julie who promptly went off to bed while the rest of us made our way to the set. God, we were a sorry sight. We looked so rough that even make up couldn't fully cover our blurry eyes and hung-over faces. As I say, I was not one of the worst ones but being on set under those hot and very bright lights trying to look all chipper and happy was not the most pleasant of experi-ences, I can tell you. At one point Andrew, the Jack Nicolson lookalike, had the misfortune of having the camera thrust right in his face with a bright spot light to boot. Having been about the worst one the night before complaining he still felt drunk and hung-over at the same time, he got over whelmed with it all and promptly threw up everywhere; splashing not only the camera man but the camera, the spotlight and the two Valinis sitting next to him. I've never seen so much multi coloured vomit and I've never seen people move so fast as those around him tried to get out of the way. It was everywhere and the most disgusting of sights. Can you imagine how those two girls felt right at that moment? Both of them started crying, poor things, as they were led away for a cleanup. Probably more like a hot shower I would imagine, I know I would have. Needless to say, Andrew was chucked off set and we all had to hang around for an hour or so whilst they got the cleaners in to clear up the horrible mess. Whilst we were waiting, I went back to the changing room to get a cup of tea and while I was making it, I could hear poor old Andy throwing up in one of the back room toilets like his very life depended on it. Luckily after everything was sorted out the rest of us went back to work and finished the second days shoot but no one would sit near or around where Andy had been sitting and I can't blame them, can you? Our flight back home was not until early the next morning and despite however hard Maxine and Julie tried to persuade us lot to go out that night, none of us did. We all had a much need early night except those two of course, party animals that they were, they hit the town once again. Still they had been asleep all day so had managed to sleep it off. However, they later told me that they had partied so much that night that they missed their fight home; serves them right ha ha!

CHAPTER 15

ALL GOOD THINGS...

All in all I worked as a Tom Cruise lookalike for about ten years in total, which for a lookalike was a very long time, and for a while there I was the only Tom Cruise so I count myself very lucky to have had such longevity. From the agents point of view it is a very cut throat business and they are all in hot competition with each other for the work as well as the next, may be younger, more lookee-liker banging on the door ready to step into your shoes. Let's not forget, at the end of the day, you are just a commodity for the use of, a tool to make money; a fun one but a money tool none the less albeit directly or indirectly through advertising, promotional work, T.V. ratings or just good old commission for the agents. Someone, somewhere, at some point, will financially benefit from employing you as a lookalike otherwise they would not have employed your services in the first place, and if a better or newer version of your lookalike character comes along that is even more beneficial to the money making machine than you are, then they are going to go with that, make no mistake. After all we have all got a living to earn but hey, money makes the world go round as they say so I don't mind; it's just the way the world works. It is not a moan just an observation and if it was not for the lookalike industry I wouldn't have had all the fun and wonderful experiences that I did so I am very grateful. Remember me saying at the beginning how the first agent said "you look more like Tom Cruise than the bloke we are currently using how'd you like all his work?" well it's my guess that that's probably what happened to me in the end.

As with most things you never just suddenly stop, (exception to the rule being what happened between me and Susan Scott which I will come to in a moment,) things just usually start to wind down as life throws you curves that make you take your eye off the ball, as it did with me, until one day you're just not doing it anymore. But you don't mind as you yourself find that you have moved on to pastures new anyway and so it was with me. So there wasn't just one thing but a series of events that lead to my demise.

The first thing to happen was that I had a falling out with Susan Scott, who as I said earlier was the most prolific of the agents and did get me the majority of my gigs particularly in the early days. It was over money; well when isn't it? I noticed with her right from the outset that she would always take a long time in paying the lookalikes for their work. Too long as it turned out; you would typically have to wait three months back then before getting paid even though she would collect the money from the client almost straight away. It was obvious what she was doing; she would put the lookalikes fees into a high yield interest account and hang on to it for months before paying out to us lookalikes thus gaining herself extra interest that should have been ours. Other lookalikes did warn me about her practices in the beginning and some of them would not work for her because of it but for me, as long as she did not go over the three month mark, I let it slide. At first I didn't realise she was doing it as she was my only agent at the very beginning and my first load of jobs were with her so I thought it was the norm. After a while I started doing more and more jobs for the other agents and would always get paid within a week or two of the actual gig so I began to notice what the other lookalike were on about. However this was the status quo between us for many a year and as she was good at getting the work so it was something I just tolerated. Towards the end of my time with her the three month mark started to extend, not just with me but with everyone. So then three months started to become four, then five, and before you knew it you would be waiting over six months. Of course, I would be chasing her up for it but her excuse was always that she had not been paid on that particular job yet which we all knew was a load of crap. What on each and every job? I don't think so! One or two may be but not all of them. It got so bad in the end that unless you hassled her relentlessly and chased her up for each and every gig, you stood the chance of not getting paid at all. Then one day I lost my temper with her over it all; she had just fobbed me off once too often. What made me lose it was not so much the actual money but her insulting our intelligence; did she really think we were all that stupid? We ended up have a shouting match over the phone. Well, within a couple of days she had coughed up on every job she owed me on and we never did business again. That more than halved my lookalike work over night. Here's a thing though; last time I checked, all these years later, she is still using my photo, albeit me a lot younger of course, on her website as her Tom Cruise lookalike and then sending in whoever it is she uses now. Cheeky cow! I discovered it recently by accident when me and my daughter Mollie were doing a bit of family research and she googled my name and sure enough on one of the searches up came her web site with me still on it. Still, looking on the funny side, it is a testament to me that after all these years she still finds it better to use my old picture than any of the others who came along after me. Think I should invoice her!

Also around this sort of time my ex wife up and left me for someone else and took the kids with her. Unfortunately it was with someone that I knew quite well, (or at least thought I did!) which wasn't very nice, who turned out to be a rather unsavoury fellow in the end. So there I was, sitting in what was the old family home without my kids around me which was now just a big empty house; which at the time knocked me for six as it probably would anyone. It all got very acrimonious for a while as these things do. There were a lot of lies and nastiness being levelled against me at the time, which did not help matters especially considering

I was not the offending party. On top of this I really had to fight hard just to be able to get proper contact with my own children, culminating in being forced to get a court order, on the advice of my solicitor, against the ex so I could see Mollie, my daughter, again. All very horrible but hay, shit happens and that's life. Anyway all that legal stuff took up a year or two and as you can imagine, that was the priority for me back then. Because of it, I was not paying much attention to other things which included the lookalike stuff and so it became a contributing factor to the lookalike demise. It was all a long time ago now and every cloud has a silver lining so once all the crap has settled and you realise what a whole new and exciting life has opened up for you, you soon move to indifference and start looking forward to your future. Another good thing to come out of all that is that a couple of years later I met someone really special, a lady called Teresa. My friends call her "an angel walking the earth" and we ended up getting married.

Although I was still doing the odd job for Maxine and Julie at this point, something else happened that help put paid to things. I started to suffer with very bad insomnia, very much more than I usually would. It was a clinical problem apparently; some kind of chemical imbalance that I had suffered with most of my adult life. Now I've never been the world's best sleeper but up to now it had never been any more than a bit of an inconvenience sometimes. As it was cyclic in nature, it meant that it would come and go from time to time, so over the years I had acclimatised to it. However around this time it had decided to really flair up and became chronic. As anyone will know that when you have a bad night's sleep, as everyone does from time to time it can be a bit hard to think straight the next day. You feel tired and ratty, and depending on how bad a night's sleep you have had, it would affect how bad you felt the following day. Now with my sleep starting to go down to under four hours kip a night for a while, I was starting to feel depressed, which is a common side effect of prolonged insomnia apparently. Then it went to under two hours a night until in the end I would be lucky to get 40 minutes and

I just could not function for a while there. It was horrible! It was scrambling my brain and it was also starting to make me feel physically ill. I started to get flu like symptoms, you know that cold and achy feeling because of lack of rest. Things got so bad that at one point I did not sleep at all for three nights running, not even being allowed my 40 minute switch off, so I just could not assimilate anything that was going on around me. I remember not even being able to drive my car at this point 'cos I just could not take in what was happening in front of my eyes and drove straight through a red light. Up till now I had never really bothered trying to go and get it sorted out because, as I say, I had acclimatised to it and it had never affected me bad enough to want to bother, until now. I was quite ill at this point which prompted me to go and get help with it and I am so glad I did. My G.P. sent me to a specialist who sorted me out in the end and these days apart from the very odd bad night, which is no more than anyone else, that problem has long since passed and if it ever did come back I now know what to do about it.

So the point being, at that time, because of falling out with the biggest agent, being ill for a bit and having to cope with the loss of my family I was having to turn down what lookalike jobs were coming my way which did not bode well with the remaining agents. They were very understanding towards me but as I say, they were quite mercenary and, with their living to earn, could not afford to turn down any job that involved a Tom Cruise lookalike while I sorted myself out. So, of course, they were turning to whoever could fill my boots. I remember seeing an advert in the stage magazine that one of the agents had put in there saying "*Tom Cruise lookalike wanted. Must be full of confidence and charisma*" that made me chuckle. I must say upon seeing that, despite all my personal stuff that was hindering me at the time, it did make me feel that perhaps they thought I must have been a hard act to follow. It was nice really considering how it had been my mate Tim who had kind of pushed me in to doing it in the first place, 'cos I wasn't really bothered myself at the start of it all. Also, considering my initial anxieties on my first few jobs about whether or not I could pull off being a lookalike as I did not think I looked much like him myself. Still in the end all that mattered was what other people thought and they were certainly happy with me.

I must draw to a close now but I would like to finish by saying that the ten years I served as a lookalike were some of the best times of my life. I am so grateful for Tim pushing me in to it in the first place. I am so grateful for fate giving me a face like Tom and grateful that I had the character that allowed me to be able to do it and enjoy it. As I say, it was not for the faint hearted. I hope that all the wonderful lookalikes that I met and had the pleasure to work with are all Ok whether they are still in the business or not and all the wonderful and colourful characters that I had the privilege to meet along the way, whether I got on with them or not (ha ha,) are all doing well. I would like to thank you for taking the time to read my lookalike memoirs and good luck to you all.

GARY.

A couple of pictures from the photo shoot at my first job
opening the UCI cinema in Cardiff Wales with Kim the
Mel Gibson lookalike.

Some of the cast and crew dressing up for the
occasion and getting into the swing of it.

Tom Cruise in town?

The man with the superstar looks.

Page 8

Search is on for star lookalikes

TOM CRUISE lookalike Gary Strohmer was searching for Dewsbury's answer to Nicole Kidman when he launched the CableTel Search for a Star competition, this week.

Tom kicked off the competition to celebrate the arrival of the CableTel movies-on-demand service, Front Row.

A CableTel spokesman said: "To mark the launch of Front Row, we want to bring a taste of Hollywood to Kirklees and find local people who look like Hollywood stars - anyone from Tom Cruise to Marilyn Monroe.

Entries must send a good quality look-alike photograph to Claire Guy at CableTel House, Market Street, Huddersfield, HD1 2EH.

Final entries must be submitted by Thursday, April 2 and judging will start at 2pm on Saturday, April 4.

So if you have you the smouldering looks of Brad Pitt, the face of Nicholas Cage or the features of Kim Basinger, CableTel wants to hear from you.

Hastings, CableTel wants to hear from you.

Tom Cruise look-alike Gary Strohmer signs autographs for fans in Dewsbury. (C130320)

Some of the papers articals from my second ever gig that they kindly sent to me for my scrapbook. It was my first sole job. You never forget your first!

Look-a-like stars wanted

TOM Cruise look-a-like Gary Strohmer was searching for Spen Valley's answer to Nicole Kidman, when he launched the CableTel Search for a Star competition.

'Tom' (left) kicked off the competition to celebrate the arrival of CableTel movies-on-demand service, Front Row.

"We are really looking forward to seeing the entrants to our look-a-like competition, and will accept anyone from dead ringers for Tom Cruise to Marilyn Monroe," said a spokeswoman for CableTel.

" We're inviting all hopefuls to send us their pictures, which will be displayed in our Huddersfield retail centre window."

The winner will spend a weekend in London and be taken to Planet Hollywood in a chauffeur-driven limousine.

Emmerdale's Malandra Burrows will be judging the entries, and all finalists will spend a day at Huddersfield's Fitness First.

Entries must send a look-a-like photograph to Claire Guy at CableTel House, Market Street, Huddersfield, HD1 2EH, by April 2.

Dolly Parton look-alike Stella Bruce serves cookies and doughnuts with Post Office pardners Olwen Mercer (left) and Gaynor McVeigh. (2134/98)

Hollywood look-alikes bring taste of America

HOLLYWOOD came to Huddersfield when Dolly Parton started working Nine To Five at the post office and Tom Cruise took on a new role as the town's cable guy.

Local cable TV company CableTel used Tom Cruise ringer Gary Strohmer to launch Front Row —its new movie-on-demand service.

The firm is looking for other Huddersfield people who resemble movie stars for a competition to be judged by Emmerdale's Malandra Burrows, alias Kathy Glover.

The winner will get a weekend holiday in London, including a limousine trip to celebrity hang-out Planet Hollywood.

At Northumberland

Gary Strohmer as Tom Cruise meets CableTel customer manager Katie Palmer. (2160/98)

Street Post Office, counter clerk Stella Bruce dressed up as Nashville's most famous daughter to serenade customers and serve American cookies and doughnuts.

The Dolly Parton look-alike was promoting the Post Office's new one-stop travel service where customers can

get foreign currency, travellers cheques and insurance over the counter.

● To enter CableTel's Search For A Star competition send a quality photograph to Claire Guy, CableTel House, Market Street, Huddersfield, HD1 2EH. Closing date is a week tomorrow.

202

Above: Some of the original photos my friend sent off
to the lookalike agents that got me started. As you
can see I didn't look too bothered at the time but
was later glad he did.

Two of the Nicole Kidman lookalikes I worked with.
I did work a fair bit with them as in the early days
of my lookalike career Tom and Nicole were an item.

Sitting in makeup before a shoot. It sometimes took hours to get made up for a five minute shot!

These are from a lookalike promotional convention down in the West Country. I told the promoters I would not be able to attend (which pissed them off a bit) as I would be on holiday with my family at the time. On the day though one of my lookalike friends phoned me up and told me that the location had changed and it turned out to be a short drive from where I was staying so I popped along anyway. Although I was not in character, as you can see, it was nice seeing some of my lookalike buddies and we all had a nice day together. There are some good examples of lookalikes having to look like one of his/hers characters.

Keanu Revees, Neo, The Matrix

Mel Gibson and Nicolas Cage lookalikes

Tina Turner

Jack Nicolson

Posh and Becks

Kylie Minogue

Angelina Jolie lookalike as
Lara Croft

Sean Connery and Groucho Marx

Warren Mitchell lookalike as Alf Garnett

Me and a bunch of other lookalikes at the
after show party in Manchester T.V. studios.

The Jack Nicolson, Bruce Willis lookalikes I worked
with when we went to Italy, with the Johnny Depp
lookalike as Captain Jack Sparrow in the background

Right: The Lisa
Riley lookalike
at another T.V.
party both a little
worse for wear!
Can you spot Pat
Butcher in the
back ground?

The girls from the agency that organised the Italy job.
They could drink any one under the table!

A couple of photos that my kids took of me standing in front of the Sky Movies poster at Basildon station. They were everywhere for a week or two. That's me jumping off the seesaw thinking about Tom Cruise in the Minority Report, hence the picture of the real Tom Cruise inside the think bubble. The poor little lad on the other end looks terrified.

I never did manage to get my hands on one of the real posters.

Instead of just looking like the actor you sometimes
have to look like one of his characters

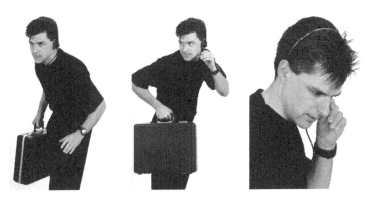

Gary as Ethan Hunt from Mission impossible

Gary as Top Gun Maveric

Anyone fancy a 'cocktail' ?

Gary as Jerry Maguire. Also a good generic look for Tom

"Show me the money!"

As one day you would be doing one character and the next day another I found it a good idea to keep a general 'Tomish' hair style that would work all round.

THE FANTASY WEDDING OF TOM AND KATIE

THE HOLLYWOOD COUPLE EXCHANGE THEIR VOWS IN A MOVING CEREMONY IN FRONT OF THEIR CELEBRITY PALS!

Above: Tom and Katie make their entrance, surrounded by celebrity well-wishers, Victoria and David Beckham, Nicole Kidman, Will Smith, John Travolta, Brad Pitt and Angelina Jolie couldn't wait to congratulate the couple. Inset: The couple's beautiful wedding rings. Facing page: Tom poses with the new Mrs Cruise, while their all their showbiz wedding guests look on

After endless rumours and postponements, Tom Cruise and his gorgeous fiancée Katie Holmes have finally married. Well, kind of. There's still a week or so to go as the most loved-up couple in America take a walk up the aisle with their adorable daughter Suri by their side and *OK!* magazine and their huge team in the UK wish them the very best of luck until then *OK!* takes readers on an imaginary yet entirely parallel

'I love this woman. I am in love. I have never been so happy'

High above the mountains of Italy, in the deep darkness of the night, was a massive space cruiser gently approaching Earth. The green-skinned occupants of the craft are all giddy with excitement as they finish wrapping their wedding gifts. It won't be long before they touch down and celebrate the union of their favourite human beings, Tom Cruise and Katie Holmes. It is such an honour to have been invited to what must surely be the biggest and most

After taking the couple's rings from a helpful alien (inset), John tells the couple it's time for them to exchange their vows so they can become husband and wife (above). After the ceremony, the couple and their guests tuck into a delicious wedding breakfast (below)

Above: Some of the pictures from the OK magazine article about the Tom and Katie Holms wedding. The lookalikes involved were Brad Pitt, Angelina Jolie, John Travolta, Nicole Kidman (Why would she have gone to her ex husbands wedding?) Will Smith and Posh and Becks and Tom Cruise with Katie Holm. As the actual Katie lookalike didn't turn up for the photo sessions this young lady had to stand in and stand on a box hidden beneath the wedding dress. I loved it, it was all so cheesy!

A promo shot of some of us 'Hollywood heavies'
as they called us.

Me with my three children, Mollie, Samuel and Ben 2006

LIVE-A-LIKE

A short story by Petina Strohmer

Bored, bored, bored.

Jim sighed and looked round the set for the umpteeth time. Nothing had moved or changed in any way. Like workmen in between temporary traffic lights, especially during the rush hour, none of the crew appeared to be doing anything either.

He glanced at his watch. "Whoo" ~ a whole two minutes since he last looked. Doesn't time fly when you're a superstar? Or when you're pretending to be one.

Jim stretched his stiff muscles. He'd been sitting in the same position too long. Nothing seemed to have happened for ages.

"I bet Jay Harvey doesn't have to hang around for hours in the heat with nothing to do." Oh no, he'd have his own air-conditioned trailer full of cold beer, pretty girls and a bathtub of Smarties with all the blue ones taken out ~ or whatever else took his temperamental fancy!

Okay, Jim *was* being paid for sitting there doing nothing whilst the production team fussed and faffed around. But not as much as Jay Harvey would have been.

But then Jim Harris *wasn't* Jay Harvey. He just happened to look like him. A lot like him. Enough to actually earn a living from pretending to be him for low-budget spoof shows and cheap commercials.

The producer appeared. "Right" he bawled. "One more time. From the top." He glanced over. "Jay" he called.

"Jim" Jim corrected him.

"Yeah, whatever" was the bored reply.

No producer would dare say that to the great Mr. Harvey!

Jim hauled himself to his feet, donned the trademark aviator sunglasses and prepared to extol the delights of dry deodorant ~ one more time.

But no sooner had he taken up position, than it all ground to a halt again. Problems with the light levels this time. Back to the dressing room ~ well, the upturned beer crate on the edge of the set again.

*

But Jim couldn't really complain. It wasn't a bad job. And it certainly had its perks.

Jay Harvey was very popular with the women. And looking like him seemed to confer similar privileges. Jim was never short of a 'lady' or two. When there was a run of Jay Harvey films on T.V., he virtually had to beat them off with a stick!

After the release of Mr. Harvey's latest film "Fallen Hero", Jim ended up exhausted and spent a week or two locked up indoors to avoid the women, both in the clubs on a Saturday night and even going round Tescos on a Monday morning. Crazy stuff.

Jim was currently a single man but he wondered how Jay Harvey's marriage weathered this level of 'interference'.

The favourite of Jim's many anecdotes on this particular subject concerned the time he was approached by an 'adult film' company to star in a porn film, as Jay Harvey of course. The rather superfluous plotline was that Harvey had been involved in a particularly sleazy Hollywood sex scandal and had been dropped from the celebrity 'A' list as a result. Now an unemployable social pariah, the only films left to him were the 'adult' variety and the rest of the picture loosely chronicalled his resulting 'sexploits'.

Jim couldn't believe the offer. Five days in L.A., all expenses paid, for a three day shoot(!) and two days holiday, at $15000 a day!

His mates, who usually teased him relentlessly about his 'job', were now green with envy. Nice 'work' if you can get it! They were even more surprised when he turned it down.

But Jim was married at the time and considered the real cost of the project too high. He would smile ruefully as he recounted that his wife left him a short time afterwards anyway.

Nevertheless, he *had* been daunted by the prospect of this particular public 'performance' anyway as well as the threat of Jay Harvey's substantial legal team. In the end, he decided to leave "The Fall and Rise of a Hollywood Hero" well alone. But it made a good bar-stool story.

*

It *was* a weird way to make a living. By day, most look-a-likes were carpenters and electricians and plumbers, sawing and switching and soldering, but by night they could find themselves rubbing shoulders with 'Mel Gibson', 'Nicole Kidman' and 'Jack Nicholson' at a 'celebrity' meet-and-greet session. And getting paid for it.

A small proportion of these people really had 'lost the plot', so immersed in their alter-egos that they actually imagined themselves to be the genuine article ~ and expected to be treated accordingly.

But most had a good handle on the ridiculous role that they were playing and became almost larger-than-life caricatures of the stars they were supposed to be.

Everybody enjoyed themselves and the money wasn't bad either.

*

Yeah, Jim thought as he prepared to leave the set of the deodorant commercial which had finally been abandoned for the day; it wasn't a bad life.

He walked down the street toward his old Ford Escort (his wife took the MG), blipping the alarm off as he went.

Two middle-aged women, walking the other way, suddenly spotted him. Their eyes widened and their mouths opened. They looked at each other then dissolved into excited whispers.

Jim always found this particular part of this type of encounter, very interesting. Were they convinced enough of his 'identity' to approach him? Would they dare?

This time they did. One of the ladies, her face flushed a deep scarlet, finally addressed him.

"Mr. – Mr. – Harvey…isn't it?

As if.

As if Jay Harvey would be getting into an old banger in an arse-end street in the back and beyond of nowhere.

Jim smiled.

"What can I do for you?" he asked in his best American accent. He practised. He was good.

"Ooh" the lady giggled. "Can I – we, have your autograph? Please?"

Jim took their pieces of paper. "Who shall I dedicate this too?" he asked.

"Angela" she cooed.

"Angel?"

"Angela" she repeated.

"Well excuse me, but you look like you were made in heaven to me, darlin' " he drawled.

Same old types of lines to the same old types of women. But it always worked.

"Oh, you" she chided him affectionately.

He signed the paper "JH" just as Jay Harvey sometimes did. No lie there either. Just another assumption.

"Thank you so much Mr. Harvey" she flustered. "We're your biggest fans."

Even though they couldn't tell the difference between the facsimile and the real thing? On the other hand, when were they likely to have actually seen the real thing in the flesh?

Once Jim thought he had seen Sean Connery coming out of a West End shop. Well, it might have been him but like most members of the public in that situation, he had simply looked twice and thought "That bloke doesn't half look like Sean Connery!"

*

Jim changed his mind. He locked the car again and headed to the nearest watering hole.

Several people looked up instinctively as the door opened. For 'Mere Mortals', usually the spectators clocked them as no-one in particular and returned to their own conversations. At Jim's local, where he was well-known, this applied to him too. But here, where appeared to the unsuspecting as a 'Hollywood Hero', the conversations stopped instead as more and more people stopped to stare.

Jim groaned inwardly. It was good to know, from a professional point of view, that he was that convincing but when all you wanted was a little peace and quiet...

Time to come clean. He smiled and held up his hands. "No" he laughed. "I'm not him. I'm just a look-a-like, filming a commercial round the corner."

The other punters looked from him to each other.

"Honestly!" Jim said, ambling over to the bar.

The customers took a last look at him and returned to their business although Jim could tell from the occasional furtive glance that not all of them were entirely convinced. So long as he got a cold drink and a hot meal, he no longer cared.

He picked up the bar menu. "A pint of lager and I'll have... chicken and chips I think" he said to the barmaid.

There was no reply.

"Yeah, chicken and chips please" he confirmed.

Still nothing.

Jim looked up. The pretty redhead was staring at him with wide eyes.

"Chicken and chips?" he tried again.

She shook her head slightly as if to bring herself to her senses.

"Leg or breast?" she said slightly vacantly.

A ghost of a smile played across Jim's handsome features. He allowed his eyes to slide over her body as she stood poised to take his order.

"Either" he smiled. "It all looks good to me!"

She bowed her head as the colour rose up her neck. She punched the order into the till, took his money and gave him the receipt, holding it between them slightly longer than was necessary.

Jim didn't know anyone here so he decided to stay with the good-looking girl at the bar. She served a couple of other people but he did not miss the twinkling glances she threw him as she worked. His food arrived and he turned his attention to fulfilling his more immediate physical needs

She watched him as he ate.

He looked up. "What?" he asked through a mouthful of food.

Her bright green eyes flashed. "It *is* you, isn't it?" she whispered.

"Hmm?"

"Jay Harvey. It is you."

He considered his reply carefully. He had had enough of being Jay Harvey for the day. But if it was going to get him through the night too...

Playing it safe, he answered with an almost imperceptible nod, much easier to deny if necessary.

Her eyes widened. "I *knew* it was" she said with great excitement.

"Shhh" he answered looking around furtively.

"Oops ~ sorry!" she giggled. "What are *you* doing *here*? You don't do commercials."

He threw a look over his shoulders at the other customers, several of whom were still throwing the occasional look back. "I can't say" he murmured.

"Oh, okay" she whispered. "New film eh?"

He raised his eyebrows.

"In this neck of the woods" she said thoughtfully. "Must be a gangster movie or something."

He let her witter on. If that's what lit her particular candle...

"Oooh" she positively shivered with delight. "I loved you in "Mob Land". You were so...rugged."

It obviously *did* light her candle then. Jim ran his hands through his carefully-styled hair, messing it up a little.

"I like a bit of rough!" she smirked.

He stroked the five o'clock shadow that was beginning to form on his chin.

"And those blue eyes" she simpered. "I'd know 'em anywhere."

He blanched slightly. "Have we met before?" he asked with caution. It was always worth checking.

"No" she said wistfully. "Only in my dreams."

He relaxed. She was pretty but obviously not too bright!

He decided to make his move. "Well, I'll happily share your pillow tonight, darlin' " he drawled.

She smiled. "I finish at eleven," she confided, "but I live on the premises. The landlord's cool so meet me round the back at half past."

He winked at her and she wandered off.

*

It was quarter to twelve.

Where was she? He wasn't used to being stood up ~ when he was Jay Harvey that is.

Then the back door opened and she appeared. "Sorry" she hissed. "Just a few things I had to…organize. Come on."

She took his hand and led him back into the building.

Well, okay ~ he figured that they'd done the chatting-up routine in the bar earlier. And the women didn't usually need much warming up to the great Mr. H!

He followed her up the narrow staircase, smiling to himself as he went. Beer, belly and a bird all under one roof ~ he liked this place.

She opened the door to her room and as he stepped inside, he was greeted by multiple images of himself in a variety of costumes and poses ~ posters, newspapers clippings, magazine articles, prints from internet sites, fan club photos ~ anything and everything.

Well, not actually *him* of course, but these were in sufficient quantities to begin to make him feel decidedly uncomfortable.

There were hundreds of them!

She smiled at his astonishment. "Impressed?" she asked.

'Intimidated more like!' he thought but he kept his cool. He wondered whether he ought to own up at this point but as she let her dress slip to the floor revealing a firm, brown body beneath, he decided to keep his mouth shut for the moment.

He might tell her when they had finished. Or he might just leave her the dream to live with.

He lay down on the bed with her and began to caress her body. She sighed with pleasure and snuggled her head into his shoulder.

"You don't know how long I've waited for this moment" she murmured.

"I can imagine."

"I doubt it" she replied.

As her face occupied his, she reached into the drawer of her bedside cabinet and pulled out a syringe. She plunged it into his neck and after an initial jolt, he became suddenly heavy and still.

She smiled. "I doubt it very much."

*

When Jim came round, he was alone and it was dark. Not sunless dark but the thick impenetrable blackness of a windowless space.

He hauled himself up into a sitting position, wincing at the painful resistance of his leaden muscles. He snorted and coughed.

An airless space too. Full of damp and decay.

Where the hell was he? He could be anywhere really. He could hear distant, indistinct sounds that may have been voices and strange thumping noise ~ footsteps? Could he be underground? And how had he got there? *Wherever there was?*

He shook his head but that just sent bolts of pain flashing between his temples. So he stayed very still and tried to cast his muddled mind back to his last coherent memory.

A girl...a room...lots of pictures...but no more. What had happened next? He could guess but unless she was exceptionally talented, *that* didn't usually result in unconsciousness.

He tried to stand. He managed to put one foot in front of him but the floor was slippery ~ with what he couldn't tell ~ and combined with his spinning head, he soon came back down to Earth.

So he just lay there and waited...and waited...and waited.

*

How long had he been sat there? It was impossible to know. Had he slept in that time?

He was certainly feeling very rough and he was dying for a drink.

"Hello?" he called out.

No reply.

"Hello?" he tried again.

Still nothing.

He sighed deeply and ran his hands across his face. How long would it be before someone missed him? And who exactly would that someone be?

Now if the great Jay Harvey was to suddenly disappear ~ that would be a very different story. There would be people out everywhere looking...

A thought suddenly occurred to him. Did this have anything to do with Mr. H? He frowned. No, how could it?

He jumped at a sudden noise above him. A metallic rattle, a wooden creak and a painfully bright shaft of light that knifed across the room.

He looked up. A silhouette stood in the dazzling doorway. It placed a cup and a bowl on the ground. "Your dinner, Jay" it said and retreated.

"No!" he yelled, scrabbling to his feet. "Don't go! Where am I? What's-" but he was plunged back into disorientating darkness as the door slammed shut.

He had seen enough to know that there was a flight of stairs in the corner of the room ~ and there was food and drink at the top of them. He edged his way forward in that general direction, scratching and scraping as he stumbled. Eventually he found the bottom stair and cautiously began to climb. There was no handrail so great care was needed on the slimy steps.

He made it to the top and began to feel around for the food. In the process, he managed to knock the cup over and the precious liquid began to flow away. He snatched it up and jammed it to his mouth but not much of the water remained. The little that made its way into his gritty throat was wonderfully soothing and allowed him to swallow the dry bread that followed.

Bread and water? What was this? Some kind of low-budget horror film? Jim's eyes suddenly widened. A film? What was that she said ~ "Your dinner, *Jay*?"

Surely not!

He felt his way over to the door and scrabbled up the wood. He hammered hard.

"Hello? Hello?" he yelled. "I'm in here. Help me!"

He stopped and listened carefully.

Nothing.

He continued to try to attraction of somebody...anybody for the next ~ well, he didn't know how long. But it seemed to be all in vain.

He sighed deeply, sank back down to the floor ad continued to wait...and wait...and wait.

*

He was returned to consciousness by the bolt sliding back behind him. He leapt up, his foot slipped on the slimy stone and he fell backwards, cracking his head, shoulders and back against the stairs on the way.

*

The bright light in his eyes was even worse than the complete darkness.

He squinted and grimaced and tried to lift a hand to shield his face ~ but found it secured tightly behind his back. For the first time, panic began to rise inside him.

Who was this person holding him captive? What did they plan to do to him? And why?

"Hello?" he tried again.

"Hello Jay" she said smoothly.

She?

Jay?

"What's going on?" Jim demanded. "Who are you? Why are you holding me here?"

"Questions, questions" the woman behind the blinding light cooed. "How about some answers instead, Mr. Harvey?"

"Who? Oh, Harvey. No, you've got it wrong, love."

"Oh, you love me now do you Jay?"

He frowned. "I'm *not* Jay Harvey" he explained.

"Of course you're not," she said, "now that *I've* got the upper hand. I know you're an actor, darling, but you'll have to do better than that."

"I'm not an actor" Jim insisted. "Well, I am but-"

She snorted. "Make up your mind!"

"I'm a look-a-like" he explained.

There was no response.

"I'm not Jay Harvey. I just look like him, a lot like him" he admitted. "My real name's Jim Harris. I'm working on a deodorant commercial just around the corner."

At least it was, if he was still in the pub somewhere. The cellar perhaps? He thought he vaguely recognized the woman's voice.

A shrill laugh ripped through the dank air. She began to clap slowly. "Well done" she sneered. "Very clever."

"But-" Jim began.

He was silenced by a swift kick to the stomach, knocking all the wind out of him.

The voice came closer. "Don't fuck me about!" she hissed. "It's not a good idea because as you can see, I have you at a distinct disadvantage, Jay!"

Jim opened his mouth to protest but quickly decided against it. She might kick lower next time! Anyway, as things stood, he couldn't know if he would be better off being Jay Harvey or Jim Harris at this precise moment in time. Best to play it safe and keep quiet; at least until he could work out what was going on.

The silence between them stretched on forever in this dark, damp, timeless place.

Eventually he cracked. "What do you want from me?"

She laughed mirthlessly. "*Now* you want to know."

"I don't understand."

"Finally got your attention have I, Mr. Harvey?"

"Sorry?"

She snorted. "Oh, you will be!"

She turned off the light.

"Don't go" he cried into the darkness. "Don't leave me like this – please."

But he clank of the door told him that she had gone.

*

He gave up trying to release his hands and feet. The struggle was only succeeding in making him sore. So he sat there and waited...and waited...and waited.

*

Eventually, she returned.

"Ooh, nasty" she cooed, examining his swollen joints as she loosened the ropes.

As soon as he felt the binds ease, his brought his fist up, catching her under the chin and knocking her back off her feet. She hit the ground hard and he raced as fast as his stiff legs would carry him, up the stairs and straight into a locked door. He howled with frustration ad wheeled round to find himself the focus of a loaded gun. In her other hand, she jangled the keys mockingly at him.

"Don't *ever* underestimate me again," she hissed at him, "or I'll kill you." The way her eyes blazed manically, he thought she just might. "Now get your arse back over here, sit down, shut up and listen."

With considerable caution, he did as he was told. In one of his many secret agent films, Jay Harvey probably would have disarmed the girl swiftly and smoothly as he passed by then swept her up in an overwhelmingly passionate clinch.

But Jim Harris didn't think he'd try to copy that particular move.

He sat down, rubbing his red wrists. "Sorry" he muttered.

She did not reply. He looked up at her. She continued to stare intensely at him.

"Please" he began.

She smiled.

"What do you want with me?" he asked again.

"Well, I think I've finally got your attention."

He nodded.

"And your respect?"

He nodded again. "Absolutely!"

"So," she began, circling behind him, "wouldn't it have been a lot easier to give it to me the first time I asked you, Jay?"

He looked confused.

"You don't remember, do you?" she went on.

That didn't help.

"I first wrote to you two years ago," she explained, "asking for an interview ~ for the exciting new magazine I was working on at the time."

"O-kay" Jim said carefully.

"I didn't expect to get far," she continued, "which was just as well because all I got in return was a snotty letter from your P.A. informing me that my publication 'wasn't important enough'."

"Right"

"But I'm a persistant kinda gal," she smiled, "so I did a little more 'research' and found out how I could contact you directly at the studio. Well, I got as far as being connected to your dressing room but then I was blocked by one of your people. He said that he'd pass on my name and number but I don't expect he did, did he?"

She looked enquiringly at him. "Annie Stone?"

He shrugged helplessly.

"Ah well, no matter. After that approach failed a few times, I dug a little deeper and managed to obtain your home address. Nice place you got there!"

"Thanks" Jim muttered.

"I must have sent you, ooh, about fifty letters at that address. Don't you remember?"

He shook his head. He could honestly say that he didn't.

"But when I received no reply, I decided to pay you a visit."

Jim groaned inwardly. He didn't like the way that this was panning out.

"Several visits actually; at all hours, in all weathers." She paused. "Thanks for finally taking notice of me."

Something in her change of tone alarmed Jim greatly.

"Thanks for calling the police. Thanks for getting me arrested for trespassing or harassment or whatever damn thing it was that I called doing my job. Thanks for losing me my place on the magazine, a job I had to work so hard to get in the first place so I ended up pulling poxy pints in a complete shit-hole of a pub in the arse-end of nowhere!"

She lowered her face to him. "Thanks a lot!" she spat.

She withdrew.

He waited.

Eventually he opened his eyes again. The barrel of the gun was pointed directly into his face.

"Don't!" he yelped. "Trespassing, harassment is one thing. Murder is something else entirely."

'You deranged bitch' he wanted to add, but in his present situation, decided against it.

"As I said," she whispered manically, "I'm the persistant type. This moment..." she closed her eyes as if she could taste it, "was most definitely worth the wait."

Jim opened his big blue superstar eyes as wide as he could.

"Annie" he implored. "Don't do it, honey."

She pulled back the hammer.

"A-Annie" he tried again. "Please..." His whole body shook. He could feel the sweat running down his face and the urine beginning to leak down his leg. Living as Jay Harvey was one thing. Dying as him was something else entirely.

"I'm not Jay Harvey," he said, reverting to his native East End accent, "and I can prove it."

She stayed perfectly still, her eyes fixed on him like a cat focuses on its prey before going in for the kill.

Slowly, he held up his hands. Both her stare and her gun remained totally static.

"Remember Jay Harvey's burst appendix last year? The news was all over the T.V. and the papers. Everywhere."

She did not move.

"Look," he said quietly, "can I show you something?"

No response.

Very, very slowly, Jim lowered his hands, loosened his trousers and pulled them down slightly to reveal his totally unblemished abdomen.

Still nothing.

"I'd have a scar, wouldn't I?" Jim reasoned. "A big one. A fresh one. Look, nothing."

For the first time, her eyes left his as she dropped her gaze to stare.

She just stared...and stared...and stared.

Jim licked his lips and swallowed. "I can understand your beef with Harvey" he went on. "He *is* a bit of a wanker after all!" He attempted a small smile.

Her stare remained unchanged.

"But I'm not him" Jim concluded. "I didn't do those things to you, Annie. I'm just an ordinary member of the public ~ like you. I'm certainly not worth throwing your life away for."

Finally she moved. She exhaled deeply and lowered the gun. To Jim's surprise, a single tear ran down her cheek.

"Oh no" she moaned. "After all this time, I thought I'd finally... Oooh" She sounded in genuine pain.

"Annie" Jim began. He reached out his hand. "I understand. Just let me go, love. I promise I won't press charges. I-"

The touch of his hand on her arm ignited a sudden, furious explosion. "You bastard!" she screamed. "You total and utter bastard! I thought I had him. I thought I finally had that stupid, self-important, over-inflated tosser within my grasp. I was *that* close," she thrust two fingers with a small space between them into Jim's face, "and then *you* come along, a mere copy of something so useless in the first place, and ruin it all!"

"I'm-I'm sorry" Jim stuttered. "It's hardly my fault that I'm not Jay Harvey or that I was unfortunate enough to be born looking like him."

"You told me you *were* him" the girl protested furiously.

"Ah, no" Jim said, a little more confident now that he didn't have a gun in his face. "I never do. You just assumed…"

He reeled back as she struck him sharply across the face.

"Shut your filthy mouth, you fucking fraud!" she roared "I'll teach you to live a lie with me!"

She picked up her glass and smashed it against the wall. He felt the razored edge slice cleanly through his cheek.

"You don't look like him any more," she crowed, "and you never will again ~ at least until I catch up with him. You needed a scar? You got one!"

She threw the keys at him at Jim. "Just fuck off" she scowled with deep resignation.

He grabbed the keys and sprinted up the stairs and out of the door before she could change her manic mind.

*

"Well, it's one hell of a story" said the policeman by Jim's hospital bedside. "Worthy of Mr. Harvey himself."

Jim felt the stitches in his cheek pull as he grimaced. "Don't," he grumbled, "I've had enough of bloody Jay Harvey to last me a lifetime!"

The policeman shrugged. "Well Mr. Harris, I hate to say it but I don't think you'll be doing any more look-a-like work now – not unless Annie Stone does get to him."

Jim suddenly looked interested. "Any sign of her?" he asked.

"Not yet" the policeman admitted. "By the time we got to the pub, she was long gone. Pity you didn't think to lock the cellar door behind you."

"I don't think so" Jim replied indignantly. "I just wanted to get away as fast and as far as possible. Anyway, I thought it was *your* job to lock up the criminals!"

The policeman ignored that. "Dangerous woman that one ~ she been done for a lot more than trespassing, I can tell you."

"Really?"

"Well, obviously I *can't* tell you," the policeman went on, colouring slightly, "but don't worry sir, we'll find her. I just hope we do before she finds Mr. Harvey."

*

In fact, Annie Stone was caught and detained the following week after she finally surfaced in another pub further up country; closer to Jay Harvey's British home.

After the trial and subsequent conviction, Jim Harris prepared to close that particular chapter of his life and move on.

Until he got the phone call.

*

Jim and Jay had never actually come face to face before.

They spent a long time gazing at the almost mirror images of themselves before either of them spoke.

"So what do you think?" Jay asked, turning his head to the side.

Jim smiled as he considered the irony of the situation.

His story, slightly modified and now entitled "Someone To See You", was being made into a film starring, of course, Jay Harvey. As the tale was being told in flashback, it began with a close-up of Jay bearing a vivid red scar across his handsome cheek.

Jim Harris was back in business.

Lightning Source UK Ltd.
Milton Keynes UK
UKOW07f1805090516

273863UK00015B/70/P